Poetic Justice

AN ANTHOLOGY OF
CONTEMPORARY MOROCCAN POETRY

www.deborahkapchan.com

Poetic Justice

AN ANTHOLOGY OF
CONTEMPORARY MOROCCAN POETRY

Edited and Translated by
Deborah Kapchan

with
Driss Marjane

CENTER FOR MIDDLE EASTERN STUDIES
The University of Texas at Austin

Library of Congress Control Number: 2019933056
ISBN: 978-1477318492

to my poet son,

Nathanaël, je t'enseignerai la ferveur

and to Thelma, who first gave me poetry.

Contents

Acknowledgments

Several competent and dedicated scholars have made this work possible. The efforts of Eman Shaban Morsi as well as Sarah Hebbouch in copy-editing the volume and contacting poets for permissions and biographical sketches were essential. When Eman took a job at Dartmouth University, Sarah picked up the work and has been unflagging in her dedication and enthusiasm. They have my deepest appreciation. Ghayde Ghraowi typed the original texts and made them accessible on the website. Kiana Karimi constructed and designed the website. Pierre Joris generously read the Introduction and made some essential suggestions, as did Jill Karin Magi, Suzanne Seriff, and my wonderful colleagues in the Gender Brown Bag organized by Swethaa Ballakrishnen at New York University Abu Dhabi. I benefited greatly from the close reading and meticulous critique of the translations provided by readers, Michael Sells and Abdelmajid Hannoum. My thanks to Jim Klosty for his visual acumen and steadfast friendship. I am grateful as well for the support of the editors of the Modern Middle East Literatures in Translation Series at the Center for Middle Eastern Studies at the University of Texas at Austin: Wendy E. Moore and Dena Afrasiabi.

I received a lot of help and guidance from Moroccan poets. Mohammed Bennis gave me a "short list" of poets for the project many years ago. While the list has expanded, his initial list provides the core of this book. An early inspiration for this project, Ahmed Lemsyeh has gone with me to track down poems at The Royal Institute for Amazigh Culture in Rabat and has put me in touch with many of the poets in the volume. He and his wife Amina Ouchelh have never lost faith in the project or in me. Our conversations about art and culture continue to inspire me. Driss Mesnaoui was also an early inspiration. His poems were the first of my translations to be published, and he and his wife Saîda Chbarbi have lent much impetus to the project over years of friendship. His poetry reading with Idriss Aissa at New York University's Kevorkian Center for Middle East and Islamic Studies (in collaboration with the PEN World Voices Festival in New York City) in 2015 was an advance celebration of this work and a memorable delight. Abderrahman Tenkoul gave me copies of out-of-print poems and introduced me to poets from Fes while I was living there. Rachid Moumni and his wife Sanae Errachidi gave generously of their time and expertise. Hassan Najmi sat with me ringing up poets on the telephone and helping me contact people I would never have been able to reach otherwise, introducing me to Moroccan painters as well. Omar Berrada generously shared the manuscripts of Ahmed Bouanani. In his capacity as President of the Moroccan House of Poetry, Mourad Kadiri met with me and reached out to other poets on my behalf. Malika El Assimi sent a doctor to my hotel room when my son was burning up with fever in Marrakech, along with a delicious couscous for the worried parents. That kindness will never be forgotten. Rachida Madani—poet-sister, kindred spirit, spiritual inspiration—what more can I say? Shokran.

Contemporary translation theory asserts that the translator must emerge from invisibility, from historical absence, in order that the power relations embedded in the text be made manifest.[1] For most of the classical Arabic-language poems presented here I have relied on the efforts of Professor Driss Marjane. Over the course of many years, Professor Marjane and I sat side-by-side translating the classical Arabic together into literal translations that I then reworked into American English poetry. Because classical Arabic poetry represents the largest source language in this volume, and because of his patience and devotion to what became more than a decade-long endeavor, Driss's name graces the cover of this book. For help on the texts of zajal in Moroccan Arabic—especially those I translated in 1994–95 when I was a Fulbright scholar in Rabat—I am indebted to El-Houcine Haddad and his great enthusiasm for popular culture. While I worked with the French poems more or less in solitude, I did reach out to my French friends and colleagues on more than one occasion to verify my intuitions. Thanks to Claire Brajon, Geneviève Massourre, Juanita Jauer Steichen and the late Mylène Salvan-Leenhardt (whose sweet memory endures). If the meaning of literature is the work a reader does while reading it, as Stanley Fish purports, the work taking place in the readings and subsequent translations of these Moroccan texts into English has been a decidedly hybrid one. Finally Idriss Aissa reminds me why we write and translate poetry at all. His inspiration guides this volume and my poetic life.

Note

1. Venuti 1992

كلمة شكر

يعود الفضل للعديد من الباحثين والمبدعين القديرين في جعل هذا العمل ممكنا. لقد كانت جهود إيمان شعبان مرسي وكذلك سارة هبوش أساسية في إعداد مسودة الكتاب للنشر وفي الاتصال بالشعراء قصد الحصول على إذنهم وعلى ملخص عن سيرتهم الذاتية. وعندما حصلت إيمان على وظيفة بجامعة دارتموث، تولت سارة بقية العمل بدون وهن في تفانيها وحماسها. لهما معا فائق تقديري. كما قام غيد غراوي برقن النصوص الأصلية وجعلها في متناول القراء على الموقع الإلكتروني. كيانا كرمي أنشأت الموقع وقامت بتصميمه. كما تفضل بيير جوريس بكرم منه بقراءة المقدمة وتقديم بعض الاقتراحات الجوهرية، وكذلك جيل كارين ماغي وسوزان سريف وزميلاتي الرائعات في "جندر براون باغ" الذي تنظمه سويتا بالاكريشنان في جامعة نيويورك أبو ظبي. ولقد استفدت كثيرا من القراءة المتأنية والمراجعة الدقيقة للترجمات التي قدمها القارئان مايكل سيلز وعبد المجيد حنوم. أنا ممتنة لجيم كلوصتي لحدة نظره وصداقته الثابتة، كما أنني ممتنة أيضا للمسؤولتين عن تحرير سلسلة الأدب الحديث في الشرق الأوسط في الترجمة من مركز دراسات الشرق الأوسط في جامعة تكساس في أوستن ويندي مور ودينا أفراسيابي على دعمهما.

لقد تلقيت أيضا الكثير من المساعدة والإرشاد من الشعراء المغاربة. فقد قدم لي محمد بنيس قائمة "مختارة" من الشعراء منذ سنوات عديدة. ومع أن لائحة الشعراء قد توسعت مع مرور الوقت لتشمل شعراء آخرين إلا أن قائمته الأولية بقيت تمثل صلب هذا الكتاب. كما قام أحمد لمسيح، وهو من مصادر الإلهام الأوائل لهذا المشروع، بمرافقتي قصد اقتفاء أثر قصائد الشعر بالمعهد الملكي للثقافة الأمازيغية في الرباط وربط الاتصال بيني وبين العديد من الشعراء الذين يضمهم هذا المجلد. وطيلة كل هذه السنوات لم يفقد هو أو زوجته أمينة أوشلح الثقة بمشروع الكتاب أو بشخصي. ولاتزال حواراتنا حول الفن والثقافة تمثل مصدر إلهام بالنسبة لي. كما كان ادريس المسناوي مصدر إلهام لهذا المشروع منذ البداية. فقد كانت ترجماتي الأولى التي تم نشرها هي قصائده. وقد شكل هو وزوجته سعيدة الشبري مصدر تحفيز كبير لي على إتمام هذا المشروع على مدى سنوات من الصداقة الرفيعة التي تجمعنا. كما أن قراءاته الشعرية هو وإدريس عيسى بمركز كيفوركيان للدراسات الشرق أوسطية والإسلامية بجامعة نيويورك (بشراكة مع مهرجان PEN Writers بمدينة نيويورك) سنة 2015 كانت احتفاء مبكرا بهذا العمل وبهجة لا تنسى.

ولا يفوتني أن أذكر عبد الرحمان طنكول الذي أمدني بنسخ من قصائد كانت قد نفذت من المكتبات وقام بترتيب لقاء لي مع شعراء من مدينة فاس حين كنت أقيم هناك. كما قدم لي رشيد المومني وزوجته سناء الراشدي بكل سخاء كل وقتهما وخبرتهما. وقد سمح لي عمر برادة بالاطلاع على مخطوطات لقصائد شعرية لأحمد البوعناني. كما عقدت جلسات مع حسن نجمي الذي قام بالاتصال عبر هاتفه بالعديد من الشعراء وساعدني بذلك على ربط الصلة بأناس لم أكن لأتمكن من الوصول إليهم بطريقة أخرى، وعرفني أيضا بالعديد من الفنانين التشكيليين المغاربة. كانت لي أيضا فرصة لقاء مراد القادري بصفته رئيسا لبيت الشعر بالمغرب الذي قام كذلك بالاتصال بشعراء آخرين نيابة عني. وقد قامت مليكة العاصمي بإرسال طبيب إلى غرفتي بفندق في مراكش حيث كان ابني مشتعلا بالحمى، وأرفقت معه طبقا شهيا من الكسكس للوالدين القلقين على ابنهما.

هذا لطف لا يمكنني أن أنساه أبدا. رشيدة مدني، أجد فيها شقيقتي في الشعر ونفس شبيهة بنفسي ومصدر إلهام لروحي. ماذا عساني أن أقول أكثر من هذا؟ . . . شكرا، شكرا.

تؤكد نظريات الترجمة المعاصرة أنه على المترجم أن يبرز من اللامرئي، من الغياب التاريخي، لكي تصير علاقات القوة المتضمنة في النص جلية. لقد اعتمدت على مجهودات الأستاذ ادريس مرجان بالنسبة لأغلب الشعر الصادر باللغة العربية الفصحى المقدم هنا. طوال سنوات عديدة، جلسنا أنا والأستاذ مرجان جنبا إلى جنب وترجمنا معا العربية الفصحى ترجمة حرفية لكي أقوم بعد ذلك بإعادة صياغتها شعرا باللغة الإنجليزية الأمريكية. وبما أن الحيز الأكبر من هذا الكتاب يحتله الشعر الصادر باللغة العربية الفصحى، ونظرا لسعة صدره وتفانيه فيما سيصبح بعد ذلك عملا امتد لفترة تفوق حقبة من الزمن، يشرف اسم ادريس غلاف هذا الكتاب. وبالنسبة للمساعدة على ترجمة نصوص الزجل بالعربية المغربية - وخصوصا تلك المترجمة خلال سنتي 1994 و1995 حين كنت باحثة ضمن برنامج فولبرايت بمدينة الرباط - فأنا ممتنة للحسين حداد وحماسه الكبير تجاه الثقافة الشعبية. ومع أنني اشتغلت على القصائد باللغة الفرنسية بشكل أو بآخر لوحدي، فقد قمت بكل تأكيد بالاتصال بصديقاتي وزميلاتي الفرنسيات أكثر من مرة للتحقق من صحة حدسي. لذا أشكر كل من كلير براجون، جونفييف ماسور، خوانيتا جاورستايكن والفقيدة مايلين سالفان-لينهاردت، التي غادرتنا إلى دار البقاء (إنا لله و إنا إليه راجعون). وإذا كان معنى الأدب يكمن في الفعل الذي يقوم به القارئ خلال قراءته له، كما يقول ستانلي فيش، فإن الفعل الذي تم في قراءات تلتها بعد ذلك ترجمات لهذه النصوص المغربية نحو اللغة الإنجليزية هو فعل متعدد بكل تأكيد. وفي الأخير، ما فتئ ادريس عيسى يذكرني بالدافع وراء كتابتنا وترجمتنا للشعر. إلهامه ينير هذا المجلد وحياتي الشعرية.

Note

1. Venuti 1992

Remerciements

Plusieurs chercheurs, dont la compétence et le dévouement sont exceptionnels, ont fait en sorte que ce projet devienne une réalité. Les efforts fournis par Eman Shaban Morsi ainsi que par Sarah Hebbouch dans la révision du manuscrit de ce volume et dans la prise de contact avec les poètes pour obtenir leurs autorisations et leurs résumés biographiques étaient essentiels. Lorsque Eman a été retenue pour un poste à l'Université de Dartmouth, Sarah a pris la relève avec un enthousiasme et un dévouement inlassables. Elles ont droit toutes les deux à ma gratitude la plus vive. Ghayde Ghraowi a saisi les textes originaux pour les rendre accessibles sur le site web. Kiana Karimi a conçu et construit le site web. Pierre Joris a eu la bonté de lire l'introduction et de faire des recommandations essentielles, de même que Jill Karin Magi, Suzanne Seriff et mes merveilleuses collègues du Gender Brown Bag organisé par Swethaa Ballakrishnen à l'Université de New York Abu Dhabi. J'ai aussi largement bénéficié de la relecture attentive et de la critique minutieuse des traductions par les lecteurs Michael Sells et Abdelmajid Hannoum. Je suis reconnaissante à Jim Klosty pour l'acuité de son discernement et pour son amitié inébranlable. Mes remerciements vont également aux éditrices de la série Littératures Modernes du Moyen-Orient en Traduction du Centre pour les Études du Moyen-Orient de l'Université du Texas à Austin, Wendy E. Moore et Dena Afrasiabi, pour leur précieux appui.

J'ai également reçu beaucoup d'aide et de conseils de la part des poètes marocains. Mohammed Bennis m'avait proposé une « sélection » de poètes il y a plusieurs années. Alors que le nombre des poètes s'est élargi avec le temps, sa liste initiale constitue toujours le noyau de ce livre. Ahmed Lemsyeh, un des premiers inspirateurs de ce projet, s'est déplacé avec moi à la recherche de poèmes à l'Institut Royal de la Culture Amazigh à Rabat et m'a mise en contact avec de nombreux poètes présents dans ce volume. Lui et sa femme Amina Ouchelh, ayant foi en l'utilité de ce projet, m'ont toujours investie de leur confiance. Nos

conversations sur l'art et sur la culture ne cesseront jamais de m'inspirer. Driss
Mesnaoui a été également une source d'inspiration pour moi depuis le début.
Ses poèmes ont été mes premières traductions publiées. Lui et son épouse Saîda
Chbarbi ont donné beaucoup d'élan au projet pendant ces années d'amitié fé-
conde et pérenne. Sa lecture de poésie avec Idriss Aissa au Centre Kevorkian
pour les Études du Proche-Orient et les Études Islamiques de l'Université de
New York (en collaboration avec le Festival PEN de la ville de New York) en
2015 a été une célébration en prélude de ce projet, doublée d'une joie mémo-
rable. Abderrahman Tenkoul m'a également fourni des copies de poèmes épui-
sées et m'a présentée aux poètes de Fès quand j'y habitais. Rachid Moumni et son
épouse Sanae Errachidi m'avaient généreusement donné de leur temps et de leur
expertise. Hassan Najmi s'est attablé avec moi pendant des heures et a appelé de-
puis son téléphone les poètes pour moi; il m'a ainsi aidée à me mettre en contact
avec des gens que je n'aurais jamais pu atteindre autrement, comme il m'a aussi
présentée aux peintres marocains. Omar Berrada a généreusement partagé des
manuscrits inédits de poèmes d'Ahmed Bouanani. Mourad Kadiri, en tant que
président de la Maison de la Poésie au Maroc, m'a reçue et s'est adressé à d'autres
poètes pour moi. Malika El Assimi a dépêché un médecin à ma chambre d'hô-
tel alors que mon fils brûlait de fièvre à Marrakech, et elle l'a accompagné d'un
délicieux couscous pour les parents qui s'inquiétaient pour leur fils. Je ne saurai
jamais oublier cette gentillesse. Rachida Madani—poète-sœur et inspiration—
que puis-je dire de plus ? Shokran.

   Les théories contemporaines de la traduction affirment que le traducteur doit
émerger de l'invisible, de l'absence historique, afin que les rapports de force en-
fouis dans le texte deviennent manifestes.[1] En ce qui concerne la plupart des
poèmes en langue arabe classique présentés ici j'ai beaucoup compté sur les ef-
forts de Driss Marjane. Au fil de plusieurs années, le Professeur Driss Marjane
et moi-même nous nous sommes réunis côte à côte pour traduire ensemble lit-
téralement de l'arabe classique vers l'anglais, pour qu'ensuite je puisse retravail-
ler cela en poésie en anglais américain. Et puisque la poésie en arabe classique est
prédominante dans ce volume, et pour sa patience et son dévouement pour ce qui
allait devenir l'engagement de plus d'une décennie, son nom honore la couverture
de ce livre. Pour ce qui est de l'aide sur les textes du zajal en arabe dialectal maro-
cain—en particulier ceux que j'ai traduits en 1994–95 quand j'avais une bourse
de recherche Fulbright à Rabat—je suis bien redevable à El-Houcine Haddad et
son grand enthousiasme pour la culture populaire. Et même si j'ai travaillé sur
les poèmes en français plus ou moins seule, j'ai bien souvent contacté mes amies

et collègues françaises afin de vérifier mes intuitions. Mes remerciements vont à Claire Brajon, Geneviève Massourre, Juanita Jauer Steichen et la regrettée Mylène Salvan-Leenhardt (qui restera à jamais gravée dans nos mémoires). Si la littérature n'a de sens que dans la mesure du travail que le lecteur déploie en la lisant, comme le prétend Stanley Fish, le travail investi dans les lectures et, ultérieurement, dans les traductions de ces textes marocains en anglais a été résolument de nature hybride. Et enfin, Idriss Aissa m'interpelle pour me rappeler la raison pour laquelle nous écrivons et traduisons la poésie. Son inspiration guide ce volume ainsi que ma vie poétique.

Note

1. Venuti 1992

Poetic Justice

AN ANTHOLOGY OF
CONTEMPORARY MOROCCAN POETRY

On Translation and Ethnography

Our business is to count the stars, star by star
to chew the wind's haughty arrogance
and watch the clouds for when they'll throw us a handful

and if the earth goes far away from us
we'll say everyone is possessed
    everyone has lost their mind
    and time, never will its letters fall between our hands
    until we write what we are

MESNAOUI 1995:73

اشغالنا نحسبوا النجوم نجمه نجمه
نمضغوا الرّيح نخوَه ع لخوا
ونحضوا لغيوم يمتى ترمي اللّقمه

ويلا بعدت الأرض علينا
نقولوا كلشي مسكون
كلشي مهزوز
والوقت عمّر حروفو ما طاحوا بين يدّينا
حتى نكتبوا اللّي بينا

shghaalna nhasbuu n-njoum najma najma
nmadghuu r-riih nakhwa al-lakhwa
wa nahdiu l-laghyuum imta tarmi l-luqma
    w-ila baadat l-ard aali-na
    nquluu kulshi maskuun

1

kulshi mahzuz

w lwaqt ammer hruufuu ma tahuu bin yeddina

hetta nkatbuu lli bina

. . . no translation would be possible if in its ultimate essence it strove for likeness to the original. For in its afterlife—which could not be called that if it were not a transformation and renewal of something living—the original undergoes a change . . .

WALTER BENJAMIN

On the Threshold of Translation: The Flesh of Imagination

The cover of this book is graced with the artwork of Moroccan creator Khalil El Ghrib. I say creator because El Ghrib does not call himself an artist.[1] Rather most of his oeuvre is fabricated of the detritus and organic matter that he finds in the streets and on the beaches of the northern coastal city of Asilah where he lives. In his studio he stores piles of paper, wire, boxes. He wades through these things as if a fisherman waist deep in the water with a hand net looking for the right catch—the one that fits his vision, his eye, his intuition. Following Benjamin's quote above, El Ghrib gives objects an after-life and in so doing translates them into another language and world.

El Ghrib also paints with watery colors and minimal lines. He gives agency to paint and to chance. The painting on the cover of this book suggests a portal, a doorway perhaps into another world, for there is no visible human habitation on the other side. The lintel casts a shadow across a threshold. Beyond there is only more color— translucent light illuminating the interior while outside a suggestion of the sea. It is a frame without a door, an opening in or out, a passageway. As a watercolor, it is sparse and unstudied. Given that the overwhelming majority of his works are found objects that he subsequently reframes, this *painting* of a frame finds particular relevance in his oeuvre.

The painting is also a portrayal of a limen, evoking for me what Sufi philosopher Ibn al-'Arabi (1165–1240 AD) has called a *barzakh*—that is, an isthmus between worlds. For Ibn al-'Arabi a barzakh is an ontological "imaginal" realm where the corporeal is spiritualized and the spiritual may become corporeal; it is a dimension where imagination "takes shape," where forms are realized.[2] There are nothing but barzakhs, says Ibn al-'Arabi, nothing but thresholds between worlds of different densities and subtleties ever unfolding.

In addition to being an isthmus between worlds, a barzakh may be marked by a *hijab* as well, that is, a veil. The portals between worlds are not always open doors so to speak, but are hidden with the gauze of in-between. Were it not so, reality would indeed be too much to bear, a clash of multiple worlds of various and precarious orders. The veils between worlds are there to protect the traveler, but they are also there to hide a reality that the traveler may not be ready to understand or assume. To veil is to contain while to draw the veil away, is to step across the threshold into another reality.

For Ibn al-'Arabi the imaginal worlds of barzakh are not imaginary—that is, disembodied and unreal—but in fact are very much a fleshly matter. "The reality of imagination is that it gives sensory form to everything that becomes actualized within it," says Ibn al-'Arabi in the *Meccan Openings* (II 375:34). It is the *materiality* of the imaginal that allows for intermingling, like the chemistry of two breaths together.

The imaginal or "barzakhi" realm has much in common with what Merleau-Ponty (1908–1961) has called "flesh" (*chair*).[3] For Merleau-Ponty flesh is an element of being like "water, air, earth and fire." It is a porous, reversible and renewable substance.[4] The human body is flesh, but it intertwines with the flesh of the world, like a pulsing rhythm or a condensation of vibrations. For Merleau-Ponty flesh is the continuity that links the perceiver's body with the world: flesh, he notes, is "a sort of incarnate principle that brings a style of being wherever there is a fragment of being."[5]

Like Ibn al-'Arabi, Merleau-Ponty is reaching for a vocabulary of the interstitial. His writing is poetic, analogical. He is creating a philosophical concept from a material all humans (and mammals) share - flesh. But he extends it beyond the human, talking about the flesh of the world and of the "ek-static" encounter of self and other, world and Being, what he calls an "intercorporeity."[6] Like a barzakh, flesh is also an isthmus, a kind of fascia or connective tissue. It creates "style" from "fragments." It traverses at the same time that it forms. It is, we might say, always *trans*forming.

I invoke these two philosophers, so disparate in time and space, because both are trying to understand the materiality of the imagination, and the relation of the visible to the invisible—themes evoked for me by El Ghrib's painting.[7] But these concepts are relevant to translation as well insofar as translations are im-

4

bued with the meaning and the *matter* of culture. Poems also present themselves as thresholds into other worlds. Sometimes these worlds are easy to access and inhabit. Sometimes they are esoteric, oblique and even resistant to entry, like veils that envelop a world or a body. In all cases poetic translations are after-lives, barzakhs that partake of the imagination of the author and that of the translator to create a third thing entirely, a style of being.[8] Poems and translations are objects that go on to live lives in the world. Both are acts of embodied imagination, depending not only on a linguistic but on an ethnographic sensibility, since words only mean through their enfleshment with the world.

Beginning with the Particular

This project began as a deep-dive into the semantic nuances, metaphors and poetics of Moroccan colloquial Arabic. In 1994–95 I had a Fulbright in Rabat. I was a new professor at the time at the University of Texas at Austin and was on a pre-tenure sabbatical to write and do research on Moroccan cultural poetics. My teachers in Folklore had taught me much about verbal genres,[9] narrative and performance,[10] as well as orality.[11] My first book was an ethnography of women's oral and embodied culture both in the private sphere (personal narratives, gossip) and more importantly for the time, in the public sphere (oratory in the marketplace, dance and song). In all of these contexts I observed, participated, recorded, transcribed and *translated*.

By that time I had already lived in Morocco for three years and was fluent in Moroccan colloquial Arabic or *darija*, having also studied classical Arabic for five years. A lover and writer of poetry, I attended a reading of *zajal*—oral poetry in dialect—in Rabat. I was immediately drawn in and began to frequent readings and festivals of zajal in school auditoriums and open-air venues in public parks. The audiences for these performances were university students and professors, high school teachers, actors, theater critics, film buffs, journalists and of course other poets—the cultural elite who sculpt Moroccan cultural aesthetics from the ground up. The audience responded to particularly beautiful or politically astute lines with expressions of "allah!" not unlike the gasps of ecstasy heard in heightened moments of Sufi ritual or musical rapture (*ṭarab*). What elicited these responses?

The answer to that question taught me why linguistic translation is first and foremost ethnographic—that is, embedded in the sensate experiences of culture.

One late afternoon in 1994 I attended a zajal festival in Rabat's central park. Ahmed Lemsyeh, the first poet to write and publish in the vernacular and an activist in the Moroccan socialist party, was on stage and read from his recently published book, *Who Embroidered the Water?* (شكون اطرز الما؟). His verses were densely weighted in the particular, replete with proverbs, song lyrics and history. He recited:

> I went down in my soul to look for the remains
> I found happiness defending spring

> I said, a head without a strategy
> deserves to be severed

> And I chanted

> Two pigeons singing, they sleep on the palm fronds
> He who doesn't love beauty, his life is lament

> He who has a little gazelle should keep his hand upon it
> One person hawks his life, another is the pawnbroker

Lemsyeh goes down in his soul [*ruh*] to look for "the remains," and what he finds are verses that exist in the oral tradition. The first of the couplets is based on a proverb: *ras bla nashwa qatiu halal*, "a head without passion, its severing is permitted." Lemsyeh replaces the letter "waw" in nashwa with the letter "ba" and alters the verse slightly: *ras bla nashba y-tsahel l-qatiae* - a head without a strategy (or "trap," presumably for one's enemies) deserves to be severed. Here he comments on the need to be attentive to the silent battle of those in power ("silence has become their weapon," he says in another line). The second two couplets recall verses from the popular song genre of *al-'alwa*, a genre performed by women called shikhat at Moroccan festive events:[12]

> Two pigeons singing, they sleep on the palm fronds
> *juj hamamat y-ghaniyu, fawq nakhla y-batu*

> He who doesn't love beauty, his life is lament
> *lli ma y-'ashq az-zin, y-ta'za fi hiyat-u*

He who has a little gazelle should keep his hand upon it
lli 'and-u shi ghaziyl, y-hat idi-h 'al-ih

One person hawks his life, another is the pawnbroker
wahed y-erhan 'amr-u u l-akhur y-twella fi-h

Employing song lyrics in the popular repertoire, Lemsyeh reframes and recycles the "remains" of oral culture into the written word, much like El Ghrib reframes his found objects. The lively responses of the audience were a reaction to this play between what can be cited (words) and the unspoken cultural and affective depths associated with them. As the late Moroccan writer and critic Abdelkebir Khatibi notes, "every language is bilingual, oscillating between the spoken portion and another, which both affirms and destroys itself in the incommunicable" (1990:20). The delight of the audience registered the recognition of their own 'bilingualism,' between the written word and the oral repertoire.

Lemsyeh's verses below, for example, play with parallel structures well known in oratory performed in the Moroccan *halqa*, the oral performance "circle" traditionally found in the marketplace:

Words are not the bed and the cover
Words are a path and people are letters
Words are not true or false
Words are a spring whose water circumambulates
Paper is a shroud sewn with white
Writing enables the eye to see
and the caftan to be dotted with life
Its clothes [are] pure, its meaning is wool
When you spin it, you find your love entangled
Bargaining is rapture, joy and fear
Wear fragrance and plane the senses
Feather the wind, leave the sky plucked
The paper's blood is mixed with ink
Its life doesn't want to stop

لكلام ما هو فراش وغطَّى

لكلام طريق والناس حروف

لكلام ما هو صَحْ أوْ خطى

لكلام عين مَاهَا يطُوف

والورقة كَفَّن بالبياض مخَيَّطة
وبالكتبة تولّي عِين تشُوف
تولي قفطان بالحياة منقطة
لبَاسو وُضُو، ومعانيه صُوف
ملّي تغزلها، تَلْقاها مِحبتك محَوْطة
متاويَة اللّيعة والفرح والخوف
تَلْبس الطّيب وبالمعاني مَقَشْطة
تْرَيّش الريح تخَلّي السحاب منتوف
الورقة دمها لمداذْ بيه مخَلْطَة
الحياة فيها ما تبغي وقوف

Compare these verses to the following well-known formulas that I recorded in the Moroccan marketplace in Beni Mellal in 1991, spoken by a woman herbalist hawking her potions:

The woman, what is she called?
l-mra ash ka-t-tsamma?

A well, and a man is called a bucket
bir, u r-rajal ka-y-tsamma dlu

The woman is called an inkwell and the man a pen
l-mra ka-t-tsamma dwaya, u r-rajal ka-y-tsamma qalim

The woman is called a field and the man the irrigation
l-mra ka-t-tsamma hawd, u r-rajal ka-y-tsamma sagiya

The woman is called a mattress and the man a blanket
l-mra ka-t-tsamma frash, u r-rajal ka-y-tsamma eghta

Clearly Lemsyeh has spent time in the halqa! He alludes as well to Sufism, to religious purification and the practice of circumambulation of the Kaaba during the Muslim pilgrimage. The associative density and parody in Lemsyeh's recycled verses present profound resistance to translation. Had I not done extensive research on both shikhat and oratory in the marketplace, these allusions and citations may have remained invisible to me. And even so, it was the affective reaction of the audience at the *performance* of these poems that first alerted me to the presence of meanings that might otherwise have eluded me.[13]

Thus began my more than twenty year inquiry into the complexities of ethnography and translation—oral, literary, cultural, linguistic, and inter-semiotic.[14]

My experiences with translation have taught me the following: 1) the *performance* context is an essential aspect to poetic interpretation, even when the event happened in the past;[15] 2) the presence of *orality* and other forms of *embodied history* abide (and sometimes hide) in the written word; and thus 3) embodied cultural knowledge is required in order for cultural depths to rise to the surface; that is, the translator must not only be bilingual, but embrace a *bi-sensoriality* sensitive to the "flesh" of multiple worlds and what lies between them. While translation is always a new creation, it is also an intimate *partage*, a meeting of flesh, a barzakh. In what follows, I demonstrate that not only does ethnography require the skills of translation, but that the art of translation itself is in its very being ethnographic.

Translation and Ethnography

La poésie est un pays heureux, "poetry is a happy land," poet Idriss Aissa often reminded me. And he is right. While translating these poems I have been immersed in an exploration of another land, the land of each poet's imagination, the land of the poem. And while not all lands are happy, poetry is a kind of alchemy that transforms even the most difficult experiences into beauty, no matter how terrifying or sublime. So that when Mohammed Khaïr-Eddine writes of the Rwandan genocide, he not only provides an implicit political commentary on the barbarism of which humans are capable, but he also attests to the ability of the poet to transform those acts into testimony, a monument to history and to the victims:

> They stink, they have nothing left—naked,
> eaten by the perennial river
> enlarged with the blood
> of innocents;—their skin sails
> bacterial
> to Lake Kivu where the scythe stands
> and the bones
> of children float, oars broken, murdered
> in the glimmers of Twilight.

Ils puent, ils n'ont plus rien—tout nus,
mangés au fil du fleuve sempiternel
grossi de sang
des innocents;—leur peau navigue,
bactérienne
jusqu'au lac Kivu où se dressa la faux
et flottèrent les os
de ces enfants, rames brisées, meurtries
aux lueurs du Crépuscule.

Is poetry a happy land even when its subject is horror? Insofar as the poet can write, I would say, yes it is.

La poésie est un pays heureux. No doubt Idriss said that in order to encourage me through the challenges and obstacles of life to find that land, to find it and re-find it over and over again; to never "lose the head (or tip) of the string," (*ttellef ras l-khayt*) as is said in Moroccan Arabic (*perdre le fil* in French), never lose the connection that conducts energy from one time and place to another, from one being to another.

Poetry is a happy land because time expands in the poem and because the poet, the translator and the reader all live within it in what Bakhtin calls the work's chronotope, the particular orientation to time and space present within the work. This immersion, however fleeting, is most often unhindered by the worries of survival, the rhythms of capitalism, the compulsion to consume and to produce. The poem is not consumed, it is shared. It is not analyzed so much as known.

Poetry is also a generous land, a landscape we inhabit as wandering Sufis at home wherever we are. On that subject, Idriss also wrote: "Our relation to place is irrational. There are things that surpass reason therein. There always remains an unknown and invincible power (magnetism, magic, gravity . . .) that ties us to a path, a dwelling, a city, a countryside, a hidden place in a residence, in a garden. . . .*We are secret characters in a grand and multi-century story that places are recounting.*"[16] For reasons that surpass reason I have been drawn to Morocco for decades, a minor character in a story whose plot I only sometimes glimpse through a diaphanous veil.

Translation is an essential part of ethnography. Some think that it is the main goal of ethnography—to make culture comprehensible to culture (not transparent but identifiable), to recognize and appreciate another's difference and thus to better understand one's own; or, as anthropologist and poet Michael D. Jackson notes, "a way of understanding the other as oneself in different circumstances."[17]

Clifford Geertz, the scholar responsible for the hermeneutic turn in anthropology and whose work also brought Morocco (and particularly the city of Sefrou) into academic purview in the United States and beyond, was well aware of the nuances and difficulties of interpreting culture. He suggested amassing a plethora of different texts—different versions of one event for example—in order to approximate "the native's point of view." For Geertz, this kind of "thick description" was the best method for cultural interpretation.

Talal Asad, on the other hand, brought attention to the differential power relations at work in any sort of translation, noting the "asymmetrical tendencies and pressures [that exist] in the languages of dominated and dominant societies." For Asad, to assume the transparent translation or interpretation of cultural or linguistic texts - however numerous or thick - is an error in ethics.[18]

If for Asad the anthropologist is often a de facto imperialist, coloring interpretations with the skewed perceptions that privilege and power bestow, the history of literary translation tells a somewhat different story. The literary translator, although no less responsible for his or her re-authoring of the text, is often erased and dis-acknowledged entirely (Venuti 2008). This may be because the most oft-translated texts are those already recognized as "classics" in their contexts of origin and canonistic authors necessarily overpower the apprenti that translate them (or so is thought). Whereas the translator of culture risks over-determining interpretations with assumptions that may be biased and positional, the literary translator often suffers from invisibility in works of literature. Where do we land?

Performance

Perhaps the best place to land is on the ground, and in the body. It is worth remembering that in the nineteen-seventies, anthropologists, ethnographers of speaking, folklorists, linguists as well as poets themselves began inquiring into the relation of form and meaning in oral texts.[19] While attending to poetics (assonance, parallelism, alliteration, repetition, etc.), they also acknowledged that embodied *performance*—the intonation and timbre of the voice, for example—played an integral part in the transmission of knowledge (including non-referential knowledge). What's more, they recognized the importance of pre-existing knowledge, cultural assumptions, aesthetics, inferences as well as gestures, to the work of translation and interpretation. Meaning emerges in performance, grounded in the body, its cultural milieux and affective repertoires.

Orality and History

But if semantic reference only accounts for a small part of communication, how translate the rest? How represent what is non-representable? What methods to employ? For scholars of narrative this is often done by drawing upon philosopher Charles S. Peirce's theory of signs. Peirce demonstrated how some signs (linguistic, gestural, sonic, visual) point to and evoke others thereby allowing the analyst to read extra-textual elements from within the text (like my association of El Ghrib's painting with a barzakh).[20] It is through a reading of the citations and extra-textual allusions (what Peirce calls "indexical" relations) that the semantic and sensate richness emerges in Lemsyeh's poetry, for example. These associations (of symbols with memory, history and aesthetics) enlarge the field of interpretation.[21]

At the same time, it is important not to discount the oral aspects of a poetic text (whether spoken or written).[22]Anthropologist Dennis Tedlock and poet Jerome Rothenberg created ways of writing on the page that evoked the rhythm and power of sounded performance, much like the *poèsie concrete* movement.[23] While these methods often privilege the sonic, they also acknowledge the import of the entire cultural sensorium, noting that language, like perception, is embodied. It indexes the tastes, smells, and touches as well as the sounds, sights and insights of its milieu.

Bi-Sensoriality

Many of these artists and scholars wrote and write under the sign of performance, examining the "performative"—that is, not only what language and other semiotic forms mean, but what they do in the world.[24] Ethnographies of speaking and of performance more generally bore and continue to bear witness to the polysemic and polysensate dimensions of poetic expression, making it clear that there is nothing transparent about cultural or linguistic translation. Indeed, it is a complicated endeavor requiring not only a certain level of bilingualism but what might be called a *bi-sensoriality* as well—the ability to share in more than one cultural sensorium, with its corresponding aesthetics, ways of being, knowing and feeling.[25]

The Promise of Ethnographic Translation

It is for this reason that translation is always ethnographic. Whether translating from the oral or the written, translation takes place in the register of parole, not langue—that is, speech and the sentence and not the abstraction of grammatical language.[26] And the complexities and idiosyncrasies of these acts of translation (what Merleau-Ponty might refer to as "intertwining chiasms") are irreducible. And yet translation occurs. And this is because translation works on a promise: one that holds that languages, although different, are allied through kinship, that they are of the same flesh.[27] This promise does not have to be fulfilled to be effective; indeed, translation contains the seeds of its own failure. As Jacques Derrida notes in his study of Walter Benjamin, a "translation never succeeds in the pure and absolute sense of the term. Rather, a translation succeeds in promising success, in promising reconciliation. . . . a good translation is one that enacts the performative called the promise with the result that through the translation one sees the coming shape of a possible reconciliation among languages."[28]

This reconciliation, like all dreams of a common language,[29] is ultimately impossible. Nonetheless, the discourse that posits the belief in and hope for a kind of utopian "transparency of codes" does important social work.[30] A promise is a "performative": it enacts rather than refers and by its very action accomplishes its goal, which is to create an intersubjective contract that is often affective and implicit rather than acknowledged and juridical.[31] But the verb to promise is also a transitive construction: I promise to meet a deadline, to arrive on time, to be faithful, and so forth. A promise engages the promiser and promisee in an affective exchange that extends beyond the moment of utterance. Indeed, a promise and a translation are akin in their assumption of an unstated trust:

"All understanding, and the demonstrative statement of understanding which is translation, starts with an act of trust," notes theorist George Steiner. "This confiding will, ordinarily, be instantaneous and unexamined, but it has a complex base. It is an operative convention which derives from a sequence of phenomenological assumptions about the coherence of the world, about the presence of meaning in very different, perhaps formally antithetical semantic systems, about the validity of analogy and parallel."[32]

As an "operative convention," translation—and its promise—takes us into the heart of what it means to be human together, co-creating "the presence of meaning" in embodied and semantic domains. This is not just a cognitive endeavor. As Benjamin notes, "translation is a mode."[33] Like music, translation is emotionally inflected, carrying mood and character, whether translating from language to language (interlingual translation) or across semiotic systems (from music to words, for example, or intersemiotic translation).[34] It makes a style of being from a fragment of being. Translation is an act that requires the translator to imagine "reconciliation" and to embody that imagination in order for alchemy to take place.

This is no doubt why philosopher Paul Ricoeur in his last work, *On Translation*, puts cultural fluency before linguistic fluency, saying that "the work of the translator does not move from the word to the sentence, to the text, to the cultural group, but conversely: absorbing vast interpretations of the spirit of a culture, the translator comes down again from the text, to the sentence and to the word" (2004: 31).[35] While it is hubris to consider the translator a guide to other worlds, perhaps she is a liminar of sorts—a facilitator between two shores. More humbly I would suggest, following Ricoeur, that translation is a *gesture* of ethnographic hospitality, an imperfect meeting where trust is enacted and a carnal imagination shared. "Bringing the reader to the author, bringing the author to the reader, at the risk of serving and of betraying two masters: this is to practice what I like to call linguistic hospitality," says Ricoeur. And it is in this hospitality that the translator finds happiness:

"The happiness associated with translating is a gain when, tied to the loss of the absolute, it acknowledges the difference between adequacy and equivalence, equivalence without adequacy. There is happiness. . . . In spite of the agonistics that make a drama of the translator's task, he can find his happiness in . . . linguistic hospitality."

Ricoeur is dialoguing with theorists like Benjamin and Derrida,[36] who discuss the impossibility of absolute translation and the mourning that follows in the wake of that acknowledgment. It is the carnality of the meeting, however, its enfleshment that makes the trope of hospitality resonate for me. Certainly translation involves "some salvaging and some acceptance of loss."[37] It is embedded in power relations that need to be made clear, rendered visible.[38] However translation is hospitable precisely because it is an *opening toward* in the face of loss and in the face of risk. It is ethnographic because it is embodied and carnal. The culinary analogy is apt; ethnographic hospitality is homely, domestic and multi-sensorial. For Sufis (in Morocco and elsewhere), taste (*dhawq*) is a central sense insofar as the taster and the tasted are one. (To taste divinity is to be one with divinity.) In eating with another, that alchemy is shared, though never in the same way. Hospitality is a way of "being with" the stranger while a *gesture* of hospitality is an embodied form of attention in motion (for gesture is never static). It is not only the basis of ethnography (where one learns the humility of the guest), but it is a primary value in Moroccan codes of honor. *Ḍiyafa*—literally "guesting"—embodies the values of generosity integral to Moroccan society. *La poèsie est un pay heureux.*[39]

Translation is not ethnography, yet it relies on an ethnographic sensibility if it is to embrace and not smother the author; nor is anthropology translation, at least not in any facile linguistic sense that assumes equality and transparency. Rather, building upon Ricoeur's notion of translation as linguistic hospitality as well as the philosophers above,[40] I suggest that ethnography and translation are twin endeavors, inseparable events, intimate paramours, *enfleshments*. Poetic translation is a happy land precisely because it is a barzakh between two, partaking of both, locatable in neither.

Might poetry provide an index to extra-textual worlds of sense and meaning-making?[41] It is my hope that this manuscript will be read not only by students and lovers of poetry, comparative literature, and Morocco, but that it will be read by anthropologists, sociologists and scholars of culture as well.

Orality, Aurality and Translation

The idea for this volume was born at the height of one vernacular movement (the emergence of Moroccan Arabic as a literary language) and ends at the beginning of another (Tamazight, or Berber as a written poetic form). While poetry in Moroccan Arabic had always been in the oral repertoire, it had never been written and published as a literary genre until 1976 with the appearance of Ahmed Lemsyeh's book, *Winds to Come* (رياح .... التي ستأتي) . By the late 1980s and early 1990s the movement was in full efflorescence and chapbooks of zajal were easily found in kiosks and bookstores in Rabat. At the time, Ahmed Lemsyeh and Driss Mesnaoui were two of the most prominent writers in this genre, along with Mourad Kadiri. I was fortunate to work with Lemsyeh and Mesnaoui personally, and with the help of El Houcine Haddad, a lover of verbal art, I translated two diwans: Who Embroidered the Water (*shkun traz al-ma?*) by Ahmed Lemyeh, and The Letter Waw (*al-waw*) by Driss Mesnaoui.[42] What's more, I worked closely with the poets themselves, interviewing them and eventually becoming close friends with them and with their families. At that time, Ahmed Lemsyeh introduced me to other writers in the Moroccan Writers' Union and I was interviewed (in Moroccan Arabic) on a special television program devoted to zajal. I had the good fortune to ride the wave of a vernacular movement at the moment of its cresting. In the wake of that wave, many poets have begun to write and publish in Moroccan Arabic. Driss Mesnaoui and others have written novels and essays in Moroccan Arabic as well. There are many festivals and forums devoted to the form, and students in Morocco now write dissertations and theses about it. While Moroccan Arabic is still not an official language, it is no longer an anomaly to read literary works written in the mother tongue.

Why is this important when the educated Moroccan speaks and writes in classical Arabic, French and more recently English, and when Moroccan Arabic and often Tamazight are spoken at home? The answer to that question lies in the meanings, textures and tastes that reside in the aural language of one's birth and home environment. These often don't exist in the "higher" and more official languages of education. These synaesthetic repertoires, sensoriums, metaphors and worldviews resonate in the embodied imagination. And it is to the embodied imagination that poetry speaks.

This is of course true for the language of Tamazight as well (with its three variations of Tashelhit, Tarifit and Tamazight). The Amazigh literary movement is much more recent, however. While Amazigh verbal art and musical genres have been celebrated in Moroccan music festivals at least since independence, it was only in 1994 that news broadcasts in the three Amazigh dialects were televised. The Royal Institute of Amazigh Culture opened in 2001 in Rabat (http://www.ircam.ma/) and Tamazight became an official language of Morocco in 2011. Now street signs and all official buildings are designated in both classical Arabic (al-Fuṣḥa) and Tifinagh, the alphabet used to write Tamazight. Tifinagh has also become the alphabet of written Amazigh poetry.*

Moroccan Poetry: from Oral to Print to Digital

When I began this project, Moroccan poetry was remarkably absent from print-media anthologies of Arabic poetry in English. And for the most part, it remains so today. In the most read volume of the 20th century, Selma Jayyusi's *Modern Arabic Poetry*, there is only one Moroccan poet mentioned (Mohammed Bennis),

---

*My thanks to Cynthia Becker for her expertise in all things Amazigh.

while Issa J. Boulatta's book, *Modern Arab Poets 1950–1975*, features virtually no Moroccan poets. This may be, in part, because North Africa has fallen outside the purview of Middle Eastern Studies. However, there are no Moroccan poets in anthologies of West African poetry either. Despite the publication in 1929 of a book entitled *al-Adab al-Arabi fi al- Maghreb al-Aqsa*, "Arabic Literature in Morocco"[43] (edited by Mohamed Ben al-Abbas Kabbaj), Morocco has until recently been neglected in studies of modern poetry in English translation.[44]

Certainly the politics of translation are implicated. Morocco, notes poet and novelist Abdellatif Laâbi, has long been on the periphery of both the Middle East and the West, adding that despite the post-colonialist moment, new forms of global domination maintain its marginality. Poet and scholar Mohammed Bennis echoes these sentiments when (speaking of Arab writers more generally) he notes, "It is significant that our great poets, thinkers and scientists remain ignored in the West. If I am the descendant of a symbolic family of modern Arab writers, whether Muslim or Christian, . . . I am also the descendant of these same Muslims and Arabs that welcomed Greek philosophy and contributed to its development at the moment when it was condemned by Occidentals. They [the Arabs] invented algebra, they are the masters of logic and astronomy, doctors, scientists, but also great mystics, the inspiration for poetic, literary and artistic modernity in Europe."[45] Indeed Europe—and the entire Western world—owes North African writers a literary debt whose acknowledgement is direly needed, especially today.

Literature always has a political valence. Even when poems do not address politics specifically, they are speaking from within a power structure, against one, or in spite of one. There is poetry that is explicitly political—prison poetry, the poetry of war, the poetry of testimony and witness to otherwise unspeakable brutalities. There are examples of those here in the poems written by Abdellatif Laâbi from prison, or those of Salah El Ouadie about the torture that took place in the prison of Tazmamart during what is called the Years of Lead in Morocco (a time under King Hassan II's rule when militants and those in opposition to the monarchy were 'disappeared'). But there are times when even love poetry can be coded as a political rallying cry, as in the poems of feminine desire by Wafaa Lamrani or Malika El Assimi. Sometimes declaring the importance of the aesthetic and waving the banners of beauty takes as much courage as armed combat.

As with any genre, Moroccan poetry has an inner and an outer orientation—structures of both internal aesthetics and public politics.[46] The inner orientation of poetry written in classical Arabic dialogues with a long history of Arab poetics in the Middle East, drawing on pre-Islamic poetry as well as contemporary luminaries such as Adonis and Darwish.[47] The outer orientation of Moroccan poetry in Arabic is deeply entwined with past and current events in the Middle East, North Africa and worldwide—Moroccan independence in 1956, of course, but also the incursion of neoliberalism, changing gender roles, the continuing conflicts in Palestine, the Arab Spring, as well as global politics.

Moroccan poetry written in French, on the other hand, harkens back to a different poetic tradition—that of Baudelaire and Mallarmé. Yet even Moroccan poetry in French is imbued with an aesthetic of difference. It is very much a poetry of resistance, even to the colonial language and culture that spawned it. As Fanon noted, "being colonized by a language has large implications for one's consciousness. To speak . . . is to exist absolutely for the other . . . it means, above all, to assume a culture, to support the weight of a civilization" (1967: 17). Laâbi echoes these sentiments, asserting that writing in the colonial language is sometimes the only way to be heard and recognized (Laâbi 2005:8). And yet in his volume entitled *La Poésie Marocaine: de l'Independence à Nos Jours*, Abdellatif Laâbi posits that languages themselves may contain a "hard nut of identity" (*noyau dur d'identité*) and asks if it is "possible, or even legitimate, to crack this nut." In this volume I do not attempt to crack this nut, so much as to infuse its materiality into English verse, to render the smells and tastes of Moroccan poetry for an Anglophone audience.

Moroccan Poetic Milieux

Translating poetry is entering into the imagination of another, its peregrinations, its childlike whimsy, its meditations and despair. Insofar as poetry is a repository for a collective spirit (and it is not always nor necessarily), translating poetry is also discerning a substrate of social ontologies, ways of being that are accrued over centuries. While romanticizing a national spirit may lead to the grossest of fascisms, it is nonetheless possible to speak of what Deleuze and Guattari call a "milieu"—the vibrations of a territory, formed by the stories that have lived there, as well as the songs, languages, idioms, metaphors and other rhythms of history that are embedded in place. Such milieux (pl.) inhabit the body just as they inhabit residences, neighborhoods, regions and nations.

> Hesperis is calling you by your name: stand up oh marble body
> Every stranger has knocked at its door, so swell with blood
> Move your wings, strike at the ships of strangers on the river's edge

Tomorrow Hesperis will decline
its doors opened to thieves, dying, disappearing
swaggerers coming in
thieves going out
deceivers rising
liars falling down
Stand up on the river bank. Your bone, your skin, your flesh is still tender
you are alive, you are so alive . . .

Hesperis and what it bore of ash, water, and lightning
the wind of wide lands that has moved the river trees
is calling you by your name

the face of dust that writing has filled
the ocean sun that has colored slopes and forests
the hand of leaves falling on you following the evening, is calling you by
     your name . . .

Hesperis is calling you by your name for every year its sons were slaughtered
     and it says:
Through the ash I saw you were fire, your fire is in you, your fire is you . . .

"هسبريس" تناديك باسمك: قمْ أيها الجسد المرمري،
لقد دق كل غريب على بابها، فانتفخْ بالدماء
وحركْ جناحيك ، إضرب على حافة النهر في سفن الغرباء

"هسبريس" غد في أفول
أشرعتْ بابها للصوص، تموت تزول
يدخل الزائفونْ
يخرج السارقونْ
يصعد الخادعونْ
ينزل الكاذبونْ
قمْ، على حافة النهر عظْمك جلدك لحمك مازال غضا،
فإنك حي فإنك حي ..

" هسبريس" وما حملَتْ من رماد وماء وبرق وشيء
تناديك باسمك،
ريحُ السهوب وقد حركتْ شجر النهر،

وجه الغبار وقد ملأته الكتابة،

شمس المحيط وما لوَّنَتْ من سفوح وغاب،

يد الورق المتساقط فوقك غبَّ المساء، تناديك باسمك. . .

" هسبريس" تناديك باسمك في كل عام، تُذَبِّحُ أبناءَها وتقول:

من خلال الرماد رأيتك ناراً، فنارك فيك فنارك فيك. . .

This excerpt, by Mohammed-Khammar Guennouni, exemplifies the genera-
tion that broke with the classical tradition while still imagining a nation. Invok-
ing Hesperis, the mythical gardens supposed to have existed on the North Afri-
can Atlantic coasts (and the name of an important literary journal dating from
the colonial period and still published today),[48] Guennouni makes oblique refer-
ence to the many waves of colonization that North Africa has endured in praise
of its steadfastness and spirit.

While the term "modern poetry" often refers to the adoption of poetic tech-
niques used in Europe in the late 19th and early 20th century, modern poetry in
Morocco rode on the wave of other modernities in the Middle East and North
Africa—responding as they did to the war of independence in Algeria, Nas-
ser's reign in Egypt, and the Arab defeats in 1967. These events had effects in
the realm of literary style as well. As Bennis notes, this poetry "erupted from the
persistent desire to demolish another poetic text . . . in a society whose material
foundations had changed. It embodied the aspiration for . . . freedom and cre-
ativity. . . . [The] violation of the traditions and the laws of the classical text de-
stroyed an assumedly eternal sacredness by inventing a poetic counter-text . . .
whose old motivations had shriveled and whose links had been cut in one way or
another from the past" (1996: 41). It is not that the music has disappeared from
these later poems, only that they developed a more line-internal rhyme that, it
may be noted, finds its equivalent in the English translation more easily than the
rhyme-ending lines (*al-qafiya*) of the classical tradition. Indeed the majority of
poems in this volume exemplify and were chosen for this modernist aesthetic.[49]

As a counter-text, modern Moroccan poetry has always been tied to a cer-
tain revolutionary spirit. This has only intensified with the waves of protests
that have flowed over North Africa, from the Jasmine Revolution in Tunisia
in 2010,[50] to the protests of Tahrir Square in Egypt and the "20th of February
movement" in Morocco, a series of protests that began on that date in 2011, and
continued into the spring of 2012. Poetry continues to be political in Morocco,
even when not explicitly so.[51]

In the decades following independence the forums for poetry were largely
newspapers and journals, particularly the literary journal *Aqlaam* (Pens)

founded in Casablanca in 1964 by A. Ben Amrou, A. Stati, and A. Boualou and published by Dar Annashr Al Maghribia, and the French language journal *Souffles* founded by Abdellatif Laâbi in 1966.[52] These journals catered to an educated elite class of politically engaged artists and intellectuals.[53] What's more, many of these authors have been published by pioneers (women and men) in the publishing industry who recognized and believed in these emerging poets. Publishing houses such as Afrique-Orient Publications (in Casablanca and Beyrouth), Al Haram Press (Tetuan), Dar Thaqafa (Casablanca), Tansift Publications (Marrakech) and Toubkal Publishing House (Casablanca) are responsible for the publication of some of the most important writers in Morocco. Despite the rising presence of Moroccan presses at international book fairs, however, these publishing houses still continue to struggle financially. Moroccan poets who write in French, on the other hand, have often sought publishers in France (La Difference, Éditions du Seuil, L'Harmattan), or have published books as cooperative ventures between two presses, one Moroccan, one French. There are also some Arabic/Spanish translations and collaborations. In 1996, the Moroccan House of Poetry was established by Mohammed Bennis, Mohammed Bentalha, Hassan Najmi and Salah Bousrif (all published here). The authors who belong to the House of Poetry include novelists, playwrights, and poets who write in Arabic, French, Spanish, Tamazight, and Moroccan Arabic.

Towards a Moroccan Modernist Aesthetic

In reading contemporary Moroccan poetry we find themes that characterize other post-colonial literatures—nationalism (and the idealism and romanticism it spawns), nostalgia in the face of urbanization, the concern with place, and with cities in particular. Moroccan poetry is often a resistance literature—to patriarchy and gender constraints, to class oppression. But the poems also respond to larger literary trends in the Arab and Western world - surrealism, for example (see the poems of Jamal Boudouma in this volume), and the development of modern or 'free' verse. Given the material conditions of life in Morocco since independence—mass urbanization, agricultural mechanization and a resulting loss of peasantry (though not a loss of poverty)—it is not surprising that nostalgia permeates much contemporary poetry. While nostalgia for the countryside is present, longings for the traditional medina, or old city, is particularly prominent, as in the poem "Scenes of the City," by Mohammed Bennis,

I went out as usual to the old city at night
the silence of the street surrounding me
and the lights of streetlamps
pouring sleep into the eyes of the alley, showering me
with their yellow pallor, as I fill up my palm
with the flowers of the wilting wind.

Then I look once more.
I gaze into the emptiness, to see you
You, my old city, I forever see you:
dust of the storms of ages
covers the balconies of your houses, the colors of paint,
clothing the plaster, whose carvings repeat the song of sadness.

Dust of the storms of ages
gathering on the bricks of minarets, and on green-roofed mausoleums
on the entrances of markets, rising
above the advance of branches.

خرجت إلى المدينة في المساء كعادتي
صمت الطريق يلفني
وأضواء المصابيح
تسيل النوم في جفن الدروب ترشني
بصفرتها فأملأ راحتي
بورد ذابل الريح.

وأنظر مرة أخرى
أحدق في الفراغ لكي أراك
وانت مدينتي أبدا أراك:
غبار عواصف الأزمانْ
علا شُرف المنازل، صبغة الألوان.
كسا جبسا، يواصل نقشُهُ ترنيمة الأحزان.

غبار عواصف الأزمان
تراكم فوق آجور المآذن ، فوق أضرحة بخضرتها ،
وفوق مداخل الأسواق ترفعها
مقدمة من الأغصان.

In this excerpt and in poems by other authors, the city is alive—its alleys have eyes, its body covered with the dust of ancient storms. It is old and tattered, bleeding with shadows, obscure and bemoaned.

Abdesselem Mousaoui gives us an example of nostalgia for a more pastoral scene, in "Forest of Letters":

> And from the ornaments of the walls
> fresh details burst forth
> and I see the threshing floor . . . over there
> And my dead father
> jumps in the midst of dust and wheat
> In his hands a mule groans from the whip's anger
> Over there a bird races from stones
> straying from my side
>
> . . .
>
> . . .
>
> I will disappear in the forest of letters
> searching for my father
> to direct him to the labyrinth . . . meandering . . .
> to tell him:
> I walked so long in your shouting voice
> I saw your palms cracked with labor
> more eloquent than the hills of books I read
> But the question that—in my childhood—bothered you
> cut its teeth in my chest, oh father
> like the scythe in your fields!

ومن زخارف الجدران
تنبجس التفاصيل طرية،
فأرى البيدر . . . هناك
وأبي الذي مات
يقفز في الغبار والقمح
وفي يده بغلة تتأوه من غضبة السوط
هناك العصفورة تسابق حجرا
طائشا من جهتي
. . . .
. . . .

سأختفي في غابة الحروف
باحثا عن أبي
لأرشده إلى المتاه...
لأقول له:
قد سرت طويلا في صراخك
فرأيت كفيك المشقوقتين من التعب
أفصح من تلال الكتب التي قرأت
لكن السؤال الذي - في طفولتي - أغاظك
قد تسنن في صدري، يا أبي
كمنجل في حقولك!

In this poem, Moussaoui recalls the *badia*—the countryside of his youth, a scene that epitomizes a generation that moved away from the land and into the cities.

Nostalgia is also present in the work of Fes poet, Rachid Moumni. The poems in his volume, *The Cradles of Descent*, are replete with allusions to Sufism (as befits a book whose subject is the city of Fes, the spiritual center of Morocco and home to many Sufi orders). What's more, they epitomize the ethnographic conundrums mentioned above: how translate the multiple semiotic and sensory systems—word, image, even smell, texture and architecture –that comprise the work? How capture the total sensorium of the poem when poesis exceeds what can be represented in words? How translate the gesture of language?

The Gesture of Language

Like many modern poets Moumni uses the space on the page to express the rhythm and movement of the poem. This can be duplicated in the translation. What resists translation, however, are the qualities that are transmitted in the writing itself—that is, in the *hand-writing*; for like many poets past and present, Moumni adopts an old form of Arabic script, a style of calligraphy that dates from at least the eighteenth century. What's more, his poems are also accompanied by paintings done in ink—each poem has its correspondent image. For Moumni, these elements are all part of an integral and inter-dependent poetic expression.[54]

There are many styles of Arabic calligraphy, each indexing a specific historical moment and school. Moumni employs a particularly Moroccan script (*khat*) that was popular several centuries ago in both scholarly and religious texts.

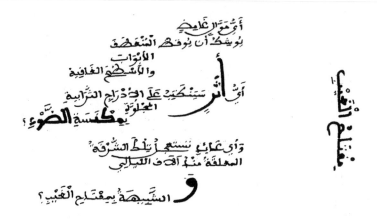

Figure 1. Calligraphy, "The Key Of Absence"

The calligraphers of the period did not "erase" the inked text, but added notes, additions, and titles in the margins, leaving a trail of their thought processes. Moumni evokes this presence of history by sometimes writing his titles perpendicular to the text (figure 1), requiring readers to actually turn the page in their hands in order to read the poem. Readers are thus involved in the tactile dance of body and text. The script Moumni employs is one that enlarges some letters in relation to others and that fluctuates in the thickness of the line. The density and inconsistency of letter size make its reproduction in type difficult. In the tension and flair of the lines, it expresses the personality of the artist. The form of both the word and the poem on the page contributes to the meaning of the poem as a whole, like gesticulation adds to language.

What's more, Moumni uses the same ink in his calligraphy that he does in his paintings. His poem-paintings are a materialization of the imaginal world of barzakh, he told me explicitly, the intermediary realm between flesh and spirit where the imagination begins to condense into material form and where material forms are spiritualized, understood as symbols on the path to gnosis.[55]

The ink painting that accompanies the poem entitled "The Key to Absence" brings the gaze into the twisting lanes of the old city. There is a doorway in

Figure 2. Painting accompanying "The Key To Absence"

the center of the painting, archways are visible, and the chiaroscuro that distinguishes the streets from the walls reflects the absence and presence that thematize the poem. In the text itself Moumni stresses the word "EFFECTS", imbuing the inked lines with the weight of history. Although the sediment of time is swept clean with light, it still lives in the hidden melodies, the shadows. Much like Bennis' "dust of the storms of ages," the traces of history are inscribed in the earth (the poem is transliterated here so that the non-Arabic speaker may 'hear' the words):

The Key of Absence

what hidden melodies
ayyu muwalin ghaamidhin

nearly awaken the twisting lanes
yushiku an yuqiẓa al-mun'atafa

the doors
al-abwaba

and the slumbering roofs
wa al-astuha al-ghafiyah

what EFFECTS will be written on the earthen stairs
ayyu ATHARIN sa yankatibu 'ala ad-draji ath-thurabiyyati

    swept clean
    al-majluwati

        with a broom of light?
        bi miknasati ad-daw'i

what returner does that balcony hasten home
wa ayyu 'aidin tast'ajilu tilka ash-shurfatu

hanging for thousands of nights
al-mu'allaqatu mundhu alafi l-layali

    like a key to absence?
    WA ash-shabihatu bi miftahi al-ghaybi?

Like many Moroccan poets, Moumni draws heavily upon Sufi symbolism and metaphor—the concept of absence as a spiritual state being particularly salient. Absence from earthly realities signals a presence to the Divine; absence is the home of the seeker—a residence whose balcony beckons. Absence lives behind the doors of the labyrinthine streets of the Fes medina (the labyrinth was also present in Moussaoui). He alludes to the pre-Islamic poetry called the Hung Odes (المعلقات) that are said to have been hung on or in the Kaaba at Mecca,[56] referencing as well the epic *One Thousand and One Nights*, which contains much poetry.[57]

I linger on Moumni's oeuvre, as it exemplifies how the reader (and the translator) must grapple with many dimensions of form in Moroccan poetry—some quite resistant to linguistic representation. It is in such contexts that discussions about the limits of translatability emerge. How create the affective depth carried by local metaphors into another language and culture? How conjure the "effects" fabricated from the smell of ink, the curve of a line, the sound-symbolism specific to a culture, the architecture embedded in the image? These questions inhabit and impel the translator, who knows that there is never fidelity between source and target text, yet who is driven by what Derrida has called "the promise of translation"—the idea of an ultimate albeit imperfect communicability. Translation requires an understanding of not only the dense metaphoric allusions informed by history and the bodily orientation of a culture (the sociocultural "habitus" in which the poem was born), but a sensitivity to the music and form of the poem, as well as the geometries that inform them. Translation is an ethnographic gesture.

Poet, novelist and essayist, the late Abdelkebir Khatibi suggests that we linger in that promise, in the "thresholds" of what remains impermeable to translation. Using the metaphor of inter-cultural love, and particularly the voice, to evoke both the desire and difficulties of such encounters, he says:[58]

The sex of a voice is like the threshold of a meeting. Sometimes, he only needed a telephone call to decide to take a car or a plane, to approach this voice, accompanying it into its mouth, its breath, its country and language of tenderness.

Le sexe d'une voix est comme le seuil d'une rencontre. Parfois, lui suffisait un appel téléphonique pour qu'il se décide à prendre la voiture ou l'avion, approchant cette voix, l'accompagnant dans sa bouche, son souffle, son pays et la langue d'attendrissement.

And further:

Mixed marriages: crossroads of beings, languages, signatures, ancestral memories. Does this woman think she has made a mistake in partners by changing continents for him? Even still 'continental drift' remains a poetic metaphor, he says to himself. A mysterious sentence: to keep as is, like an incomprehensible word, slightly insane. (Aimance, p. 96, 104).

Les mariages mixtes: croisée des chemins entre les êtres, les langues, les signatures, les mémoires les plus ancestrales. Croit-elle, cette femme, s'être trompée de partenaire en changeant de continent pour lui? Il se dit: Même la "dérive des continents" demeure encore une métaphore poétique. Phrase toute mystérieuse: la garder telle quelle, ainsi qu'une parole incompréhensible, légèrement insensée.

Khatibi invokes the voice as a symbol of sex and as a threshold; the voice, which is always sonic, always ineffable, is both a unique signature and a barzakh that traverses; the voice calls him across mediation (a telephone) and impels him to travel (in transport) to meet it. Khatibi is well-known for employing bilingualism as a metaphor for the encounter of differences. The "threshold of meeting" he describes is also the threshold of translation—the place of "continental drift" where meetings but also partings take place, the floating away of the same land to become different bodies. The ambiguity of the French is noteworthy: "*la garder telle quelle ainsi qu'une parole incompréhensible, légèrement insensée.*" . . . *keep it/ her as is, like an incomprehensible word, slightly insane.* Is it the sentence, the metaphor or the woman herself who is baffling? It may be all of the above. And it is from this mystery of ineffable unknowing that poetry and its translation emerge, what Benjamin refers to as "the unfathomable, the mysterious, the 'poetic,' something that a translator can reproduce only if he is also a poet."

Gender and Genre

Thresholds of all kinds exist in the poetry in this anthology, including the thresholds challenged and crossed by women writers. Against the patronization present in the male voice (*keep her as she is, like an incomprehensible word, slightly insane*) the poems by the women poets in this volume are "writing the feminine body into being," as Hélène Cixous exhorts women to do. The poems are self-conscious creations of the feminine subject, where the subject is not "an entity half-concealed behind events, but a changeable formula for managing oneself during them."[59] These poems sometimes read as anthems to feminine desire, but also lamentations of the feminine soul, as in the poem "My Name is Rain" by Malika El Assimi. In this poem, the female protagonist changes her name, thereby transforming herself, and by extension her gender, into another entity. The author plays on the meaning of her name—Malika—which means "queen/ sovereign," but also the "owner" or "possessor":

My name is Rain

I changed my name a while ago
When the storms
Hurled branch to branch
When the winds
Drove masses of clouds from over the sea
So that sorrow would sail away from the flowers
I named myself the waters washing the branches and the trees

Sweeping away dirt from inside the hearts,
From cloth and stones . . .
I decided to be called . . .
"Rain"

*   *   *

I own nothing but my torment
I own nothing but estrangement from loved ones
                                          and friends
I own nothing but the cries of my childhood
                                          and my melancholy
I own nothing
I will never be the Owner
My name is Rain . . .
Pouring down to water the earth holding the lover
A body I see in my dear strange dream
And with spring I continue to plant
Bunches of flowers in its soil
From my fertile and happy name

My daughter who was to be born from my blood one day
I kept this name to call her: my daughter Rain
But I will die no matter how long I live like a dog . . .
                                          and there will never be
A child of mine named: Rain
I love the breeze of freedom
Like a lonely wild cat
Running from forest to forest
Fleeing people and chains
And I am the rain . . .
Pouring my dewy drops on the earth
I will make blossoms grow, spreading them over the lover's body
So that it remains with the flowers . . .
Clothing it in spring, in the fall, in the summer-time
The perfume of flowers singing for him so he won't be alone
I have decided I would be called . . .
"Rain"
*   *   *

اسمي مطر

غيرت اسمي منذ حين

حينما العواصف

تقذف الأغصان للأغصان

حينما الرياح

تسوق من فوق المحيط كتلة السحب

لتنزح الأحزان من فوق الزهور

سميت نفسي كالمياه تنظف الأغصان و الشجر. . .

و تكنس الأدران في القلوب

و الثياب و الحجر. . .

قررت أن أدعى. . .

((مطر))

*   *   *

ماذا ملكت سوى عذابي

ماذا ملكت سوى اغترابي بين أحبابي

و أصحابي

ماذا ملكت سوى بكاء طفولتي

و سوى اكتئابي

أنا ما ملكت. . .

و لن أكون مليكة. . .

إسمي مطر

يهمي فيسقي تربة تحتها الجسد الحبيب

جسد أراه بحلمي الغالي الغريب

و مع الربيع أصر أن أزرع. . .

على حصياته باقات ورد

من إسمي الخصب السعيد

بنتي التي كانت ستخرج من دمي في ذات يوم

خبأت هذا الاسم كي أدعوها: يا بنتي مطر

لكنني سأموت مهما طال عمري كالكلاب. . .

و لن تكون

لي طفلة باسم: المطر

أهوى نسيم الحرية

كالقطة البرية المتفردة

تجري من الأدغال للأدغال

هربا من الإنسان و الأغلال

و أنا المطر. . .

سأصب قطراتي الندية في التراب

و سأنبت الباقات، أفرشها على الجسد الحبيب

لكي يظل مع الزهور. . .

تكسوه في فصل الربيع، و في الخريف، و في المصيف

يشدو له عطر الزهور فلا يظل هنا غريب. . .

قررت أن أدعى . . .

((مطر))

If calligraphy acts as a signature for Moumni, the name—the very proper name that Derrida asserts cannot be translated—can nonetheless be changed, and this is in part because El Assimi refuses "ownership." Rather, the notion of the subject is a malleable one for El Assimi, a more liquid and mutable substance like rain. Women poets write their own identities into being. They can also write their desire, as this excerpt from Wafaa Lamrani attests:

Getting Ready for You

For the stranger inhabiting the depths of my vows
his oboes resounding in a ferocious heartbeat
his earth cleansed with the seduction of murder
For his wound　　　his feasts
For the language of his things
Once in a poem
　　I consigned a jasmine to the loneliness of his forests

For the salt of his desires in my blood
For my old wine dream
For our night that wasn't
　　　　the affection in my heart pulsing
Let my sweetheart come to me
whispered an iris slumbering at the flowing
　　　　dawn
I will get tomorrow and yesterday ready
my visions, my orbits, my magic
my lofty loneliness
my breath, the fragrance of the meadows

my beauty and my desires
the celebration of words, my henna
my gusts and my breezes

Let the harvest come
I will ready my wheat for it
His absence like his presence is peopled and ripe
Time, the senses, conscience overflow with him
The copper coffee pot
my desk, my balcony, its flower
the desolate pillow, the mirror, the cloth
the thyme of his country and the splintered sky of the heart
        As if I had whispered him
Like my shadow
I slowly return to him

هيأت لك

للغريب الضارب في أغوار نذري
لمزاميره الطالعة من ضراوة الخفق
لأرضه المجلوة بفتنة القتل
لجرحه   لأعراسه
للغة أشيائه
لياسمينة أودعتها عزلة غاباته
ذات قصيدة

لملح شهواته في دمي
لحلمي النبيذي القديم
لليلتنا التي لم تكن
حفي نبضي
ليأتني الحبيب
همست غفوة قزحية عند فجرها
الساحي

سأهيىء آتي و أمسي
رؤاي مداري و سحري
وحدتي الشامخة

أنفاسي عطر البراري
زينتي و اشتهائي
احتفاء القول حناياي
عصفي و انسيابي

ليأتني الحصاد
سأهيء له قمحي
آهل و يانع كالحضور غيابه
طافح به الوقت الحواس السريرة
ركوة القهوة
شرفتي المكتب وردتها
الوسادة الموحشة المرآة الثوب
زعتر بلاده وسماء القلب المشروخة
كأني همسته
مثل ظلي
رويدا أفيء إليه

Unlike the absence thematized in Moumni's oeuvre, it is abundance that characterizes the poems of Lamrani. Her poems are exercises in excess, her larger oeuvre expressing sexual desire in more explicit terms than those exemplified here. Indeed the poems in her book are accompanied with erotic ink drawings by Moroccan painter al-Malihi. There is no ambiguity in the sexual connotations in her oeuvre. In this regard, Lamrani is speaking feminine desire into being, just as men have spoken their desire (homosexual and heterosexual) into being for centuries of romantic poetry.

Of course not all women's poetry is romantic. Rachida Madani writes in French about inequities, torture, as well as social and gendered injustice. This is an excerpt from her book *Wounds in the Wind* (*Blessures au Vent*, page 112–13):

I leave them the period
the comma
all the punctuation
and know-how
for a while now I've no longer surprised myself
no longer questioned myself
no longer stopped myself
   I am no more a poet

than I am the oasis and the doe
that you dream of
Pilgrim my old brother

My words have become livid
on the milky way of your fantasies
insomniac city
where I lose my name.
I hug your walls
my delirium conjugated with your fountains
my mouth on the mouths of your sewers
where I vomit the detritus
of an aborted poem
from where
a cry decomposing in my entrails
climbs to the sky
the one spontaneous cry
of a destroyed woman
emptied of herself
    agonizing.

Woman
I haven't finished dreaming of my childhood
haven't finished lifting each star
on the path of expectation
sentinels watching over my cemeteries
where I sit without counting
the tombs
without saying anything
watching for your return
Pilgrim my old brother.

Je leur laisse le point
la virgule
toute la punctuation
et le savoir-faire
depuis longtemps je ne m'étonne plus

ne m'interroge plus
ne m'arrête plus
    je ne suis plus poète
    que je ne suis l'oasis et la biche
    dont tu rêves
    Pèlerin mon vieux frère.

Mes mots sont devenus livides
sur la voie lactée de tes fantasmes
cité insomniaque
où je perds mon nom.
Et que je rase tes murs
mon délire conjugué à tes fontaines
ma bouche à tes bouches d'égout
où je vomis les détritus
d'un poème avorté
par où monte jusqu'au ciel
le cri décomposé de mes entrailles
le seul cri spontané
de la femme détruite
vidée d'elle-même
    agonisante.

Femme
je n'ai pas fini de rêver mon enfance
ni de lever chaque étoile
sur le sentier de l'attente
sentinelles veillant mes cimetières
où je m'assois sans compter
mes tombes
sans rien dire
guettant ton retour
Pèlerin mon vieux frère.

In Madani, nostalgia, the city, gendered poetics, as well as searing metaphor come together as beautiful social critique.

Conclusion

Modern Moroccan poetry is a particularly heteroglossic genre, laden with poly-semic turns of phrase and allusions to historical and present events. It is also dense with puns, which, as Bourdieu notes, depend on a shared *habitus*, a shared past of collective memory and language.[60] In *her* book entitled *Poetic Justice: The Literary Imagination and Public Life* philosopher Martha Nussbaum demon-strates how literature can shape the cultural and moral imagination in profound ways, exerting a vital impact on public discourse, law and debate. Through a re-structuring of the senses, literature provides a model for public empathy and so-cial ethics.[61] This is a testimony not only to the value of the Humanities in higher education but to the value of literature to social life more broadly. It is particu-larly applicable to the Middle East and North Africa where poetry maintains a vibrant oral and written life in festivals and public readings. When politicians seize and close down the House of Poetry, as they did in Morocco in 2009, we know that poets are doing something right! (It was subsequently reopened.)

Largely thanks to the internet, Moroccan poets now speak to international audiences in journals such as *Banipal* (http://www.banipal.co.uk) and *Arabic Lit-erature in English* (http://arablit.wordpress.com). Well-known poets like Mari-lyn Hacker have brought Rachida Madani to English-speaking readers. Pierre Joris and Habib Tengour have opened a millennium of North African poets to the world. In Nathalie Handal's work, *The Poetry of Arab Women: A Contempo-rary Anthology* (2001) two Moroccan poets are included. International poetry festivals like the PEN World Voices Festival in New York City have welcomed Moroccan poets and writers, as has Poet's House in New York. The journal *Souf-fles* is still being published.[62]

The poetic translations in this book of *Poetic Justice* are a contribution to these ongoing endeavors. They by no means represent a history of Moroccan po-etry. Indeed, with a few exceptions, the youngest generation of poets are *not* rep-resented here. That is a future project. In addition and despite dogged efforts, poems in Tamazight are few, though I have been able to include works already translated into French by Amazigh poets. The reader is directed to the *Insti-tut Royal de la Culture Amazighe* (IRCAM) for more works by these and other authors.

Poetry is a passion and not an enterprise. This volume is necessarily incom-plete. But it is, as the Sufis say, a "taste" of an oeuvre unknown to many, and it will hopefully instill appetite rather than satiate it. The "letters of time" have fallen into the hands of Moroccan poets, as they translate and write what they and their readers *are*. I am deeply grateful to all the poets who have enriched my life in profound and magnificent ways, both through their oeuvres and with their friendships.

Addendum: To the Poets

I have taken your words into my body, where they have become infused with another scent. What is the odor of two breaths, the taste of barzakh? These poems are an alchemy. I have sometimes changed your passive tenses into active verbs, your objects into subjects. Do not look for words in their original order. These poems bear your name, but they are not the ones you have given birth to. They have ventured out into the world, taken lovers, had their hearts broken, sailed on imaginal voyages. You may not recognize them now, weary, creased from squinting in the sunshine, spotted with age. But they recognize you. And that's what matters.

ملحق: كلمة موَجَّهة للشعراء

لقد حضنْتُ كلماتكم في دواخل جسدي، حيث أصبحت مُفعمة بعبير آخر غير عبيرها. فكيف يكون الطيب المُنبعث من نَفَسين؟ ما هو طعم البرزخ؟ هذه القصائد ضرْب من الخيمياء. لقد قمت أحيانا بتغيير أفعال مبنية للمعلوم إلى أخرى مبنية للمجهول، وأثبَتُّ عن فواعلِكم مفاعيلها. فلا تبحثوا عن كلماتكم في ترتيبها الأصلي. صحيح أن هذه القصائد تحمل أسماءكم، لكنها ليست تلك التي منحتموها الحياة. لقد قامت كلماتكم بجرأة المغامرة في الدنيا، عاشت تجربة العشق، وانفطرت قلوبها عند كل فراق، وجالت في رحلات الخيال. قد لا تتعرفون عليها الآن، وهي مُرهقة، مُتجعّدة القسمات من فرط الحوَص في ضوء الشمس، وقد غدت برشاء مع تقدم العمر. لكن كلماتكم تتعرّف عليكم. وهذا هو الأهم.

Addenda: Aux Poètes.

J'ai pris vos mots dans mon corps, où ils se sont imprégnés d'une odeur autre. Quelle odeur se dégage de deux souffles, le goût du barzakh? Ces poèmes sont une alchimie. J'ai parfois transformé les phrases passives en actives, les objets en sujets. Ne cherchez pas les mots dans l'ordre original. Ces poèmes portent vos noms, mais ils ne sont pas ceux auxquels vous avez donné naissance. Ils se sont aventurés dans le monde, ont pris des amants, leurs cœurs ont été brisés, ils ont navigué sur des bateaux de l'imaginal. Il se peut que vous ne les reconnaissiez plus, fatigués, plissés d'avoir trop regardé le soleil, tachés par l'âge. Mais ils vous reconnaissent. Et c'est ça l'important.

Notes

1. https://www.youtube.com/watch?v=suIQZ1jrTu4, accessed September 13, 2018.

2. This is not a Platonic model where ideals precede forms or where mind precedes or is separate from the body. Ibn al-'Arabi stresses the materiality of all ontological realms—corporeal, imaginal, spiritual, and everything in between.

3. Not skin (*peau*), which although it may act as a sonically permeable envelope between self and world in infants is nonetheless a border, a marker of separateness; but flesh (*chair*) See Anzieu 1985.

4. "The flesh is not matter, it is not mind, is not substance. To designate it we should need the old term element in the sense it was used to speak of water, air, earth and fire; that is, in the sense of a *general thing*, mid-way between the spatio-temporal individual and the idea, a sort of incarnate principle that brings a style of being wherever there is a fragment of being. The flesh is in this sense an "element" of Being. . . . If we can show that the flesh is an ultimate notion, that it is not the union or compound of two substances but thinkable by itself, if there is a relation of the visible with itself that traverses me and constitutes me as a seer, this circle which I do not form, which forms me, this coiling over of the visible upon the visible can traverse, animate other bodies as well as my own."

5. This continuity is marked by chiasms—intersections and differentiations. Chiasms are like veils that envelop a world or a body, but that may be pierced, broken open, touched and transformed. If chiasms are like skin, worlds themselves are incarnate, elemental, flesh.

6. "One's own body is in the world just as the heart is in the organism" Merleau-Ponty writes in the *Phenomenology of Perception*. PP: 245/209).

7. Both philosophers however are grappling with the paradox of separateness and unity, of distance and proximity (*tanzih* and *qarb* in Arabic).

8. For Merleau-Ponty flesh is the continuity that links the perceiver's body with the world in what he calls an "intercorporeity." This continuity is marked by chiasms—intersections and differentiations. A chiasm is based on the double helix of genetics, it is one strand made up of two coils. If for Ibn al-'Arabi there are nothing but barzakhs, for Merleau-Ponty, there are nothing but chiasms, what he also refers to as the "thickness of flesh between the seer and the thing." Merleau-Ponty ibid 1968:135. There are also many resonances here with Karen Barad's notion of an "agential cut"—the way experience is intersected in any given time and place to produce a phenomenon she calls an "intra-action" Barad 2007.

9. Roger Abrahams 1976, 1983; Dan Ben Amos 1976; and later Joel Sherzer 1983; 1987; 2002.

10. Bauman 1984.

11. Mills 1991.

12. Women performers are called shikhat in Morocco. They perform a genre called al-l'aita. See Kapchan 1996 and 2002.

13. In the nineteen seventies, anthropologists, ethnographers of speaking, folklorists and linguists began inquiring into the relation of form and meaning in oral texts. While attending to poetics (assonance, parallelism, alliteration, repetition, etc.), they also acknowledged that embodied *performance*—the intonation and timbre of the voice, for example—played an integral part in the transmission of knowledge (including non-referential knowledge). Indeed it was at this time that scholars working in the realm of pragmatics elucidated the importance of *language in context*, demonstrating that communication and interpretation are context-driven; that is, they depend on pre-existing knowledge, cultural assumptions, aesthetics and inferences as well as gesture and its environment. Meaning emerged in performance, grounded in the body, its cultural milieux and affective repertoires.

14. Roman Jakobson defines three kinds of translation: intralingual, a "re-wording" or "interpretation" of verbal signs with others in the same language; interlingual, a translation of verbal signs of one language into another; and inter-semiotic, which he defines as a "transmutation," and an "interpretation of verbal signs by means of signs of non-verbal sign systems" (Jakobson, Roman. 1966/59. "On Linguistic Aspects of Translation" in Reuben Brower (ed.), *On Translation*. New York: OUP, pp. 232–9.)

15. Roman Jakobson called this the "narrative" as opposed to the "narrated" event (1971). See also Bauman 1986; Briggs 1988.

16. "Notre relation aux lieux est irrationnelle. Il y a des choses qui dépassent la raison dedans. Il reste toujours une force incomprise et invincible (magnétisme, magie, gravitation..) qui nous lie à un chemin, une demeure, une ville, un campagne, un coin retiré d'un domaine, d'un jardin . . . . nous sommes les personnages secrets d'un grand récit multi-millénaire que se racontent les lieux" Aissa, Idriss. (personal communication 2016).

17. Jackson 2012:8.

18. It is worth noting that working with authors who write and publish their own cultural and poetic texts is different than "translating" the tacit meanings of culture in both participant observation and then in the narrative rendition of experience to follow. There is a more equal playing field for one thing, and perhaps more accountability in the process.

19. These scholars were influenced by the work of Russian linguist Roman Jakobson, as well as Lévi–Strauss' work on native American myth and Sapir's on Native American languages.

20. An example of this is Steven Feld's work among the Kaluli, of Papua New Guinea where he demonstrates that certain sung phrases are "iconic" not only of birdsong, but of the ancestors (Feld 1985). Anthropologists also applied Peirce's concept of indexicality (a sign that points to another) and iconicity (a sign that resembles another) in their analysis of cultural texts. See Silverstein 1966; Feld 1985; Peirce 1982; 1998.

21. For a recent example see Kohn 2013.

22. While it was impossible for Dell Hymes to attend a performance of a Chinook ritual at that time, for example, he nonetheless attempted to reanimate the text by reading its performative qualities. Through an analysis of repetition, he reconstructed the poetics of the performance and thus (in part) a Chinook verbal aesthetic.

23. See Henderson 2017.

24. The term comes from J.L. Austin's book *How to Do Things with Words* (1960) and the development of Speech Act Theory, which examined not just what words mean but what they do in the world.

25. Kapchan 2017.

26. Voloshinov 1973.

27. Benjamin 1969.

28. Derrida 1985:123.

29. Rich, Adrienne. 1978. *Dream of a Common Language*. NYC: Norton.

30. Crapanzano 2004; see also Muñoz 2005.

31. Austin 1962.

32. Steiner 1998:193

33. Benjamin 1969:70.

34. Jakobson 1960.

35. "What is "the spirit of a culture"? How come to know it? How presume to translate it? These are large and existential questions and largely ignore that all translations—whether linguistic or cultural—"domesticate" the source text; they carry "an ensemble of values, beliefs, and representations that are inscribed in language without the user's awareness or control." Venuti 2018 p. ix. Venuti further notes that "the claim of value-free translation research is spurious. Any theoretical discourse creates translation as an object for a specific kind of knowledge through the ideas and methods that characterize that discourse." Venuti 2018: x. Yet while philosophers ponder these paradoxes and conundrums in abstraction, ethnographers tackle them in the practices and performances of everyday life.

36. See the work of Benjamin 1968; Steiner 1975; Derrida 1985.

37. Ricoeur 2006/2004.

38. Venuti ibid.

39. Ricoeur 2006/2004: 21. Education is the cornerstone of participant observation, the method of the ethnographer. Tim Ingold argues that education, and not ethnographic inscription, is the goal of anthropological field work. https://culanth.org/fieldsights/841-enough-about-ethnography-an-interview-with-tim-ingold, accessed September 13, 2018.

40. Namely Ibn al-'Arabi (ibid) and Merleau-Ponty (ibid).

41. In fact this is precisely to what the field of humanistic anthropology aspires. Founded in the 1970s, the website of the flagship journal of the same name declares that humanistic anthropology "draw[s] on the creative humanities not only as data but as inspiration and genres for anthropological production, but it also demands the rigor of the sciences of humanity. It values work that bridges disciplinary splinterings to bring out the various processes of living as humans in the world, explicitly including the ac-

tivities of anthropologists. It recognizes that human reality is a relational and proces-
sual thing-in-flux in which we creative primates actively participate and that our work
has consequences in the world. It thus includes the potential to change social and phys-
ical environments through improved understandings of the diversely multicultural and
polyvalent nature of our world. Trademarks of humanistic anthropology include em-
phases on writing and the creative use of language, with concern for the relevance of
the discipline for the broader human world." *Humanistic Anthropology* publishes poems,
narratives, stories as well as translations that create knowledge aesthetically as well as
theoretically. (As its late editor, Edith Turner exhorted me, "enough analysis!") See also
Jackson 1995, 2012, 2103; Pandian and Mclean 2017; Stewart 2004; Taussig 1006; 2015;
Rosaldo 2013; Stoller.

    42. Kapchan 2000.

    43. Literally, Arab Literature in the Furthest West North Africa .

    44. See Joris and Tengour 2013; Handal 2001; Laâbi 2003; Madani 2006, 2012
along with a spate of online publications. Another anthology of Moroccan Literature in
Arabic entitled Highlights of Moroccan Poetry in Arabic Literature (النبوغ المغربي في الأدب
العربي) was edited by Abdellah Guennoun (1908–1989) in Tetuan in the Spanish-
administered zone in 1934. The circulation, sale or exhibition of this book was explicitly
banned by the French military administration in the rest of Morocco in a statement that
was issued in a newspaper. (My thanks to Driss Marjane for bringing this to my
attention.)

    45. "Il est significatif que nos grands poètes, penseurs et hommes de sciences restent
ignorés en Occident. Si je suis un descendant d'une famille symbolique d'écrivains arabes
modernes, musulmans et chrétiens, sans aucune différence, je suis aussi le descendant de
ces musulmans et de ces Arabes qui ont donné l'hospitalité à la philosophie grecque et
contribué à son développement, au moment où elle était condamnée par les Occidentaux.
Ils ont inventé l'algèbre, ce sont des Maîtres de la logique et de l'astronomie, des méde-
cins, des savants, mais aussi de grands mystiques, des inspirateurs de la modernité poé-
tique, littéraire et artistique en Europe." In *Les Plis Infinis de la Parole* Entretien avec Mo-
hammed Bennis, Dec 2013. translation Kapchan.

    46. Medvedev, P.N. and M.M. Bakhtin. 1978. *The Formal Method in Literary Schol-
arship: A Critical Introduction to Sociological Poetics* Baltimore and London: The Johns
Hopkins University Press).

    47. For the influence of pre-Islamic poetry on Moroccan poetics, see Bennis: http://
www.amourier.com/580-dans-les-plis-infinis-de-la-parole.php, accessed August 23,
2016.

    48. "Hespéris began in 1921 as a merger between two older serials, "Archives Berberes"
and the *Bulletin de l'Institut des Hautes-Études Marocaines*. In 1960, it merged with an-
other serial, "Tamuda", to become "Hespéris-Tamuda", a journal that is still published to-
day." http://amirmideast.blogspot.com/2012/05/open-access-journal-hesperis-archives
.html, accessed October 22, 2014.

    49. In the first decade of this project I was often confined to the poems I was able
to access either from archives, from dusty chapbooks found by chance in bookstores, or
from type-written pages conveyed to me in person or by mail.

50. The Jasmine Revolution began after the self-immolation of Mohamed Bouazizi, a fruit seller. This act sparked protests and civil disobedience that eventually led to the ousting of president Zine El Abidine Ben Ali and then to democratic elections.

51. Poets recite verses in Moroccan Arabic during the protests in Casablanca: https://www.youtube.com/watch?v=ecxJPQNUKu0, accessed May 9, 2016.

52. Indeed, the Moroccan Ministry of Culture has published a volume explicitly entitled *Diwan Sh'ir Maghrebi Romansi, A Volume of Moroccan Romantic Poetry*, edited by Abdeljalil Nadhem (also director of the publishing house Dar Toubkal).

53. Poet and literary scholar Mohammed Bennis notes in his dissertation that before 1964 only three poem collections had been published—one by Mohamed Sabri, one by Abbdelkrim Tebbal, and another by Mohamed El Maïmouni.

54. Calligraphy is not only a highly developed art form in the Islamic world, it is a spiritual discipline as well. Despite that fact that writing is only a substitute for the voice in the Islamic tradition (the voice considered the unmediated link to the soul), calligraphy is considered closer to the soul than other forms of print because it is written by hand. Calligraphy represents the "autograph" or "signature" of the author (Messick 1992).

55. Moumni's book is also on YouTube with audio-visual accompaniment. https://www.youtube.com/watch?v=9g-1kajxCtU&feature=youtu.be (accessed September 21, 2016).

56. Sells 1989.

57. Pinault 1992.

58. Khatibi 1990.

59. Goffman 1986/74: 573.

60. "If witticisms strike as much by their unpredictability as by their retrospective necessity, the reason is that the *trouvaille* that brings to light long buried resources presupposes a *habitus* that so perfectly possesses the objectively available means of expression that it is possessed by them, so much so that it asserts its freedom from them by realizing the rarest of possibilities that they necessarily imply. The dialectic of meaning of the language and the 'sayings of the tribe' is a particular and particularly significant case of the dialectic between *habitus* and institutions, that is, between two modes of objectification of past history, in which there is constantly created a history that inevitably appears, like witticisms, as both original and inevitable" (Bourdieu 1990:57). Puns are particularly present in the genre of zajal, but the close cultural reference is present in all the poetry, whatever its language of composition.

61. Nussbaum 1995: xv.

62. http://www.lehman.cuny.edu/deanhum/langlit/french/souffles/.

Works Cited

Abrahams, Roger. 1983. *The Man-of-Words in the West Indies: Performance and the Emergence of Creole Culture*. Baltimore: Johns Hopkins University Press.

————. 1976. The Complex Relation of Simple Forms. In Ben-Amos, Dan. 1984. *Folklore Genres*. Austin: University of Texas Press, pp. 193–214.

Anzieu, Didier. 1985. *Le Moi-Peau*. Paris: Dunod.

Barad, Karen. 2007. *Meeting the Universe Halfway: Quantum Physics and the Entanglement of Matter*. Durham: Duke University Press.

Bauman, Richard. Bauman, Richard. 1986. *Story, Performance, Event: Contextual Studies of Oral Narrative*. Cambridge: Cambridge University Press.

————. 1984. *Verbal Art as Performance*. Prospect Heights, Ill: Waveland Press.

Bauman, Richard and Joel Sherzer, Eds. 1974. *Explorations in the Ethnography of Speaking*. New York and Cambridge: Cambridge University Press.

Ben-Amos, Dan. 1976. Analytical Categories and Ethnic Genres. In Ben-Amos, Dan. 1984. *Folkore Genres*. Austin: University of Texas Press, pp. 215–242.

Benjamin, Walter. 2013/1968. "The Task of the Translator," In *Illuminations*. Translated by Harry Zohn, edited and with an Introduction by Hannah Arendt; preface by Leon Wieseltier. *Illuminations: [Essays and Reflections]*. New York: Schocken Books, 2013.

Bentalha, Mohamed. 2010. *Lectures Critiques de la Poèsie Marocaine Contemporaine: Analyse et Evaluation*. Casablanca: Fadā'āt Mustaqbaliyyah.

Bennis, Mohammed. 1979, *Zahira ash-shi'r al-mu'asir fi l-Maghrib* (The Phenomenon of Contemporary Poetry in Morocco). Rabat: National Archives.

Bennis, Mohammed and Jacques Ancet, 2016. "Dans les plis infinis de la parole," Entretien réalisé pour la revue *Europe*, par Jacques Ancet avec Mohammed Bennis http://www.amourier.com/580-dans-les-plis-infinis-de-la-parole.php, accessed September 28, 2016.

Boukous, Ahmed. 1995. *Societé, Langues et Cultures au Maroc*. Casablanca: Annajah al-Jadida.

Bourdieu, Pierre. 1990. *The Logic of Practice*. translated by Richard Nice. Palo Alto: Stanford University Press.

Briggs, Charles. 1988. *Competence in Performance: The Creativity of Tradition in Mexicano Verbal Art*. Philadelphia: University of Pennsylvania Press.

Cixous, Helène. 1991. *Coming to Writing and Other Essays*. Cambridge, MA: Harvard University Press.

Chittick, William. 1989. *The Sufi Path of Knowledge: Ibn al-Arabi's Metaphysics of the Imagination*. New York: State University of New York Press.

Christian, Barbara. 1988. The Race for Theory. *Feminist Studies* 14 (1): 78.

Crapanzano, Vincent. 2004. *Imaginative Horizons: An Essay in Literary-Philosophical Anthropology*. Chicago: University of Chicago Press.

Derrida, Jacques. 1985. *The Ear of the Other*, trans. Peggy Kamuf. Lincoln & London: University of Nebraska Press.

Deleuze, Gils and Felix Guattari. 1987. *A Thousand Plateaus: Capitalism and Schizophrenia*. Minneapolis: University of Minnesota Press.

Elinson, Alexander. 2013. "Darija and Changing Writing Practices in Morocco," *International Journal of Middle Eastern Studies* 45: 715–730.

Poetic Justice

Ennaji, Moha. 2005. *Multilingualism, Cultural Identity, and Education in Morocco.* Springer Publishing, p. 127.

Feld, Steven. 1982. *Sound and Sentiment: Birds, Weeping, Poetics, and Song in Kaluli expression.* Philadelphia: University of Pennsylvania Press.

Goffman. Erving. 1986/74. *Frame Analysis.* Boston: Northeastern University Press.

Handal, Nathalie, editor. 2001. *The Poetry of Arab Women: A Contemporary Anthology.* Northampton, MA: Interlink Publishing.

Hymes, Dell. 1981[1975]. "Breakthrough into Performance." In *In Vain I Tried to Tell You*: Essays in Native American Ethnopoetics, 79–141.

———. 1964. "Introduction: Toward Ethnographies of Communication". *American Anthropologist.* 66 (6): 1–34.

Jackson, Michael D. 2013. *Lifeworlds: Essays in Existential Anthropology.* Chicago: University of Chicago Press.

———. 2012. *Between One and Another.* Berkeley and Los Angeles: University of California Press.

———. 1995. *At Home in the World.* Durham: Duke University Press.

Jakobson, Roman. 1978. *Six Lectures on Sound and Meaning,* Cambridge, MA: MIT Press.

———. 1971. *Words and Language.* The Hague: Mouton de Gruyter.

———. "Linguistics and Poetics", in T. Sebeok, ed., *Style in Language,* Cambridge, MA: M.I.T. Press, 1960, pp. 350–377.

Joris, Pierre. 2014. *Barzakh: Poems 2000–2002.* Boston: Black Widow Press.

Joris, Pierre and Habib Tengour, Eds. 2013. *Poems for the New Millenium: The University of California Press of North African Literature.* Berkeley and Los Angeles: University of California Press.

Kapchan, Deborah. 2017. "The Challenge of Bi–Sensoriality," *Society of Ethnomusicology Student News* 13.2. https://cdn.ymaws.com/www.ethnomusicology.org/resource/group/dc75b7e7-47d7-4d59-a660-19c3e0f7c83e/publications/SEMSN13.2.pdf

———. 2015. Body. In *Keywords in Sound.* In Novak, David and Matt Sakakeeney, eds. Durham: Duke University Press.

———. 2015. "Slow Activism: Listening and Lingering in the Longue Durée." *International Journal of Middle Eastern Studies* 48: 115–119.

———. 2008. The Promise of Sonic Translation: Performing the Festive Sacred in Morocco. *American Anthropologist* Vol 110 (4) : 467–483. [Reprinted in Frank Korom, editor, *The Anthropology of Performance* pp. 217–233. Wiley-Blackwell. Reprinted as well in *Practicing Sufism: Sufi Politics and Performance in Africa,* ed. Abdelmajid Hannoum. London: Routledge, 2016.]

———. "Translating Folk Theories of Translation," In Rubel, Paula G. and Abraham Rosman, Eds. *Translating Cultures: Perspectives on Translation and Anthropology.* Oxford: Berg. pp. 135–152.

———. 2001. Performing Depth: Translating Moroccan Culture in Modern Verse. In, *Colors of Enchantment: Visual and Performing Arts of the Middle East,* edited by Sherifa Zuhur, Cairo: American University in Cairo Press.

———. 2000. "Driss Mesnousi: Zajal" *Méditerranéens* 11 (Winter 1990–2000): 45–47.

Khatibi, Abdelkebir. 1990. *Love in Two Languages,* translated by Richard Howard. Minneapolis: University of Minnesota Press.

Kisliuk, Michelle. 2017. "Writing the Magnified Musicking Moment," In Kapchan, Deborah, Ed. *Theorizing Sound Writing.* Middleton, Ct: Wesleyan University Press, 86–114.

Kohn, Edouardo. 2013. *How Forests Think: Towards an Anthropology Beyond the Human,* University of California Press.

Kusserow, Adrie. "Anthropoetry," In Pandian, Anand and Stuart McLean, Eds. 2017. *Crumpled Paper Boat: Experiments in Ethnographic Writing.* Durham: Duke University Press, pp. 71–90.

Laâbi, Abdellatif. 2017. *In Praise of Defeat: Selected Poems.* translated by Donald Nicholson-Smith. With an introduction by Pierre Joris. Brooklyn: Archipelago Books.

———. 2005. *La Poésie Marocaine de L'Indépendence à Nos Jours.* Paris: La Difference.

———. 2003. *The World's Embrace: Selected Poems.* San Francisco: City Lights.

Lakoff, George & Mark Johnson. 1999. *Philosophy in the Flesh.* New York: Basic Books.

Lévi-Strauss, Claude. 1958. *Anthropologie Structurale (Structural Anthropology,* trans. Claire Jacobson and Brooke Grundfest Schoepf, 1963).

MacDougall, Susa. 2016. "Enough about Ethnography: An Interview with Tim Inglod. Dialogues, *Cultural Anthropology* website, April 5. https://culanth.org/fieldsights/841-enough-about-ethnography-an-interview-with-tim-ingold.

Madani, Rachida. 2012. *Tales of a Severed Head.* Translated by Marilyn Hacker. New Haven: Yale University Press.

———. 2006. *Blessures au Vent.* Paris: La Différence.

Magidow, Melanie Clouser. 2016. "Trending Classic: the Cultural Register of Moroccan Malhun Poetry," *The Journal of North African Studies Vol.* 21, Iss. 2.

Medvedev, P.N. and M.M. Bakhtin. 1978. *The Formal Method in Literary Scholarship: A Critical Introduction to Sociological Poetics* Baltimore and London: The Johns Hopkins University Press.

Merleau-Ponty, Maurice. 2002/1962. *Phenomenology of Perception.* Translated by Colin Smith. New York and London: Routledge and Kegan Paul.

———. 1968/1964. *The Visible and the Invisible* (Alphonso Lingis, Trans.). Gallimard. 1969. *Visible and the Invisible.* Evanston: Northwestern University Press.

Messick, Brinkley. 1993. *The Calligraphic State: Textual Domination and History in a Muslim Society.* Berkeley and Los Angeles: University of California Press.

Mills, Margaret. 1991. *Rhetorics and Politics in Afghan Traditional Storytelling.* Philadelphia: University of Pennsylvania Press.

Narayan, Kirin. 2007. *My Family and Other Saints.* Chicago: University of Chicago Press.

Nussbaum, Martha. 1995. *Poetic Justice: The Literary Imagination and Public Life.* New York: Beacon Press.

Pandian, Anand and Stuart McLean, Eds. 2017. *Crumpled Paper Boat: Experiments in Ethnographic Writing.* Durham: Duke University Press.

Peirce, Charles Sanders. 1998. *The Essential Peirce*. Volume 2. Eds. Peirce edition Project. Bloomington IN: Indiana University Press.

———. 1982– *The Writings of Charles S. Peirce: A Chronological Edition*. Volumes 1–6. And 8. Eds. Peirce Edition Project. Bloomington I.N: Indiana University Press.

Pinault, David. 1992. *Story-Telling Techniques in the Arabian Nights*. London: Brill Publishers.

Ricoeur, Paul. 2006/2004. *On Translation*. Translated by Eileen Brennan. Introduction by Richard Kearney. New York and London: Routledge.

Rosaldo, Renato. 2013. *The Day of Shelly's Death: The Poetry and Ethnography of Grief*. Durham: Duke University Press.

Rothenberg, Jerome and Diane Rothenberg, Eds. 1983. *Symposium of the Whole: A Range of Discourse towards an Ethnopoetics*. Berkeley: University of California Press.

Rubel, Paula G. and Abraham Rosman, Eds. *Translating Cultures: Perspectives on Translation and Anthropology*. Oxford: Berg.

Sadiqi, Fatima. 2003. "Women, Gender and Language in Morocco." *Women and Gender*, Volume 1., p. 354.

Salah-Dine Hammoud, Mohamed (1982). "Arabization in Morocco: A Case Study in Language Planning and Language Policy Attitudes." Unpublished PhD dissertation for the University of Texas at Austin, Available from University Microfilms International, Ann Arbor, Michigan.

Sapir, Edward (1921). *Language: An Introduction to the Study of Speech*. New York: Harcourt, Brace and Company.

Sells, Michael. 1989. *Desert Tracings*. Middleton, CT: Wesleyan University Press.

Sherzer, Joel. (2002). *Speech Play and Verbal Art*. Austin: University of Texas Press.

Sherzer, Joel. (1987). "A Discourse-Centered Approach to Language and Culture." *American Anthropologist* 89: 295–309.

———. (1983). *Kuna Ways of Speaking: An Ethnographic Perspective*. Austin: The University of Texas Press.

Silverstein, Michael. 2003. "Translation, Transduction, Transformation: Skating "Glossando" on This Semiotic Ice," In Rubel, Paula G. and Abraham Rosman, Eds. *Translating Cultures: Perspectives on Translation and Anthropology*. Oxford: Berg, pp. 75–108.

———. 1976. "Shifter, Linguistic Categories and Cultural Description," In Basso, Keith H.; Selby, Henry A. *Meaning in Anthropology*. Albuquerque: University of New Mexico Press.

Slaoui, Mohamed Adib. 1986. *Notes from Moroccan Poetry: A Historical Study 1830–1960*. Rabat: Afrique Orient Publishers.

Steiner, George. 1975. *After Babel: Aspects of Language and Translation*. Oxford: Oxford University Press.

Stewart, Kathleen. 2004. *Ordinary Affects*. Durham: Duke University Press.

Stoller, Paul. 2008. *The Power of the Between: An Anthropological Odyssey*. University of Chicago Press.

———. 1997. *Sensuous Scholarship*. Philadelphia: University of Pennsylvania Press.

Taussig, Mick. 2015. *The Corn Wolf.* Chicago: University of Chicago Press.

———. 2006. *Walter Benjamin's Grave.* Chicago: University of Chicago Press.

Tedlock, Dennis. 1983. *The Spoken Word and the Work of Interpretation.* Philadelphia: University of Pennsylvania Press.

Toadvine, Ted. 2018. "Maurice Merleau-Ponty," The Stanford Encyclopedia of Philosophy. Edward N. Zalta, Ed. https://plato.stanford.edu/entries/merleau-ponty/, accessed September 2018.

Venuti, Lawrence. 2018. "Introduction: Conditions of Possibility," In *The Translator's Invisibility: A History of Translation.* New York and London: Routledge.

———. 1992. *Rethinking Translation: Discourse, Subjectivity, Ideology.* New York and London: Routledge University Press.

Voloshinov, V. N. 1973. *Marxism and the Philosophy of Language.* Boston: Harvard University Press.

Many of the poems in their original language can be found at
www.deborahkapchan.com.

Abdelghani, Mahmoud

Mahmoud Abdelghani (born in 1967 in Khouribga) lives in Rabat where he works as a professor of modern literature at Mohammed V University. His major publications in poetry include: حجرة وراء الأرض (*A Room Behind the Earth 1998*); عودة صانع الكمان (*The Return of the Violin Maker 2004*); أرض الصباح (*Land of the Morning 2007*); كم يبعد دون كيشوت؟ (*How far is Don Quixote? 2007*). Mahmoud Abdelghani has translated much of his poetry into English and Spanish.

Flowers

Soon snow will fall
on the stone inhabiting my heart
and I'll sleep with a kiss in my mouth
warming and protecting me
from the attack of my pain
making me dream
of the abyss below
And the flowers in my hand
to whom will I offer them?

Stars Scolding Me

I returned to my house
to replace the walls
that used to eavesdrop on me.
The small rocks were silent

and the open windows
closed by time.
It was a difficult task,
days sleeping in the walls
clouds hidden in stones.
I put new doors on
sunless rooms
and looked for memories
shattered on the tile.
I labored, lost
under the stars
that were watching and scolding me
from a distance.

Oh, White Page

Tell them oh white page
that we have lived together in a certain
place
similar to the heart
and mind.
Tell them that heavy rain
poured from my fingers.
Let them know
we have talked of everything
each of us
looking for his place in the other.
Tell them
that when the mind chatters
and spits out ideas
it sees you as if
it had known you before it was born.
Tell them that the poet's heart
circles you attentively
And when it bids you farewell
you follow him like a piece of moonlight.

You are the face that he alone reads
and will continue forever to be.

From Age to Age

This language delivered me from the pain of
the road that thirsts for walking more
than the foot, as Satan's wine thirsts for
grief. Once, like a Tuareg in the desert,
I crossed an intractable abandoned garden.
Turning towards the grass of childhood
that rises on its own like laughter I said,
as I pass from age to age, I refuse to live in
its memories.

Achaari, Mohamed

Mohamed Achaari (born in 1951 in Zerhoun) is a poet, a politician and a novelist. He works as a journalist for several newspapers, including the daily *Al-Massae* (The Evening). His major publications include: صهيل الخيل الجريحة (*The Neighing of Wounded Horses* 1978); عينان بسعة الحلم (*Eyes the Size of a Dream* 1981); سيرة المطر (*The Biography of Rain* 1988); يوم صعب (*A Hard Day, A Collection of Stories* 1992); مائيات (*Watercolors* 1994); حكايات صخرية (*Stone Tales* 2000); القوس و الفراشة (*The Arch and the Butterfly* 2010), among many others.

A Russian Doll

Night is an oversized coat
    like the overcoats of soldiers
trees hide in it
fields and seas
lies
and songs
a heavy body walks in it
dreams hide in it
    fears
    desires
    and dirges
carried by a weary soul
rays hide in it
extinguished planets
straying comets
and a heavy night
like the overcoats of soldiers

A Lesson in Bitterness

Bitterness is not a strange bed
not the residue of a dark day
not poems that save us from gloom
Bitterness my friend
is a train passing with dreamy eyes
and a face that almost speaks of hopelessness
so that your butchered heart leaps
and wet butterflies flutter around your pulse
All the burdened ceilings fall in upon you
and the distances and pavements flee from your feet
Bitterness my friend
is returning to a room that seizes upon the sound of
your steps
and runs away terrified
while you pursue its trace inflaming the wind
only to discover a rider on horseback
who travels behind dreamy eyes
and a face scattered in the whistle of a train.

A Balcony over Asphalt

A window falls from a building
onto the scorching street
where people walk on their dreams
more than on their feet
It clatters down with pots of basil
its curtains opening like a caftan
revealing the white breasts
of a woman who looks out
It falls without glass
without shutters
like a silent lake
where the viscous eyes of
a woman watering basil
splash
behind blue curtains
like migrating fish

A Stone Tale

A restless story dozes by my side
Nothing is clear but a woman
who almost kills herself
to be rid of her husband
because she loves another man
Since the first day she knew love
she has loved no one but him
But since the first day she knew marriage she has
known
only the other
She wants nothing the way it is
She wants to leave him
A traditional tale indeed . . .
But whatever the woman does
she will not leave her husband
It is too late
the two men have aged
And love is no longer a man
but a story
Nothing in it is clear but a woman
If she could find it within herself
she would escape the tale
release her life to the wind
embrace her lover's neck on trains
in cafés
sleep on his chest in parks and airports
astound him
and be astounded by him
play with his love
bow her head to his silence
pour down from his clouds
become perplexed in his longing
kindle her fire with his madness
and waste away for him
If she could find it within herself
she wouldn't sleep by her husband's side
like a widowed tale.

Adnan, Taha

Taha Adnan (born in 1970) grew up in Marrakech. He is a Moroccan poet and a writer. He has lived in Brussels since 1996 working for the Ministry for Francophone Education. His publications include: Transparences (*Transparencies* 2006); Je Hais l'Amour (*I Hate Love* 2010); Bye Bye Gillo (2013); Bruxelles, La Marocaine (*Brussels, The Moroccan* 2015); Ton Sourire est Plus Beau que le Drapeau National (*Your Smile is More Beautiful than the National Flag* 2016).

Rendez-Vous of Arab Love

My sweet,
Why did your suspicious telephone stubbornly refuse to answer?
I arrived at the rendez-vous on time minus two cigarettes
The *Café de l'Opera* was jumping as usual
The clients were a little too gallant for my tastes
Among them I seemed like a spot of oil
On a white shirt

A Flemish woman disguised as a baroness in a classic film
Observed me with suspicion clutching her handbag between her arms
Me, I pretended not to see anything
And threw back one beer after another

As if I had just escaped from a desert of thirst

My doe,
Beer costs three Euros here
Why are you so pitiless?
Can't you find something less expensive than the terrace of this bar?

A gypsy with a malevolent bearing asks me to buy a rose.
But you, where are you my flower?
Where are you?

Even the sun checks in timidly
So that my glass glints from time to time.
Why don't you brighten my face?
You, oh light of my eyes?

My beauty
After numerous glasses and seven cigarettes
The sun eclipsed
    And I could only do the same.

Adnan, Yassin

Yassin Adnan (born in 1970 in Safi, Morocco), is a writer and prominent television host. He received a bachelor's degree from Cadi Ayyad University, Marrakech in English and has a diploma from the Faculty of Education in Rabat. He's been a member of the Moroccan Writers' Union since 1994. As a journalist, he has been heavily engaged with the Moroccan cultural scene since the 1990s, publishing literary magazines and hosting the television programme مشارف (*Heights*) from 2006 onwards. He has written books of poetry, short story collections, and non-fiction works, including a study of the writer Fatima Mernissi. His debut novel *Hot Maroc* (2016) was nominated for the Arabic Booker Prize. His publications also include: بقايا نساء و *Mannequins* (*Mannequins and The Remains of Women* 2000); رصيف القيامة (*The Sidewalk of Resurrection* 2003); فرح البنات بالمطر الخفيف (*The Girls' Delight in Seeing Light Rain* 2013).

Fishermen in Harvesting Clothes

Sailors with earthen temperaments
emigrated here years ago
burying the butts of their destinies
in the waves
They never forget
their fathers were peasants.

They don't often think about God but
they fear death
so memorize the shortest holy
verses

You know their customs well
You are familiar with their secrets
the winds
of their twists and turns
their drunken friendships
from all that wine
and their straw hats.

You were among them
when they gathered in a circle at night
around their cold
lethargic light

You've memorized their sad songs
—the ones that don't sound like
shepherds' songs—
and their tall tales about big fish
even though they catch only small.

When the weather is a dog
they run like squirrels
to their warm tree trunk
at the gates of the port
and chat for hours
as if words were the lungs of the world
and their gatherings the breath of life.

The fishermen . . .
are not always sane

Once they threw their bodies one after
another into the sea
under God's sky
empty of stars.
No one paid attention to that.
No one ever pays attention to their
misery
or their little joys.

The fishermen . . .
are the ocean's wide-open eyes
over the world's harbors
the eternal keepers of the shrine of
wakefulness

(when do they ever sleep?)

When they return home
at the end of the night—their wives
slumbering—
they plant themselves within them
haphazardly
and because the women are used to it
they sleep without underpants.

In the port
they forget they have wives and children
and talk only about big fish.
They also forget that only small fish
await them
but they talk incessantly
and chug their wine out at sea.

You see them roaring like waves
exchanging greetings
and obscene insults as they smoke.

Their large lungs breathe out clouds
like the smoke of ships fleeing the fog,
and talk friendship with Korean sailors
on the high sea.
Even when they head back to their
homes
at the end of the night
they soon return.

With the reflexes of thieves
they pull out of their women
turn the key twice behind them
and go back to the arms of their
immense
azure sea.
Those fishermen . . .
surely exaggerate
when they talk about themselves
as if fierce mainland ghouls
daily invade the sea
to punish the deeps.

Of course they exaggerate
because when they, separately, come
back home
at night from the port
each one of them looks afraid and
nervous
like a frail young tree
grown naked in the wilderness.
But they are brave when they are
together
good-looking like children in their folly
and their straw hats.

(Asfi, September 1997)

On the Way to the Year Two-Thousand

In the year two-thousand
many things will happen to this world
the school teacher
with the embroidered
white veil
and pious eyes

told us
one rainy afternoon
She told us:
The voices of soothsayers will become
white
and Jesus will appear
with a beard of light
He will walk among people in the
markets
bare-footed
The mountain
kneeling down at the entrance of the
town
will burst open
with a winged she-camel
Young girls will be born with golden fins
exactly like sea nymphs
Our eyes will gradually rise
to settle high overhead
and we will see the transparent
steps of God
bending down
as if they were the air.

In the year two-thousand
the school teacher told us
—as the rain pecked at the windows
and the cold sneaked into our little
bones—
God will be close by
and we will send off this ferocious world
to its last abode
in an exalted funeral

I didn't wait long
Or rather
How I waited

And now after all these winds
I see the sands
licking their fire at the foot of the
mountain
And the storms swathing
their secrets
outside the walls of history
I didn't come here by chance
I crossed
seas and oceans
I knew dull evenings
and satisfied mornings
I knew naked love
and impromptu picnics
I knew one-night stands
in the tent of the moon guarding lakes
I knew sleep
in train stations
I contracted secret deals with joy
in the back streets
of life
smuggling the stars
of my first sky
unnoticed by the guards of the season.

I didn't come here by chance
I crossed seas and deserts
I saw corpses hanging down
from wire cables in abandoned towns
I passed Yazidi Kurds
with the picture of the devil
on the walls of their shrine in northern
Iraq
who suddenly started reciting their
sacred legend
to naked grandchildren

I passed Algerian women roaring
with life
hiding pleasures and cigarettes in their
bosoms
before going out to the boulevard
with stiff faces suitable only for curfews

I passed fishermen's wives in the
North Sea
whose
displayed fish for sale
didn't look like fish.
My life that I dragged behind
like a raw-boned she-camel
down the soul's slopes
is still panting behind me indifferent
to the winds of endings
And here we are as we have always been
No wings have grown from us
The shadows
haven't turned away from our steps
I have crossed the wastelands of life
running after
the way to
the year two-thousand
and now
after all these trenches
that time has dug inside me
Nothing has happened. Nothing.

(Marrakech 2001)

Aissa, Idriss

Idriss Aissa is a Moroccan poet who was born in 1956 in Kénitra, Morocco. He received his bachelor's degree in Arabic Literature and a Diplôme des Etudes Supérieures Approfondies from the Faculty of Letters in Rabat. He is a retired teacher. He joined the Moroccan Union of Writers in 1990. He has published his poems in newspapers including البلاغ (*The Communiqué*), الاتحاد الاشتراكي (*The Socialist Union*), and أنوال (*Anoual*). His publications include: امرأة من أقصى الريح (*A Woman from the Farthest Wind* 1990).

The Wild Book

Is it a grove of palm trees
before our eyes, or a book
with a text of wandering plants
in the blur of dawn
where light knows a path

its lines a southern wind
with thirst and mirage in its margins?

How do we read it, and recover the memory of palms
when they rise up in splendor
a celestial body whirling
turning around nothing but its own solitude?

We forget
so to remember, like those resigned humble ones who lost
the maps of oases

in order to enter the ceremony of absence.

Palm

O distant palm grove that
rises behind the door's arch

we see you still and hear the fronds
quietly creating winds
for a wind to come.

Stand, resist. Hold up
space
Travel in a whisper
as an oriole with its
pervasive song
lights
upon a tree
turning into a thousand orioles

and abandons itself.

Elegies for Mina

To my mother's soul in its blessed journey across the supreme universe, out there.

1

A white horse
shaped with wakefulness and distance
its haunches illumined by presence

descended from its wandering in memory
from its journey of the eyes to you
it walked towards your hands in the stillness of the trees
as if it recognized them by their gestures and their smell

as if you carried its manger and trough
and spliced its mane together with the morning

it came close to your room while you slept
the fragile curtains of the room slept
and the wind in the acacia garden fell silent
When the night spread over the walls
it did not remove its palms from over the windows

nor from over your eyes.

2

The horse came
from a wild land inhabiting your cousin's dream
It advanced before she could recount it

without a saddle or a bridle
whinnying in the direction of your pillow

you slept far from pendulums and clocks
as you looked higher up
waiting for the last raven

that hovered in the world beyond

3

As if the horse's streaming and perfected forehead
hung down over your pillow and face
and your eyes took you away
toward the one and only light that brings all ways together
in the earth's disarray

4

As if you had not slept
we always return to emptiness
where your hands support the air
your shrouded body undulating
like a river detained in its bed
as if you had not departed
and the horse had not skirted the garden's night
amplifying the darkness in the tree trunks
near your house

5

I am no longer shaded by the tree of motherhood
A desert has covered my lips

in the face of death
words have wings of salt and sand
　　　　　　　　　　　　and here I am again stuttering
on the thresholds of ash

6

Pain is an untimely sun
that surprises the balconies, the doors and walls
blind-siding the one who sees enough shadows
to ask what is hidden by light
What is it about my hands that darkness calls out to them?

7

The book is open until its end
placed at the edge of understanding
an eddy whirling nomads around in the wasteland
drawn tightly towards the vast expanse
they swerved from the star's landing

the paths confounded by their feet
　　　　　　　　　　　and by the necks of the beasts
the road they trod left them with one smell:
　　　　　　　　　　earth and old clothes
　　　　　　　　　　rising from the bottom of the coffin

8

A week went off towards the steepes
where shepherds and nomads kept silent
and your perfume hovers around the rooms

Come back to the old butter jars
that you prepared in the name of God for guests

and wheat blessed with your presence
spread over the rooftop on sheets

one part for the sparrow and another for the wild dove
Come back to the rolling pins and looms
the wheels swathed with skeins of wool
that you spun with your eastern hand
walking about praying in the center courtyard
like dervishes bringing the edges of the world together under their sleeves
snatched by a night trip to the light

9

Your hands, carrying the candlestick of motherhood
advancing despite the night
left no solitude in the world

10

There is no contradiction between day and night
in your eyes staring
toward what sight cannot grasp
there is no difference between earth and sky
bird and stump
on your palms stretched towards absence
the universe is one in your rest
doubled, multiplied and boundless
and the instant that took you away
has become your captive for ever

Nathaniel

I put on a veil, the woman says,
and entered the garden
the tomb of Sheikh Muhayddin Ibn al-'Arabi
my son Nathaniel was beside me
attentive, dazzled like a bird taking its first breath
delighting in the blessing of feathers
I stood still, anticipating the gift:
silence like a pearl

I cover its light with my hand
knowing I am before
the door
that no isthmus, no barzakh, separates from the guest . . .

she recounted this as I urged her
to stay in the Damascus of her mind
returning to me only in voice
as if she was setting out in a mist
a candle waving from the top of a hill
her eyes see farther than eyes see
her hand going through her hair
we walk together
as if she took my hand to a visionary garden
I bridle despair
with the voice of a woman describing light
footsteps opening onto other footsteps
the beast of my heart that before had hurtled me
into the stormy jungle of trance
following, its forehead touching me
its hoofs light on the path

. . . the fragrance I smelled then
was not from the earth
pervasive, nameless,
it descended on its own
and you know he is there,
dressed in serene infinity
enlightenment is a gentle hand on your shoulder
you see as if in a dream
and the world grows in your sight
 as you look down from the paroxysm that is you
and say, "I am content with what comes
because I am here
and beatitude is a verdant palm
that in my moving hands
becomes a fan over the sleeping
I fear I know the world

as a blind man who comes to meet passersby
embracing them with two strong arms
and then retreating back into the trench
to wallow in the mud with his clothes on

All of life is surmised in a happy tear
you can give it away for a glistening grain of seed
or covet it to become strong
You say:
I have forgiven the sun for giving me shadows
and the earth that is but a maze
for the amusement of night and day
filling people's pockets with rotten pits
and stones
I have forgiven the world residing in its trench
a path edged with berries
and flowering ash that sends off its first blossoms
here where the summer plays its embers
before you get to the path of the jacaranda
and go up to the studio of a painter friend
A mystery? the woman asks
or a magnet pervading his knotted hands
he sits calmly
so that his loneliness leans its head on his thigh
at the humble grave
where the one who talked to light still remains
he swears he did not seek a way
only the one swayed by light
leading to the door of the living
that meets it in peace
He named it the way of the door

I let go the beast's bridle
and said to my sister in vision
and to the pearl that her hand enclosed forever:
"yes, it is him
only he is the soul."

Akhrif, Mehdi

Mehdi Akhrif is a poet, a translator, and a Professor of Arabic Literature. Akhrif has published وردة في الرماد (*A Rose in Ash* 1980); باب البحر (*The Gate to the Sea* 1983); سماء خفيفة (*Low Sky* 1989); قبر هيلين (*Helen's Grave* 1998); ضوضاء نبش في حواشي الفجر (*Desecration Noise at the Edges of Dawn* 1998), and other poetry and prose.

Lightning without Rain

Sleeplessness
and an old song
leak
from the fissures of languor.
Luminous stones
hit the windowpane.
Handicapped sentences
circle me
around the ceiling.
Shall I fill the tune with laughter
or with an obscene love poem?!
—my vision doesn't come—
Oh brother of stone
Oh mouth that's in my mouth
Dispel this languor
at once!

Women

I have a night
forged of the ruins of a tower
of incense and orphans.
I have towers that made me beautiful
before my death was born.
I have a night in me
                        clothed with every wind
And a night seen
by the hoopoe that rises from
                        the rim of my glass.
I have women
who gather kindling from the ashes of
words
And women
igniting with agony
on the mirrors of words.
I have women who safeguard my despair.
They are the orphan's flowers.

The Notebook of Loss

In the notebook of loss
I built
a heaven the size of the sphere of the
universe
with letters
                made of the sweat of hell.

In the notebook of loss
I mourned my skeletal friends
to the end of all questioning
shrouding them
with solemn insomnia
and silence.

Oh letters
of a cold chord
holding the sea and the journey
in white spots
in my mouth

Oh notebook of loss
that I carved
with the blazing noon
I seized the ink's soul
to speak . . .
And when I was about to exist
                in its vast blueness
                my visions evaporated . . .

Alahyane, Ayad

Ayad Alahyane was born in 1970 in Asehnan, a small village in the south of Morocco. He is a high school teacher of French in the nearby town of Belfae. He obtained a master's degree in Amazigh language and literature and a doctorate degree in Amazigh-French comparative linguistics from Ibn Zohr University in Agadir where he also teaches Amazigh language classes. His poem collections written in the Amazigh language include Wes sa Ignwan (*The Seventh Sky* 2010); Tga Tguri Tislit Ig as iD Imilcil (*The Word is a Bride and the Night is its Wedding Feast* 2011); AjnDiD n Twargiwin (*Stings of Dreams* 2014). Ayad Alahayane won the Royal Institute for Amazigh Culture literary prize in 2013.

Dark Night

Dark night
My friend the night
I give you my hearing
You give me your ear
I talk to you
Though you are completely deaf
Black night
I ask you
What is the point of lengthening
The night for the sick
The night that is for lovers
I am in the lap of darkness
I have no one to talk to
Even in the light
I am dressed in shadows
Black night
My friend the night
Won't you lengthen my time
Shake up my side
Even if the heart beats
It can't give life to anything
Dark night
Make it so the day doesn't peel off
Tie it firm, fasten it
So it can't run away
So it can't lie

Arouhal, Khadija

Khadija Arouhal (born in 1979) is a poet originally from Mirleft near Sidi Ifni on the southern coast of Morocco. She won first prize in the 2M Creative Amazigh Literature Competition. She hosts the television program *Amiri* on the Moroccan Amazigh TV Channel. She also won the Amazigh poetry Prize awarded by the Matoub Lounes Foundation in Algeria in 2013. Her publications include: Azawan n'Urmmad (*Music of Pain* 2009); Tandra n'Ifssi (*Murmuring of Silence* 2011); and Tfras (*Traits* 2018).

Flight

Hide me oh flower
under your leaves!
Save me from cold
so that I feel the heat!
Quench me with a drop of dew.
Spare me from thirst!
Mirages
could never slake my yearning.
Separate me oh flower
from lies!
I am haunted by fears.
Make me rejoice.
The laughter of tickling makes me tired!
Elucidate for me oh sun the way
because my sight is worn
from stargazing!

I am tired of darkness.
Take me
Oh horse of Ounamir
because the foot gets weary
the way is endless
the heel bruised
the gravel
has no mercy!
Lift me up!
Raise me!
Will I find Tanirt
waiting for me?
Will I find
peace among the stars
and a path without thorns?
Will I find a land where rights
exist?
I would like to forget you oh earth.
I would like to forget myself
but
that will never make me fall
even if the heart dies of pain
even if I die
of nostalgia, oh mother!

(Translated from the Tamazight by Mohamed Farid Zalhoud)

Ammach, Jamal

Jamal Ammach is a Moroccan poet. Born on December 27, 1957, in Marrakech, he has a bachelor's degree in History and works as a teacher trainer for the Ministry of National Education. With others, he was involved in the publication of أصوات (Voices) magazine in 1992 in Marrakech. He is a member of the House of Poetry. His writings appear in daily newspapers like العلم (The Flag), الاتحاد الاشتراكي (The Socialist Union), and القدس العربي (Al-Qods Al-Arabi) and in magazines such as كتابات معاصرة (Contemporary Writings) and آفاق (Horizons). His major works include: اشتعال الثلج (The Blazing of Snow 1998); خطوات تتقدم الموكب (Steps Heading the Procession 2005), and حارس النبض (The Pulse's Guardian 2010).

Sentences Refusing Love

Coming from nests of scorching heat
exasperated by the bus
and its stumbling dry engine

You left in a hurry
didn't drink your usual black coffee

Exasperated by your face in the mirror
and the glass
broken with rancor

You lingered too long on a rotting
banister
looking at your absent face
in the mirror
looking at my face
on a page of the newspaper
or on top of a snowy mountain
surveying the place
with exuberant eyes

Surveying me, your ephemeral talk a kiss
unnoticed by those passing by

Desire passes stealthily
like a lifetime
on a carriage without lights

Stealthily you pass, a dark passion
in a dark tunnel

Coming with a white thread
and a scarf torn
by bodies
cities
stairs

Passing through gardens of illusion
sauntering close to you
far from the lighthouse in the harbor
bothered by the sting of words

Stealthily we pass through
the isthmus, the barzakh,
meeting hand in hand
water in water

We pass through with one face
without names remembering us

Only the thrum of a melody
or the bursting of a heart
on a drowning sky

Coming from the darkness of the horizon
to the door of darkness
take off your shoes
there are letters
there's blood that drove two hearts apart
long evenings
candles that burned the depths of night
burned the whole night
burned sentences
refusing love.

There are words that steal away the silver
depths from me
and there is a child who shares with me her love
. . . .
. . . .
She leaves and I don't see her
straying over winding paths
in the chill of deserts

She goes
to the
remotest of places

Coming
from distant waters
journeying in the blueness of my unexplored frontiers
Oh one who knows the beat of her heart,
lead me there!

Azaykou, Ali Sedki

Ali Sedki Azaykou (1942–2004), also called Dda Ali, was a Moroccan Amazigh (Berber) poet, historian, philosopher and critic. He was also an Amazigh activist and greatly influenced the Berber cultural movement. Born in the village of *Igran n'Tuinght* in the High Atlas Mountains in the surroundings of Taroudant, Morocco, he began his education in his native village and completed his studies in Marrakech at the national teacher training college. His works include: Timitar (*Signs: A Collection of Berber Poetry* 1988); Relation de Voyage du Marabout de Tasaft dans le Haut-Atlas (*The Voyage of the Marabout of Tasaft in the High Atlas* 1992); Petit Dictionnaire Arabe/Amazigh (*Little Arabic-Amazigh Dictionary* 1993); Izmulen (*Scars: A Collection of Berber Poetry* 1995); Histoire du Maroc et ses Possibles Interprétations (*The History of Morocco and its Possible Interpretations* 2002); L'Islam et les Amazighs (*Islam and the Amazigh People* 2002); Quelques Exemples de Toponymes Marocains (*Some Examples of Moroccan Toponyms* 2004).

Wells of Thirst

Years instilled
in thirsty wells
The pain of days cultivated
in hearts
watered with a drizzle of life
with the venom of exodus
Laurier-rose and colocynth
however futile
are abundant here

81

The years summon us
but we don't know for whom
Dancing, searching
avoiding tears
with incandescence, clamor and song
We forget little
The mute talks to the deaf
and reason ends
hanging
on the roots of thirst

(translated from Tamazight into French by Mohamed Ouagrar)

Words

Amazigh is my verb.
no one understands it
bearer of so much meaning
who can dance on it?
alone I hold fast to it
my verb suspended
like a rope around my neck
my language still alive
continues to speak
in the middle of the deaf; it is not tired
the thirsty word must
quench our thirst

Amazigh is my verb
no one wants it
some say "it's just a dream"
abandoning me
some say:
"it will never come true"
others say,
"your verb carries a painful past
suffering no one wants to share"

Amazigh is my verb
it wants to break the time of silence
embrace hearts
like galaxies
uniting
in the heavens

(Translated from Tamazight into French by Fatiha Lasri 2009)

One

I made a dream of my love for you
and dived in
having created wings I flew
away
the earth itself doesn't carry a burden as heavy
as that in my soul
can space contain it?
yes, I built habitations on the
stars more beautiful than
every paradise
I no longer see anyone, there is only
you and me
when I wanted to take your right
hand
we straddled the breeze
and set off for the Milky Way
we blazed with love and
disintegrated
but then you changed that fascinating
face exchanging it for a bitter one
unknown to me
you lacerated my chest
extinguishing that heart where you lived
you threw it into darkness . . .
but I opened my eyes and saw the dream dissipating!

(4/3/ 1971)
(translated from Tamazight into French by Mohammed Khaïr-Eddine 1980)

Azrhai, Aziz

Aziz Azrhai (born on November 4th, 1965 in Casablanca) is a Moroccan poet and press consultant. He obtained his bachelor's degree in Ancient History in 1990. He was in charge of the cultural section at the weekly النشرة (*The Bulletin*) for seven years. His major works are: لا أحد في النافذة (*Nobody at the Window* 1998); في انتظار الأموال الغير الطائلة (*Waiting for a Little Money*). He has been a member of the Moroccan Writers' Union since 1996.

Childhood Nursery Rhyme

To wake up at home, or almost.
To spill out over the ground
as if you didn't exist.
To get hungry and find nothing.
To have bowels play
like an accordion.
To eat and not get full.
To sleep below an imaginary ceiling
with holes.
To have joy come over and over again
in a painful rhythm.

This is one of the new and improved
versions of childhood.
With the addition in my case
of cold.

The Last Confessions of a Rhinoceros*

For mature reasons of social-class
I read books I don't finish
and generally dream of women of paper.
I have a jocular nature, difficult to understand
even though I'm realistic
I don't run
after dreams
(with an ostrich's legs)
My dreams are tame and easy
Moreover, they don't go to sleep hungry
for ideas
like one who climbs the void replete and predatory
I defer my friendships
until the end of life
when I'll be worthy
of the architecture of cancer.

Because my desires are tired of me
I don't know how to be of use to the world
Sad and thick
I don't want to understand
(Understanding too much hurts the imagination)
Because of a certain dietary condition
I don't read about causes
And I don't let my odiousness sleep in sadness
the night before.

*

I am not ardent enough to be beneficial
And there is nothing I can restore

---

* The poet has used a less common word for the animal (*khirtīt*). The most widely used name is *waḥīd l-qarn*, literaly the *one-horned* [animal]. The same term is used to refer to "horn" and "century" in Arabic.

My fear of happiness is a thorny issue
That's why I don't walk before meditating
with all my senses
I can for example understand something
other than ideas
such as not lending my nerves
to hopeless chatter
or I can be sad just like that
merely for the sake of the herd
And with rare ease
I can be recalcitrant
And this is saying little.

My convictions are always liquid and fragile
So I don't even go regularly
to religion
I prefer as much as possible not to understand
My head accidently fell down
between two horns
My heart is weak and cowardly
And precisely because of this infirmity
I like poultry
and ambiguity
and the proletariat
I actually get sick
on Labor Day.

I am the rhinoceros
an animal with a tongue
My appearance can still deceive
for another century
even though I am frightening
and don't laugh
My sadness is always in need of herds
And friendships that do not exceed the bounds
of caution
I seldom do

The fingers that I customarily hide in the sand
are drowning in kindness
that overtakes me
Reckless and repulsive fingers
but they are always mine
How can I jump for joy
without scattering the earth?!
Someone is in my hand
It may be none other than myself
But I am absent and copious
How did I get
all this expertise?!

Because I am sad with all this food
I always forget to be sated
My hunger is huge and loose
and has teeth
When I confess my wisdom
it's because I am the lone horn of this century
I'm ageless
That's how I see things
And forget.

*

Oh!
What a nice idea
this world!
"It's just that I missed the chance to be an angel"

Barakat, Ahmed

Ahmed Barakat was born in 1960 in Settat, Morocco, and died in 1994. He worked as a journalist and received the Union of Young Writers Award in 1990. He published two anthologies: أبدا لن أساعد الزلزال (*I will Never Give my Support to the Earthquake* 1991); and دفاتر الخسران (*Notebooks of Loss* 1994).

Caution

. . . as if I were walking in an atomic storm
where a long nuclear winter prevails, the petals
of fire stridently blossom, the birds emerge
from their high holes and linger for a long while
on the horizon, here light equals shade, the
current of death, the road that always retreats
of its own accord! Smoke rises from the
low ruins, things scattered about, metal wheels
compacted with reckless violence, old photos
laced with black blood strewn on ceramic tiles
and nothing else but the remains of a few
shocked men.
What place is this
where I walk
and want to sing?!

The Afternoon Wind

This is not the desert.
This is the cloak of a dead Sufi
And those are his bones tossed by the afternoon wind.

I heard

I heard the warrior commanding his shadow
heard the burial grounds returning the echo

but the drums
and the cymbals of the band
were eulogizing dust.

Bassry, Aicha

Aicha Bassry was born in Settat, Morocco in 1960. She holds a bachelor's degree in Arabic Literature from Mohammed V University, Rabat. She worked as a teacher, then as an editor of a magazine of education at the Ministry of National Education. She is a member of both the House of Poetry in Morocco as well as the Moroccan Writers' Union. She is also the vice president of the International Association of Literary Criticism in France, and a judge in many literary committees. Her major works are: مساءات (*Evenings* 2001); أرق الملائكة (*Angels' Insomnia* 2002); شرفة مطفأة (*Dark Balcony* 2004); ليلة سريعة العطب (*A Frail Night* 2007); حديث مدفأة (*Fireplace Chat* 2007); صديقي الخريف (*My Friend Autumn* 2009); خلوة الطائر (*The Bird's Seclusion* 2010); درس في الرسم (*A Lesson in Drawing* 2013). Her fiction publications include: ليالي الحرير (*Silk Nights* 2013); and حفيدة كريطا كاربو (*Greta Garbo's Granddaughter* 2015), which won the international Kateb Yacine Prize for novels.

Shama

She pointed
her little finger:
I want this grape.
"It's not real
my darling."
I want the pomegranate.
"It's not real
my little one."
She banged the floor
with her feet

She scrawled with her fingers
She lay her head down on her tear
and she slept.
When she woke
she stretched out damp
like the morning dew
and with a child's innocence
she confessed
"Mom
I ate the painting
in my dream."

Exercises in Solitude
« Every woman for herself »

Getting out of bed
without searching for the arm that embraced your night

Going into the bathroom
without tripping over wet towels
or missing his toothbrush

Staring at the mirror
and combing your hair
as you shake the snow off your heart
You fix the collar of your dress
and flatter yourself
« How lovely I am without a man's gaze »

Telling the sun
« Good morning light »
without drawing the curtains over chronic grief

You enjoy the monotonous rhythm of coffee bubbles
as it simmers in the silence of the spacious house
without moving your hand on the weariness of silk muttering—
« Why didn't I put out two cups ? »

You look out the kitchen window
at a lonely woman across the way
waiting patiently for someone not coming
without whispering to yourself
« That lady looks like me »
And indifferently you look away
from the scene of two lovers pelting one another with passion
without being pricked by longing

You start your day with silent coffee
and no tears

listen to the morning news
without recalling yesterday's dreams

You watch the weather forecast
without wondering if the rain storm
will annul the evening date

You sit at your desk
scolding your fingers as they
check email or Facebook
Meanwhile, diving deep into the white page
to begin a poem
in praise of solitude
But, on one condition -
To not start crying.

The Mythology of Flesh

If I had had the intuition of a she-wolf
As I have been accused
And pretended the wolf had eaten me
I wouldn't have been eaten twice.

Had I screamed,
« O, God! These are not my sins; I haven't committed any.
It's the snake that tempted me »
when I was stung at the hole twice,

had I denounced Adam,
and pointed my accusing finger at him:
« This is also your own creature, O Lord, and he ate of the apple. »
I wouldn't have been thrown on earth with a double hemorrhage,
one in the uterus and one in the heart.

Had I blasphemed against myself,
and given birth to myself in the basin of seduction,
I would have been crowned queen of Eros
And owned my body.

Had I not removed the fig leaf,
my only cover,
and thrown it in the face of the devil,
I would have been a tree in the promised paradise.

Had I been more careful and cunning,
I wouldn't have given birth to a man who would enslave me.

Had I been Atum* I would have created myself alone
and there would have been no first woman
nor any first man,
nor any perpetual infidelity.

---

* Atum, a self-created Greek god thought to be perfect because a hermaphrodite.

Had I been malicious,
as I have been stigmatized
I would have torn the garment of my beloved
from the front
so people would have believed my passion.

Had I stood at the gate of death,
and with the courage of one used to swinging back and forth with it
cursed Hades and all its names.
I wouldn't have been dead between two lives.

Can I really be myself
when I haven't yet existed?

Benchemsi, Rajae

Rajae Benchemsi (born in 1957 in Meknes) is a Moroccan writer. Benchemsi studied literature in Paris and wrote her thesis on Maurice Blanchot. She has published collections of poetry in Morocco and in France. Rajae Benchemsi is also the host of a Moroccan television program on books. Her own books include: Paroles de Nuit (*Night Lyrics* 1997); Fracture du Désir (*Fracture of Desire* 1999); Marrakech, Lumière d'Exil (*Marrakech, Light of Exile* 2003); and La Controverse des Temps (*The Controversy of Times* 2006).

from *Night Lyrics* (Paroles de Nuit)

scarlet and alone
caressing at day's end
the vast and imperceptible
liquid of former dreams
the sun
unappeased and decisive fire
lacerated from its wings
truncated and inconsolable
in an extinguished sky
close and without horizon
disappears from the gaze of the earth
into the origins of the world

an infinite whirlwind

in the darkness of long ago
the walls sweat
drifting scraps of memory
hang from old sighs

remnants of a summer unlived
slowly warm the penetrating humidity
from which exhales harsh and indolent
a vast black smoke

the dead with a breathless gaze
lift the shadowy thickness
from their heavy eyelids

from the somber recesses of the earth
cold and poignant
comes the pale glow of day

Benjelloun, Abdelmajid

Abdelmajid Benjelloun (born on November 17, 1944 in Fès) is a poet, a novelist, and a retired law professor. He is a founding member of the Moroccan House of Poetry and is the president of the Moroccan chapter of PEN International. He is the author of numerous books of history, fiction, poetry and aphorisms. His numerous publications include: Les Sept Cieux Apparents du Mot: Aphorismes Poétiques (*The Seven Apparent Skies of a Word: Poetic Aphorismes* 1993); Mama (2002); Rŭmi ou une Saveur à Sauver du Savoir, (*Rumi, or A Flavor to Savor from Wisdom* 2009).

Do with words what silence does with the storm
What transparency does with stones at the bottom of a stream
What clear stones do at the bottom of a brook
What the hand does with the sky
What my memory does for deceased loved ones
What music does with my soul
What my heart does with all those I love

Do with words what truth does with reality
What dance does to nymphs
What the rain does to the black pavement in the dead of night
What infinity does with our days
What silence does to stone
What immobility does to rocks
What the angel does with our pure hearts

Do with words what the last wave does to the beach
What old age does with childhood
What the song does to love that has died
What poetry does with CREATION
What the dawn does with the daytime
What our traveling conscience does in dreams
What life does with death

Do with words what the fresh flower does to the desert
What time does with the infinite
What time and infinity do together
Do what the word does with the word

from *Aphorisms of Love* (2009)

Often I prefer the promise of young girl's dance to her embodied dance. Often I prefer the promise of young girl's dance, exiled in the losses of my never-realized loves, to her embodied dance.

Here are my Days

Here are my days
My beauty of happiness
My sparkling spell gone missing
My fifth of jubilation
My biting fairy
My monarch's cry
My melancholy legend
Resigned to our difference . . .
My persistent substance
My exhilarating solstice
My suitcase of absolute charity
Here are my days
My beauty of happiness

Here are my days
My beauty of happiness
My neurasthenic boat
My ideal weakness
My jubilant spell
My suitcase of clarity
My splendor and feast

Benjelloun, Abdelmajid

Abdelmajid Benjelloun was born in Fez in 1918 and then moved with his family to England where he spent his childhood. He came back to his hometown and went to Al Qarawiyin University. He went to Al Azhar University in Cairo and obtained a bachelor's degree in Literature. He also obtained a degree in Journalism. He was one of the founders of the Arab Maghreb Office in Cairo in 1947 and was its secretary general. He took part in the Afro-Asian Bandung conference in 1955 to defend the cause of Morocco's independence. After Morocco's independence, Abdelmajid Benjelloun worked as editor in chief of the Independence Party's daily العلم (*The Flag*), and was a state minister in 1958 and then ambassador in Pakistan in 1962. He was diplomat at the ministry of Foreign affairs until he died in 1981. He wrote an autobiographical novel in two volumes in 1957 and 1968, في الطفولة (*In Childhood*), and in 1963 he published a poetry anthology, براعم (*Blossoms*), where his previously published poems were collected. Abdelmajid Benjelloun is also author of two collections of short stories and several other books.

Dawha

When the beautiful dawn breaks
casting its light on the plains
sending its breath among the fields
it wakes up the birds in the middle of the *dawha*
—and the tree resounds with joy
as if a soul were concealed in its branches
unseen by eyes in the dawn's splendor.
We hear it though concealed
a resounding melody, a spirited tone—it's all
magic, magnificence and rapture.
That is how the darkness around me dispelled
and my heart became infatuated in love,
a resounding melody, strong and overflowing.
That is how I became like the *dawha*
all the chords of my heart vibrating
like a tall, luxurious tree.

Ben Jelloun, Tahar

Moroccan writer Tahar Ben Jelloun was born in 1944. He has published numerous novels, poetry collections and essays. He was awarded the Goncourt Prize in 1987 for La Nuit Sacrée (*The Sacred Night*) and the Impac Prize in 2004 for Cette Aveuglante Absence de Lumière (*This Blinding Absence of Light*). The following poems are excerpts from Clair-Obscur, Les Pierres Du Temps et Autres Poèmes (1995. Paris: Éditions du Seuil).

When light springs from the cemetery where our
    ancestors stubbornly die
trancing in its wake the alleys of our childhood
When it gets up like a morning on fire in a turbulent
    sky
don't be impatient
If some darkness holds you back
captive to your ignorance
just know that hands can explore the shadows
and know as much as eyes
(p.9)

The night in us since birth
brightens the dream where butterflies lose their
    colors
On our sheets the crumpled wings of day
push against the resinous tree
In the silence of wandering mornings
washed with doubt and shadow
we rise in the immensity of the secret

our heritage, our passion,
to utter the incomprehensibility of the world
(p. 10)

Water likes this country only from time to time
It is attentive to the brightness of the moon and waits in
the heart of the wind
Prayers go up to the sky abridged by the sun
And the desire is so great just to sleep under a tree
the horse is left in the meadow,
to dream the world to where?
To slash the long days of drought,
to paint the wait behind our misery
and to signal to the wanderers that it's time to return
home
(p. 12)

The passion for origins
is a tree
it follows you in your travels
in your wanderings
when you are tired
you lean against its trunk
when you want to sleep
you shake it
and ripe dreams fall in your
sleep like the fruits of childhood
(p. 18)

The eastern wind of Tangier and Martil
raises an army of sparrows and
moths
pushing them towards the sun
The peasants of Fahss
fly away, their white haiks
swollen like the sails of boats.
They slide on the foam

and sing the love of the saints.
The western wind of Tangier and Martil
makes passions fall.
Men talk in cafes.
Little toads fall from their mouths.
The children pick them up to grill them on the
coal.
When they laugh
birds chirp
in their voices.
The people of the north bend down
when the wind passes.
(p. 21)

In a dark street of Fez
a kid on a reed calls himself a rider of the Atlas
he draws trees on the walls
fruits are breasts
some are lemons
others dried figs
He runs and calls for the rain
for fear of losing his harvest.
(p.26)

Benmoussa, Ouidad

Ouidad Benmoussa was born in 1969 in Ksar Al Kabir. She is a board member of the Moroccan Writers' Union and a member of the House of Poetry in Morocco. She was vice president of the House of Contemporary Art in Asilah and also worked as counselor at the office of the Minister of Moroccan Culture. She was a journalist for 10 years for the widely read newspaper العلم (*The Flag*). Her major publications in poetry are: لي جذر في الهواء (*I Have a Root in the Air* 2001); بين غيمتين (*Between Two Clouds* 2006); زوبعة في جسد (*A Storm in a Body* 2009); كدت أفقد نرجسيتي (*I Almost Lost my Narcissism* 2010); ألهو بهذا العمر (*I Toy with this Life* 2014).

Another Saturday

I open the door
and hang my exhaustion behind it
surrendering my body to the endless
desires of the bed
Neither I nor
my senses sleep . . .
I content myself bejeweling the ceiling of the room
with dreams of love
and sweet whispers . . .
my dreams have grown old
no warmth
scatters what has gathered behind
the door of brave exhaustion
and cold lives . . .

my morning is damp
and my fatigue still blooms behind the
door
and as for me,
the desires of the bed talk to me
I surrender my body to them
and sleep . . .

Old Age

Like this . . . all of a sudden
the bushes of the garden are unveiled
naked in the tremor of rain
they presage a wilted autumn.
Yet from a corner on the balcony
I ponder the bushes of the garden
they are not unveiled
they are not naked
and they don't presage any autumn . . .

The Path of the Cloud

Until now your vision hasn't been clear to me
Until now your reach hasn't healed me
I follow your footsteps
I vanish in your clear crystal
I offer you the flow of my passion's secrets

And I name you:
My little sister in the journey
O cloud in the distance

Another Pathway

I am there . . .
my soul exhorted me, and I said:
The blue of the sea is the soul's blue
The water of the source the soul's water
The anarchy of the body . . . the soul's anarchy
The path to truth is itself the truth

So why look outside
when
everything leads back to the soul?

Bennis, Mohammed

Mohammed Bennis (born in 1948 in Fez) is one of the most prominent modern Arab poets and the first Moroccan poet whose poetry appeared in anthologies of Arabic poetry outside Morocco. He is now a retired university professor of Arabic poetry at Mohammed V University and lives and writes in Mohammedia. He has many well-known essays and poem collections, among them: في اتجاه صوتك العمودي (*Towards your Vertical Voice* 1980); كتاب الحب (*The Book of Love* 1994); كلام الجسد (*The Body's Talk* 2010); هبة الفراغ (*The Gift of the Void* 2007); سبعة طيور (*Seven Birds* 2011)

Me, Not Me

I am the Andalusian residing between the
delights of meeting
and the wheezes of parting
I am the phenomenologist
from Cordoba
abdicating every ministry and power
I am the one raised on women's laps
and between their festive hands
They were the ones who taught me poetry, script
and the Qur'an
From their secrets I learned what others
hardly knew
I am the one who says: death is easier than
parting

108

That is my sacred law
To confess to the ardent lovers
In Baghdad and Fez
Cordoba
And Kairouan
To accompany the teardrop deep into its
whispering doubts
to bless the flower between lover and loved one
and to write to you
about this seed that is enough
for everyone who is
between the paths of listening and seeing
and in the presence
of madness.

Scenes of the City

I went out as usual to the old city at night,
the silence of the street enveloping me.
The lights of streetlamps
pouring sleep into the eyes of the alley, showering me
with their yellow pallor, as I fill up my palm
with the flowers of the wilting wind.

Then I look once more.
I gaze into the emptiness to see you.
You, my old city, I forever see you.
Dust of the storms of ages
blankets the balconies of your houses, a hue of colors
clothing the plaster whose carvings tirelessly repeat the hymn of sadness.

Dust of the storms of ages,
gathering on the bricks of minarets, on green-roofed mausoleums,
and on the entrances to markets, rising
above the advance of branches.

Dust of the storms of ages
on window panes that reach the ceilings,
extinguishing a star that melted on the doors and walls.

I drag my steps.
My cane-like shadow bleeds. My pond floods with wounded trees.

I walk on the echo of my silence.
The scarf of dust of the storms of ages
turning into moss upon the cracks
as if the constant coming and going of women without light
has risen up from the depths of night
as if the clouds of the rivers of day
have set out by night behind the walls
and never rained down, here, on my home.

Dust of the storms of ages
multiplies in your sirocco night, so listen to what is scattered in the sacred
    quietness:
verses that shed light on the mourning of my cursed tear.

People pass in front of me.
I see coral
fading in the trembling of words
and smiles.
Even people's steps
are wrapped in the dust of the storms of ages.

(1968)

The Road to Words

1.

Lonely, I went out in search of copper cities.
My blood filled with a dream that bloomed between Damascus and Fez.
I went out, all of me yearning
for a new morning. But I had no news of Alborak*
landing in my homeland, knocking on my door,
carrying me—like a baby—to my mother's smile as
she sleeps with me in bed, to the tremor of warmth at dusk.
So I enveloped myself in jasmine, becoming water that ripples among the suns.
I went out because I was still the prisoner of exile,
aspiring to stir the letters of destiny.

2.

I left behind me pillars of ash
and what insomniac nights had scattered.
First the extent of my vision
climbed up my chest like a flame. It was hope.
It was yearning, sprouting quick flashes of the sign
like water shivering with cold in the morning.
The profuse rain of expression showered down.
There were no more veils
between me and my premonitions,
no thirst or wounds.

3.

I abandoned my darkness to wander,
the glitter of a cloudless day taking me away.
I was the sunset and I was the evening,
believing what the songs in the air promised

---

* Alborak, the name of the creature on which the Prophet Muhammad made his ascension to the seventh heaven.

and what rippled, pure, over the voice of the soothsayer.
Water sprang out in the darkness of the deep
as she streaked the sand with lines, laughed, read my picture in her sand
and blew the seeds of fertility
into my shadow.
As if kingdoms of my joy
promised their children lilies, while they whirled around the thresholds of the
     orbits.
As if the lights of many candles
emanating from the soothsayer's tower
were swept away by the palm of a child fastening his bags
for the day of return.

4.

I knew nothing but the way to you.
Paths that rise over the mountains, far away, to bend down over you.
But my old wind has aged at your feet.
The water of the shores receded with the magic of incense.
Fire bruised my vessel, and resurrection is
a pole of salt that I shrouded with earth
and buried without a prayer. At the borders of a mirage
my shadow was torn apart: I cry no more.
A pickaxe is cleaving the sky's rock with its blade.

5.

A pathway of light comes within earshot.
Features of a land of tryst and peril
roar up in its docile horizon.
How can I turn the wings of your love away from the heart?

I went far from you in order to reach my future in you.
And here I am learning the secret of my hands.
I build towers of pride, and in my mind I start
by crushing skulls: " Oh! One of my own,
abandon the sun and jasmine

and a nation that proliferates in the shells of nostalgia.
Abandon the name and the homeland.
Abandon the witches,
and the language on which wailing women rest their heads."

6

Through the wall
ropes of the wagons crack.
And I listen.
These are your labor pains, saddling up the horses with light.
So be my wineglass, and be my fire.
Be for me a grapevine that rests its head on the sun of the fields,
a dream that comes over and over again on the wagons of day.

(August 16, 1967)

Whose face?

It is the shadows alone
that guide me to you with the sweet taste of
echo.
Emeralds
and lilies
and a burning whose merciful water I drank
from your hands.
Here I am running after the moon's
undulations,
looking to you
and taking two steps,
my lips snatching
desire
from your lips.
Truly, I began in you, I journeyed and I saw
an ocean illuminated with metals,
with the stars
and tempests of human nature.
I contented myself
with slumber on the luster of your knees,
yearning,
enlarging the call.
When I am closer I to you
a scream
I hear lifts me
and a flower
precedes me to the air of your shoulders.
The morning's blood,
my blood that I offered to your shores,
tells me that the song
is the song of azure
that flows from your feet.

Whose Will and Testament?

A dove's nape
a voice stretches out its hand
as if it were a candle in a field of fog
A voice says
if I had the orbit of a meteor
I would complete it
in a single gasp of awe
If I had a will and testament
tattooed with henna's desire
I would write on the blood of branches
in all seasons
The beginning of love is
a game under the lovers' roof
They discover its path
by chance, when they first discover
a dove
they laugh
Love falls down on you like a flower
coming from the farthest uncharted regions
of stillness
Love hides its river
from me and you
One step
then two steps
it lights its longing in you
One tear
then two tears
The angel's voice
leads one lover to the drunkenness of perdition
and another to the point of madness
The sweetheart's voice alone
houses me in its dome
I bequeath my body to its dying ember

Bentalha, Mohammed

Mohammed Bentalha (born in 1950, Fez) is a poet and a retired professor. He is a founding member of the Euro-Mediterranean Network of Poetry, the House of Poetry in Morocco and the Moroccan Literary Alliance. He is also winner of the Argana International Poetry Prize awarded by the House of Poetry in Morocco. His publications include: نشيد البجع (*The Swan's Song* 1989), غيمة أو حجر (*A Cloud or Stone* 1990); سدوم (*Sodom* 1992), and قليلا أكثر (*A Little More* 2007).

Below an Oil Painting (During a Reception)

The living were playing
while the dead
soon got fed up with a life of trifling
and returned
each to his barracks
I mean: to his body
drumbeats in the air.

El Dorado
Café-restauarant-bar

Beside the sea
Leg over leg
And solo music playing
We are in April
And in the back
Wine for two
To the poet, and the health of the dead
And to the alchemist, may he approach life
And forget elixir

Berrada, Omar

Omar Berrada is a poet, translator and curator, and the director of Dar al-Ma'mûn, a library and residency for artists and writers in Marrakech. He is developing a writing practice that integrates and hybridizes English, French and Arabic. His publications include *The Africans*, a book on racial dynamics in Morocco. He co-edited with Erik Bullot, *Expanded Translation—A Treason Treatise*, a book of verbal and visual betrayals and co-edited with Yto Barrada, *Album—Cinémathèque de Tanger*, a multilingual volume about film in Tangier and Tangier on film. (Omar Berrada's poems are the only ones in the anthology written in English, and remain un-translated.)

Pax Babeliana

> The ghost city is a field of rubble but at night it rises up and up, re-erects its towers by night, its people its murals its bridges.
> MARIE BOREL, *WOLFTROT*

> I'd speak if I wasn't afraid (. . .)
> FANNY HOWE, *INTRODUCTION TO THE WORLD*

A town full of holes
Monumental latencies
Ruins in reverse

In the Odyssey there is a pig
that speaks fluent Greek

Time is officially ended

> La nuit après l'amour
> L'aube avant la mort
> La tradition se retire
> Un désastre nous dévore

> Mystical tide
Unholy tongue

I've spent a lot more time in my life swimming than writing
and I get cold, writing, a lot more quickly.

In the confusion
  I seek
provisional light

    In the confusion
    I speak

لخولة أطلال ببرقة ثهمد

  Ruins

        appear

أطلال . . . تلوح

  and fade

تلوح

          Speaking in tongues

In Navajo there are three hundred fifty-six conjugations of a verb that
translates as 'to go,' she says.
  'To be' hardly even exists.

une folie sous surveillance
C'est le réel qui polyglotte
Palindromes et bienséance

The trace of a tattoo
on the back of a hand

لخولة أطلال ببرقة ثهمد
تلوح كباقي الوشم في ظاهر اليد

The trace of a tattoo
  appears and fades

          On ne coupe jamais
          la main des artistes

In the desert
lightning is elegiac

يا بارق يا حارج يا ثهمد

In the desert
literature is civility

          est une manière   أدب

I'd speak if I wasn't afraid
of inhaling

يقولون لا تهلك أسى

Don't lose yourself
in grief
      I follow
myself fleeing

          fuir, là-bas fuir
      a feeling

le pays qui me ressemble

in the Odyssey
there is a fawn
that speaks
fluent Greek

We embraced the world
before we knew it
Your ignorance will be your foundation

يقولون لا تهلك أسى
وتجلد

True fiction
          false reality
Exit myth

Below the Hafa café
a highway was built
Tarmac ashes
Magic rubble

          Exit the sea
          Gone with the sun

لكل علم وعمل بقايا وخفايا

Our fantasy found a form
in geography

          Sous les pavés
          l'asphalte

عرب وعجم وكلام وخمر

An erotics of words and wine
in يمن or in عراق
A Babel of sighs and brine

Il n'y a d'originel
que le malentendu

En choeur on ventriloque

We are the earth
et la terre n'est pas si ronde

Get me a map, now

"Nadie le vio desembarcar en la unanime noche"

Light
in itself
is silent

And this mirror is a masterpiece

Du lumineux
et de l'obscur
le mélange
seul signifie

Finally all reference vanishes
Your ignorance will be your foundation
—a sacrifice of matter

لخولة أطلال ببرقة ثهمد

تلوح

كباقي الوشم في ظاهر اليد

I'd speak
if I wasn't afraid
of inhaling
a memory

ذكريات . . . تلوح

All the Birds
(for Sarah)

1.

So many tombs
in the life of the self
Protect and save
Project and stave
off the time when
evening loosens
the gilt of her locks
Stanford, Clotsky
what's with the Ts
the terrible Ts
the vertical bars
of a wooden crib
the linear chain
of authorities
family, religion
sacred transmission
the past speaks
in silence
Identify, then multiply

Half of me comes from here, half from everywhere

2.

Night paints a shadow
into your heart
a word hides a word hides a word
            hides a silence put
                    your hand here I'll
put my hand there
something marvelous
is bound to happen
larger than life
lines unhinge
the signs no

harm intended
Heretical healing
devotional treason
Humble humble reader
your gracious likeness I shall seek

Something heavenly has wounded the soul

3.

In the Odyssey
is a crow that speaks
fluent Greek
Let us rename all
the birds my love
a dictionary of silent screams
and the world will fly
to our hearts' beating

The poem, the dream: our very lives

4.

Musiqa, musiqa
A button pressed
another turned:
she sways in circles
Velvet goldmine
Celtic dreamlands
it is we who fall
asleep to a film
soundtrack

A sheep by any other name . . .

5.

Long fingers holding
fast metal needle
black fabric fainting
from a sewing machine

logic of production logic
of collapse a plummet
into darkness
while in the courtyard
a plum tree grows
Technicolor puppets
Is that all
that heaven allows?
they know nothing
of gravity so says Kleist
they know nothing
but gravity:
take the stick out
puppet falls flat

Her experience of scale is always paradoxical

6.

You talk in your sleep
arms raised high above
your breath
a dance of hands
in silent air

Voices of the psyche racing through the flesh

7.

The museums there are empty
shells so said the scholar
from Syracuse lovely
outside ruins inside
Preserve and educate
is what we ask of you
engage and transform
Instead you lie quietly
out of date in
dejection unworthy
of thy name break

our hearts we
who believe
and remember
even the past
needs to breathe

Home is an intimate stranger

8.

Words erect
a barrier
at the core of intimacy
a tremor breaks the surface
with a life of its own
Some mornings are hard
and these are healthy
horizontal yearnings
now standing to shower
heads not our own
feel the pull of
gravity within us
we want to live
like trees
It is snowing
inside your body
and tamaas in your tongue
has a secret meaning

Can we share solitude without loneliness

9.

The cold
from the small of
your back
my hand
away
will blow

If we go to Texas we will come back naked

Bouanani, Ahmed

Ahmed Bouanani (1938–2011) published one novel *L'Hôpital* (The Hospital)—a cult classic of contemporary Moroccan literature—and three books of poetry: Les Persiennes (*The Shutters*), Photogrammes (*Picture Frames*), and Territoires de l'Instant (*Territories of the Instant*). He also directed several short films and one feature, *Mirage*, widely considered a milestone in North African cinema. In a sense, however, Bouanani's oeuvre is still forthcoming: his death uncovered dozens of completed yet unpublished manuscripts, spanning many genres—poetry, fiction, plays, film scripts, essays, history books, as well as drawings and graphic novels. He shunned the limelight and, unless friends forced his hand, avoided sending his work to publishers. Paradoxically, this obstinately silent writer was part of a most vocal generation of artists gathered around the journal *Souffles*, to which Bouanani was an early contributor. He was obsessed with the preservation of collective memory, and with the project of telling a people's history of Morocco beyond official narratives, be they colonial or post-colonial. Combining high literary standards with constant political concern, his work was important for rethinking North African literary and cinematographic modernity in relation to oral traditions and popular culture.

P.S. (a letter for Touda)

We have to wait for another light
for all other suns
to be extinguished, for the earth's grass
to dry up and die once and for all,
for the shutters of a non-existent home
to open, sphynx-eyed,
on the sick memory of silent memories;
We have to wait for another past
sharpened like a trap full of
new corpses, that
unrolls its ugly toothless ghost face
on the deserted road before me,
sick of children,
of faces with dead smiles and hearts
in sarcophagi ceaselessly crying
in rhythm with a great silence.
We have to wait for a fraudulent poem
for the page to be embodied
in the light and silence so coveted.
Somewhere there are navigators
in the galaxy of my blood that scan
the endless night, without parchments or
kaleidoscopes,
between the lines of Capricorn and Gemini.
What mythic road do I take,
free of vain vocabularies and
inconstancy?
Will it be said that my rainbows
hide the treasures of kings, crazy with lies?
I see myself in this century
of fear,
ardently straddling outrageous ideas,
microscopic desires above the
landscapes of my dreams. This disembodied
country kills its ancestors in the sky of the future.

Territory 1
Description 1

The walls hide horizons that sketch
wild flowers, flowers
from a country of midnight.
Unlocked places—their veins
swollen with the blood of fruit—hear
the invisible galleons passing
dragging seaweed and stars
in their wake.
Dawn refuses to break.
The sky closes, eyelids torn by
silently murderous thunderstorms.
Yesterday's houses
fall one by one.
Like a trammer,
I trace, at some cable-lengths in the mine
of my interior, a storm
in the sun.

Fable

In the dead gardens of the poem that possesses me
I know that a sky in the form of a living bed
will easily contain my silences, my myths
forged in the same clay as a god dreaming
of unbearable interstellar shipwrecks

the fable of the world that tells my heart
about the red flame of legendary amazons
that it revives in the middle of our fear
so there are no longer any futures without faces:

My illiterate warrior ancestors
nomadic in their pieces of land
feel the freshness of moons at their feet

I hear them chanting when they pray
incomprehensible verses of the Quran
their dreams always stopping in front of the Black
Stone I see them, crazy skeletons coursing
through the limbs of paradises of sadness
From petals of blood they plait shrouds
dying once more for the love of fauns
and gorging without a single respite until night
surrounded with manuscripts and illuminations

Who will tell their naïve truths?
the defeats gloved by deep burns
that old ones never discuss?

Their tomblike identity has been erased
for so long
May the red flame of legendary amazons
live in my heart.
May it revive in the midst of our fear
So there are no longer any futures without faces

into silence

I know I will not die in Casablanca
Yet my dreams my dreams of childhood
will survive oblivion like an Inca treasure
in this land of frightening silence

Even the hummingbird no longer believes in songs
All day he looks at the clouds
angry, waterless, rolling along
black electric shivers smeared with images

oaks, cedars, palm trees and poppies—
that tender red that cradled the dew—
they no longer remember the times when echoes
lived on the flanks of exorcised mountains

There is nothing on the terraces now but lizards
turbaned and sated their dead legends
dressed in the dust of the Alcasars
their giant armies like bumble bees

I will leave on camelback in the late afternoon
scribbling fairy-tales in the sand
surrealist enigmas and fables
smuggled from paradise

In tears the only thing left for me to do
to cling to the thunderstorms' mane
to write an ultimate wild poem
I know I will not die in Casablanca

(7/2/92)

Boudouma, Jamal

Jamal Boudouma was born in 1973 in Midelt, Morocco. He is a poet and a television presenter living in Paris. Some of his works include: الديناصورات تشتم ستيفن سبيلبيرغ (*Dinosaurs Insult Steven Spielberg* 2001); and نظارات بيكيت (*Becket's Glasses* 2006). He's also author of a book about immigrants in France: كيف تصبح فرنسيا في خمسة أيام . . . و من دون معلم (*How to Become French in Five Days. . .and without a Teacher* 2011).

Cartoons are in my house

Wonderful things happen at seven o'clock in the morning:
The hen comes down from the clock on the wall and grains scatter
The clock's scorpion hands turn in reverse
They sting my feet and laugh out loud
The hen lays a breakfast: a cup of coffee, a croissant and a newspaper
I wake up frightened and shout: Where are the colorful stars that were over
　　my head?
The hen shouts: Didn't you like the sky and the winged angels? Didn't you like
　　the white clouds?
The scorpions shout: Didn't you like the shy electricity pole? Didn't you like the
　　stork over the post office building?
I shout: I want the stars, I want a flower, I want rain and the faces of the ones
　　I love . . .

I open the room's window to let the air in
I see myself sitting on the terrace of the café opposite my house
without a moustache, without a hat and without hands

smoking a thick cigar and smiling
I smile
I greet myself and return to sleep
Very often the greeting falls down on the sidewalk and shatters
When it doesn't break, an obese man I know walks by
and crushes it with his heavy shoes
I feel distressed
When the obese man doesn't come by, an old woman appears walking slowly
    dragging a funny dog
The dog pisses on the greeting
The dog turns into a zebra but the old woman is oblivious
The old woman's eyeglasses resemble the bottom of a glass
and her face, a rusty frying pan without eyes
and the funny dog wasn't a dog from the start
and didn't change into a zebra . . .

I get up from the table to gather the splinters of the greeting
In the middle of the thought I realize that I am without hands
and I return from whence I came like a soldier who didn't carry enough bravery
    in his sack
A sallow tree sprouts up on the wet spot of greeting
and friends of mine from the university who have since died sprout up
The sidewalk splits apart and their heads come out
Their bodies are lithesome and are covered with blood and dirt
They wipe off the dust with their hands, the blood disappears and the truth
    emerges
They walk away in opposite directions, smiling as if wonderful things were
    happening

A young girl walks by with shabby clothes and wet matches
She asks the blind beggar under the sallow tree: what time is it?
The blind man points in the direction of my room
I close it quickly and throw myself under the bed
I tremble and the kitchen utensils fall down with my old convictions,
the walls crack up
The girl comes in without knocking at the door
She puts her boxes of matches near the stove to let them dry

Her soul dries up and she cries
She pretends she escaped from a cartoon
She says she got tired:
There was no reason for her wealthy father to suddenly die
as early as the first episode
She didn't have to live in an orphanage
The director was a rough woman without a heart and she had a long black coat
The children were devils with white wings
And after all they were not drawn as they should have been
while she sweeps the floor and cleans the room and prays to God and
    studies . . .
and in the end she is free and she doesn't want to be with them until the end

The blind beggar comes to my room
He takes out two glutinous eyes from his pockets
He puts them on his face as it was agreed he should
He says that he too was an important person
before the clock hands turned in the opposite direction
He is proud to be a blind beggar under the sallow tree
and not an employee in the bank
He regrets that Chantal involved him in worthless matters
He really loves Chantal
but Kundera is selfish and writes only to torture people
He takes a rest in my room
A sallow tree grows up beside my bed
He is an arrogant beggar but we listen to him
We die and stand up
and he is still repeating that he is happy to be a blind beggar under a sallow tree
and not a poet
All of a sudden, the stove stands up with a match in its hand threatening us
The girl laughs
The blind beggar laughs
The walls laugh
The house goes up in flames
I shout:
You scoundrels . . . I want the stars that were over my head!

Mischievous Boys Torturing the Morning in the Bathrooms

The teacher of Arabic
sings and throws fish out the window
hurls old school songs at the afternoon
stars sprout from his striped jacket
and the class catches fire
a teacher without a message
a teacher without stamps or an envelope
without a conscience
a teacher inflicted with a knife's scar on his forehead
he's an expert at swindling
his dreams are wet
and flat
he leaves his head on the wooden desk
and walks toward the window
A teacher without a head walking about between the rows
while the mischievous ones laugh
they piss on his dreams
they slip on them and blow up the rainbows

Mischievous pupils
with white wings and heavy school bags
plucking out the hair of the leap year
they hang the months on a broom stick and sweep
they spread their souls on the classroom wall
they torture the morning in the toilets
they laugh

The morning arrives with ragged clothes
it sits in the back row
complains and moans
the teacher's dreams have dried up and come down with the flu
the morning talks to itself
and wipes its tears with a handkerchief
the pupils play tricks on the sun
they tuck their noses into boxes of matches
and pull out clouds from the teacher's ass

the stars on his back die out
then he rises lightly toward the sky
like a striped hot-air balloon
he goes higher up
and bumps against the ceiling,
with spirits and flying saucers below,
the pupils bounce up and shout: he's falling down, he's falling down . . .

They take their trousers off and shower life
their white wings are broken
their teacher rises up while they fall down
no mountains are on their shoulders
no snow in their dreams
they repair their impaired souls
jumping from one age to another
they peer stealthily at the school mistresses' underwear in the school yard
they uncover the future's pudendum
and they laugh
the mischievous boys laugh

(Casablanca, August 2004)

A Dead Man Holding a Rose and Laughing

At ten o'clock at night
A devilish spirit sneaks into my room and sleeps in my bed
I jump with fright
I hide behind the curtains
I tremble
I stay awake the whole night
The light hurts me
I realize I have ascended to heaven and come back
I realize I am dead holding a rose and laughing
My face disintegrates but the red rose doesn't wilt
I sit down on the air
and I don't think:

Who has made eternity awful like this?
Some kind dead men arrive
dragging lifetimes of smoke behind them
the way a reckless athlete drags a heavy truck
What is this flock of souls doing in my house?
They enter through the walls and suffer torment
They look at me and I ask them about my friends and my family
about Zahra
about my future that is bleeding
They tell me about things that will happen in the past
I believe them
like guests who have come from a distant village
exhausted by the sun and forgetfulness
I smoke a cigar and I don't care

I go to the toilet
I find someone else pissing in my place
I don't find the toilet
I realize I don't have a bladder
The guests are sitting on air
They are hurting the back of the riding beast
They chat as if we were alive
I make coffee for them
I put grains of poison in it
so they will come back from the dead
I serve cookies to the curtains
They don't come back
Rather, they melt as the body of the sun grows bigger
They go away and leave me alone
I fall apart
The light hurts me
The greetings they left behind the door when leaving hurt me
I sigh in regret for the air they didn't take with them:
Without air they will die much more
I choke instead of them
I crawl on my belly like a silkworm
and I don't get anywhere

At night
the same spirit comes again
and the next morning I wake up as another person
I speak English and I insult Arabs
On the third day I wear the skin of a bull
An iron ring hangs down from my mouth
The rivers and the sounds of Koalas hurt me
I climb the ladders of civilization
I fall down and don't get up
Humankind comes and scatters around
while I am asleep as if in a long springtime
and I wait for you
You were not with them
You were not in the song
We didn't meet in eternity's elevator
You left the stars in your house and you didn't feel regret
You didn't kiss me on my mouth
so that I would wake up from sleep
And the stone covering my old face breaks
You didn't repeat the magic words at the entrance of the cave
I searched for you in the future and in the past but you were not there
You chose the path of the afternoon
and you reached love at night:
Have you come to put the seven skies in order and go back?
Evil spirits eat the seeds of sorrow
in order to forget the night
while I am behind the curtains
The houses have slept
and the stars that you have forgotten in your house are hurting me
The dead men are still looking for their souls in the woods
They wander about and they insult the fog
Their bodies are exuding blood
and nostalgia

Bouhlal, Siham

Siham Bouhlal was born in Casablanca and has been living in France for twenty-five years. She received her doctorate from Paris-Sorbonne University. She has dedicated her career to translating medieval texts, writing and translating poems. In recent years, she has taken part in different poetry festivals: *Les Derniers, Les Voix de la Méditerranée, Poetry Festival of Pescara* in Italy, and *Arte del Viaggio Arte dell Incontro*. She has published: Le Livre de Brocart ou la Société Raffinée de Bagdad au Xe siècle (*The Book of Embroidery or the Refined Society of Baghdad in the Tenth Century* 2004); L'Art du Commensal ou Boire dans la Culture Arabe (*The Art of the Commensal or Drinking in Arab Culture* 2009); and Poèmes Bleus (*Blue Poems* 2005).

from *Body of Light (Corps Lumière)*

To no longer see you
Is to seek your breath in particles of air
Your skin in each grain of sand
Your taste in each tear
Behind each tree your shadow

To no longer see you
Is to run into the void to follow your steps
Turning my head everywhere behind your eyes
To curl up my body leaning on your arm

To no longer see you
Is to listen to your voice a tambourine against my soul
To open all the doors of time on your silhouette

To no longer see you
Is to disrobe my heart and wait for you under the sheet
Scrutinizing my hands replete with your smell

To no longer see you
Is to stretch out on the ground and whisper your words
To take any handful of earth and blow on my lungs
Spying on the buds that will carry your face

To no longer see you
Is to dress the wind in hope and let it go
To fertilize the water of streams with sorrow and
Let none of them drink

To no longer see you
To no longer see you
Who would understand ?

from *Dying Alive* (*Mort à Vif*)

Surging forth from the darkness
You lit a fire in the sky in the sea in the center of the earth
You poured light on my darkness
Injected life in the cadaver disintegrating in me
Like a gushing forth
You took my buried ardor and threw it at me
Pulled up my heart from the heart of the void
And stuck it in my chest
Like a gushing forth from the shadows
You rained ink on my breath
And redrew its forms
Like a gushing forth from the shadows

You threw two die in the air
And gave eyes to my sight
Like a gushing forth from the shadows
You pulled a lock of hair from the infinite
And redrew my veins
Like a gushing forth from the shadows

You brought your mouth to my kiss
And made it find its lips
Like a gushing forth from the shadows
You stole two pebbles from the moon
And placed two dots on my chest
Like a gushing forth from the shadows

You
Emerged
And
Drank
  The
    Stream
      That
        Poured
          From
            My
              Breast

Boujbiri, Mohamed

Mohamed Boujbiri (born on April 25, 1955 in Azilal, Morocco) is a retired high school teacher. His major works include the poem collections عاريا . . . أحضنك أيها الطين (*Naked; I Hug You O Clay* 1989); كما لو أن الحياة كانت تصفق (*As if Life were Applauding* 2017); and an autobiography, العبور (*The Passage* 2017).

Spirits

Spirits
suspend their shadows on the thread of memory
Spirits
held captive by the presentiment in the womb of dusk
like a lotus flower
at the end of night
waiting for the rays of sanctity to break
* * *
Spirits
come close to dinner tables when evening approaches
Spirits
whenever the situation calls
approach, translucent, like moaning
or in-between joy
and weeping
* * *
Spirits
at times come for this whiteness
at times from the caves of the ancestors

and from the valley of wind-born dust
Spirits
are forever returning and do not die
Spirits come
just for this emptiness

(Autumn 1998)

Boussrif, Salah

Salah Boussrif was born in Casablanca in 1958. He has a doctorate degree in Arabic literature. He is a founding member of The House of Poetry in Morocco and was the president of The Moroccan Writers' Union branch in Casablanca. His publications include: فاكهة الليل (*The Night's Fruit* 1994); ديوان الشعر المغربي المعاصر (*Anthology of Modern Moroccan Poetry*, co-edited with Mostafa Nissaboury 1998); شجرة النوم (*The Tree of Sleep* 2000); حامل المرآة (*The Mirror Stand* 2006); شهوات العاشق (*The Lover's Temptations* 2006); and many other poem collections and essays.

Sheer Mirage

Your perfume
   is
      nothing
         but a spark of lightning
           or a whim of ink
              that illuminated
                 the whiteness of my delusions
                    and became a   sheer   mirage

Erasure

No way
for words to be a minaret

my eye lying down its water
strewing me about
erasing my limbs
I am obliterated
become dust in the air

Would I then quake the way the earth does
Would I change the shape of the air
and the color of ash
Would I

satiate my thirst
me, the one filled with the breaths of thirst

I'll incline towards the impossible
Maybe I'll drop anchor
at the farthest sky
and thereafter
the earth will be my refuge

Chebchoub, Fatima

Fatima Chebchoub was born in 1952 and died in 2006. She served as director of the Tanet Show Company for Mass Media, and was a professional script writer. With the support of UNESCO, Fatima Chebchoub directed two short films on rural women and their difficult living conditions: لا أمي يزة (*No, Mother Yezza* 1996); and الرخصة (*The Permission* 2000). Her poetry, written in Moroccan Arabic, is found in two collections طبيق الورد (*Little Vase of Roses*) and التهليلة (*Exultation*).

Little Vase of Roses

O one dominating his peers
saddled with formidable pride
O one surveying a garden
whose grasses are a saturated forest
O one pouring old wine cooled
From the spring of his eye
My thirst is a turbulent sea that isn't quenched
My illness has increased and is incurable
Oh little vase of roses
When he laughs his teeth are jewels
My eye is falling today
Sliding and blind for you
Seeking the favor of a tender heart
I'm the one in need
O faithful heart without treachery
I've come of my own accord without apology
Or if you consider it a blow

out of the head of the casket it came
It stirred grief
and swore and menaced only me
It planted a blade in my heart
blunt, rusty, and twisted
My burden has grown heavy beyond belief
My cloak has tightened beyond patience
A fiery affliction came
Black and bitter like a hadja gourd
I never thought it would grow
to become a curled viper
that kills me each day
a hundred thousand times without mercy
Without you I've become vanquished
Your shackles are stronger than I am
I couldn't free myself from them
Its chains are locked around me
Its fire is locked patterns
whose bars are burning and rude
There's no way out
other than your hands, you the ear of hope
unchain my irons with fulfillment
and reunite me with serenity
Bring back to my eyes a gaze
bewildered and assuaged by your beauty
Restore to my heart an hour among your magnificent hours
My mind and spirit will be in peace
and my soul will expire in glory
I will say that my fortune has become rosier
for the sweetheart has kept his promise to me
even if I've come without apology
just with a look and a gaze
He understood my intentions all at once
and lay my head on his chest

Chouhad, Ali

Ali Chouhad is a Moroccan Amazighi singer-artist. His long musical career gives him an incredible celebrity in Morocco. A specialist in the Archach style (fine rain), his songs are full of sweetness, philosophical depth and hope. Awarded many times, this singer, still alive, is a reference of engaged Amazigh song.

Oh poetry!

Oh poetry!

Verses do no harm to garner blame
They make no one a gainful income
It's not idleness that makes such beauty
But standing in the court of the gifted
It takes two hands to hold this pillar
And the one-armed soul has only to lay down his burden

Oh poetry!

I still scold only this heart that adores you
The whip of misfortune cooks me on all sides
Forehead dry, from ember to ember I move
My eyes, oozing with blood, shrivel
Devoured by mice, my rotten fines
Yet the wild birds still sing canticles!

Oh poetry!

I hug my patience between my tired arms
Living or dying too much no longer makes my heart contract
My zeal alone is enough for me to finish this path
The work of verses neither dries up nor dies

Oh poetry!

How much time do I need to warn
the herd that rushes to the summit
I have no more worries, I no longer expect the worst
Let them fall into the abyss without any rescue

(Translated from Tamazight into French by Hassan Oumouloud)

El Aoufi, Boujema

Boujema El Aoufi was born in 1961 in Taza, Morocco. He is a poet, translator, and art critic. He began writing and publishing poems and articles in 1986. His early writings drew a lot on visionary and mythological material, but he later departed from this tendency, and assumed a "new poetry" posture characterized mainly by a concern with ordinary language and everyday life. In 2001 he received the Shariqa award for Arab creative writing, awarded by the Ministry of Culture and Communication in the United Arab Emirates. El Aoufi is a member of both the Union of Moroccan Writers and the House of Poetry in Morocco. He published two books of poetry, بدايات شيقة (*Thrilling Beginnings* 2001), and أصدقاء يغادرون حنجرتي (*Friends Leaving my Throat* 2001).

Baghdad a City Enriched by Uranium

- 1 -

"the best thing that a deserter does: leave his legs behind" (Mohamed Serghini)

Letter:
Soon
we will set Baghdad free from its name
and return purified to Philadelphia . . .
- the soldier writes to his sweetheart -
keep:
our rendezvous for dinner . . .
the evening kiss . . .
the newspaper with my photograph . . .

and leave the door of the house ajar
I will return soon
to continue fighting the war on despots from my room!

- 2 -

A child's expressionless face
limbs ripped apart by a rocket-propelled grenade
cleans his flesh of the raiders' nails . . .
and screams:
Oh God! Oh Ali!
Pain enriched by sobs
His mother dirties her face with the wounds of Hussein
pointing to the one who hid the projectile in the child's toy!

- 3 -

    Go back to where you came from, you Sumerian bird. There are no trees in my homeland that are suitable for nests. Nor is the air here spacious enough for your flapping wings. Errant bombs. Gardens trembling. Ripped up in my hands. The sky here is too blue. The crops no longer own the trees. They are inhabited by snipers and spies. There remains nothing in my homeland to shade the heart. The earth is a plague.

4.

Come here, my son!
Lie down here between my bones
The coffins are generous
The vultures scrutinize the hair of their prey
Sleep here: between our two graves
So invaders won't wake you
while the country dozes in your eyes . . .
Nothing is more beautiful than dying strangers . . .
Take that splinter
And draw your colorful dreams on my cheeks
And the names of graves looking for occupants . . .
Nothing is more beautiful than dying without a brother:
We are the last strangers!

5.

I will not fill
my lungs with arsenic this morning
I will not pour more white lead into my coffee . . .
There is already too much eloquence in my blood
Too much smoke
And too many voices of newscasters
To remember the image of the killer
And to choose my preferred means of death!

6.

   The pits here are ravenous. Their appetite is expanding. The trucks are well
equipped, the earth stalled by insomnia, punished by an insolent soldier. This
deserter's eyes wouldn't have betrayed him if white heat hadn't reached the
threshold of the scream. The trees are changing their course. The children are
beheading the sinner with pick axes, silver-plated so their desire does not cause
them pain. There is no hint of victory for us. The fall is certain.

7.

On these television screens
Are these roundtables
or
graves?
The diggers prepared them with care
In order that compassion fit our skulls
The executioner greets his victim!

8.

Now
The rockets can sleep
The wind has muted their nuclear sound

9.

Those who know are content with silence. God's creation will return to the
kingdom of ants. The remains of corpses to their sellers. And the dirt to its
infirmity. Those who died died. Those who escaped were saved. We who have
no ally but the pillar of wind, what should we do so that the fearful deserve
their death? How did we build steel crematories for the earth? We are the last
destitutes.

10.

Baghdad
Is without a sky
Naked as my hand . . .
Baghdad glistens in the dust
Breathing splinters
Awaiting the next missile . . .
A war, live,
The picture an exercise for the apocalypse!

11.

A man pained by tears
The wars settled in the folds of his life
He whips his picture with an old shoe
And thinks about the dictator . . .
How did these defeats grow worse between his fingers?

12.

This heart is as obstinate as a gasp. There's nothing in the heart for Baghdad
but what saves my name from the general's shoes. The news is armored.
Piercing my chest. Bombarding my tear ducts. And raising sun-dried graves in
Victory Square. The hours are armored. The night bites my fingers. The statues
are scratching their skins. Pissing on the heads of survivors. And deserters.
Come let's chew the gum of the news reports. And enjoy the scenes of Baghdad
cuddled by uranium. We'll build ceremonies for Baghdad. And winged statues

that intelligent reports cannot topple. Baghdad, the city of God and palm trees
and thieves in tales : more frail than the texture of the story's weave. It fell like
a stranger betrayed by his feet. Baghdad the first sacrifice. Lady of eulogies.
Fashioned by the general to be a city of paper.

13.

Now that
The earth has become tumorous for her own
Historians have gone on their way
And us, what shall we do
With the armies this war has left in our sad homes ?
With the wardrobes of our clothes and the dining rooms ?
What shall we do with the politicians and analysts ?
With screens that flourish with destruction ?
Where shall we throw away the remains of rotting bodies?

14.

Regrets:
Dear Victoria:
(the soldier writes to his sweetheart)
    We didn't find the Baghdad that's in the story. Another city is in
our hands. I'm sorry I can't make it. I will not come back before the fall of the
next Baghdad.

These Odd Probabilities

Probability 1

These
words that won't reach you,
their trails are probably of
lead, that's why they melt quickly
in the first utterance I send to you!

Probability 2

This
glory is not mine. I try
to fix it firmly at the top, and not to obey the hand
of force! I'm not someone
frightened by the abyss: I'm one
made dizzy by heights!

Probability 3

In order to flay this skin that I loathe
I have two choices:
either change the name of the crust, or
praise its color with words, then
I may become another person
without regret!

Probability 4

This
race that the city desires,
with real racers, and referees
whose impartiality is beyond doubt, may
be just a façade for the victory of the only
player!

Probability 5

So often
this fast train has passed us
stopping only to empty its entrails
of wind, it didn't have seats
for those returning and no windows
to make time humane, its whistle
resembled a blade, that's why
we thought all its passengers were
murderers!

Probability 6

This boy
always looks at his toy with suspicion,
trying to give it a form other than the one
fashioned by the hand of its maker, and when
the toy doesn't change in his hands
he demolishes it with skill and ambiguous innocence.
That's why we, whose childhood
has grown old, let the toy be killed
on our behalf!

Probability 7

On
my other side, there may be
one who resembles me, but with one probability
that leads to the same conclusion: it's
always me that person resembles!

These probabilities:

It's probable:
that the house will become a grave for you . . .
that this loss won't lead to concord . . .
that no rain falls this year . . .
that the earth suddenly alters its orbit . . .
that all the shadows fall down wounded . . .
that there is no rule . . .
that the air gets poisoned between your hands . . .
that I will soon look out upon my loneliness . . .
that angels will visit me at home . . .
It's very probable:
that we'll never attain
solid ground!

El Assimi, Malika

Malika El Assimi (born on December 23, 1946, in Marrakech) is a Moroccan poet and politician. She is also a university professor at Cadi Ayyad University in Marrakech. In the early 1970s, she edited and published the magazine الاختيار (*Choice*) and co-edited الثقافة المغربية (*Moroccan Culture*) magazine. Her own books include كتابات خارج أسوار العالم (*Writings Outside the World's Walls* 1988); as well as أصوات حنجرة ميتة (*Voices of a Dead Throat* 1989) and شيء له أسماء (*Something with Many Names* 1997), among others.

My Name is Rain

I changed my name a while ago

when the storms
hurled branch to branch
when winds
drove masses of clouds over the sea
so sorrow would sail away from the flowers
I named myself the waters washing the branches and the trees
sweeping dirt from inside hearts
from clothes and stones . . .
I decided to be called . . .
"Rain"

*   *   *

I own nothing but torment
I own nothing but estrangement from loved ones

and friends

I own nothing but the cries of my childhood
                          and melancholy
I own nothing
I will never be *Malika,* the Owner
My name is Rain . . .
Pouring down to water the earth holding the lover
a body I see in my sweet strange dream
And with spring I continue to plant
bunches of flowers in its soil
from my fertile and happy name

My daughter who was to be born from my blood one day
I kept this name to call her: my daughter Rain
But I will die like a dog no matter how long I live . . .
                          and there will never be
a child of mine named: Rain
I love the breeze of freedom
like a lonely wild cat
                  running from forest to forest
fleeing people and chains
And I am the rain . . .
Pouring my dewy drops on the earth
I will make blossoms grow, spreading them over my lover's body
so that it remains with the flowers . . .
clothing it in spring, in fall, in summer
The perfume of flowers singing for him so he won't be alone
I have decided I would be called . . .
"Rain"
*   *   *

Oh my friends!
Excuse me if I
Don't respond to your call
I don't remember my former name
With the trembling of branches,
With the embrace of grasses in the meadows,
With the white and fatuous spring
In the world of women

Oh my friends!
Excuse me
If I don't recall my former name
When spring came, I picked bunches of flowers
And scattered them in my room
Everyplace and everywhere
And I knew that my name was . . . . "Rain".

Creation

At night I throw off
My shame
Bursting open my sun
So completely
My madness goes crazy
A wild
Blaze inhabits me
I rise like waves at high tide
In rough seas
My tempests swell
One after another
My light gleams
I sparkle
Like lightning running
Out from behind the clouds
I blaze
With God's light
And ponder my temptation
I sit on the throne
Mistress of creation
On the breast of the star
My madnesses and arts are perfected
The lord of the woods
Roars
In all of me
In my hidden places

My lion
Roars
In rapture for the red star
That pierces the horizon

Something with Many Names

In the dusk of the moons
I was born
Dawn was
Looking down on the worlds
And the chest of the night
Was tearing its clothes in torment
* * *

Poor relatives sat down
On the doorstep of the Lord's earth
The birds of paradise sang in the wombs
The holy branch leaned over
To shade this earth
It put forth leaves
Of silk
And white roses
* * *

The day of birth . . .
I was thunderstruck
Mount Toor rose up
Followed by verses of light
And the face of God
I heard the Great Voice whispering:
"Oh, servant of the earth
Walk towards the pond, to the water
Towards the blueness in the eye of the griffon
You will find people weighed down by the burden of the earth
But don't be sad
In your right hand, you have
Clouds

In your left hand, you have
Earth
Don't begrudge them water
As the earth lies fallow "
* * *
The Lord talked to me
The next day
The branches cried from extreme sorrow
Sins spread over the world:
—"Pray, daughter of breeze and tempests
Your prayer will cool hell's woe
Your prayer will dispel the gloom and sorrows in this world"
I prayed
And the gloom didn't dispel
And His ample mercy did not come down
On this tormented world
And I'm still struggling those who seize the prayer niche
When I want to pray
While they keep guard at the mosque's door
This world wasn't purified with my prayers . . . !
And I'm still praying.

El Hajjam, Allal

Allal El Hajjam was born in 1949 in Meknes, Morocco. He earned his doctorate degree from the school of Arts and Humanities in Meknès. Formerly a professor of Arabic language at Al Akhawayn University in Ifrane, Morocco, he also taught at other universities in Meknes and Rabat before he moved to the USA where he is a senior Arabic lecturer at Emory University, Atlanta. El Hajjam's publications include the poem collections الحلم في نهاية الحداد (*Dream at the End of Mourning* 1975); and في الساعة العاشقة مساءا (*At the Night's Hour of Love* 2001), among many others.

Ghailan's Morning

Ghailan has his morning fruit
                    fresh from the mountains of innocence
like the odor of grass when blown by a breeze
He wakes up his school books from their sleep
His playful steps bursting wild
from inner springs

The nightingale's radiance lights up
                    over the branch of an olive tree
          Amid blankets he crowns himself king
          He is taken astray by a flower
          that has moistened his workbook
He wakes up the sun from its sleep
          yawning drunken redolent with fragrance

          as it rises, stumbles, gets up
          it caresses his school bag

As he wakes up his pencil case
the pencils exchange insults with tales of excited colors
before the small whispers pick up:
      Khalil's dream chasing the promise of butterflies at daybreak
In a twinkle of an eye, he has landed
      from the heights of lofty clouds
to his assignment in grammar, writing, drawing
      and the language of love.

Khalil's Evening

O my little friend
When I contemplate the snow turning green during my slumber
becoming green between the building and the guardian oak
I imagine the palm of sleep's hand picking a quarrel
at your eyes and a phantom clasping your waist
as a candle burns far away, its blueness mixing
with green in the thick clouds
their breath dripping tears
    one tear, two, three, then twenty
      fading away little by little
      and then the brigades of the moon attack.
It's almost midnight . . .
Won't you listen to me? . . . night has grown dark
The clock hands have to come together, there's no more time
      to spin the threads of wakefulness
Wrap yourself with a happy dream in your bed
and come over to the song of lavish tenderness
Take your book and read a poem
    and let the whisper of the soul roam
over there, in the courtyards of princely imagination . . .
It's time for the pampered nightingale to silence her chatter
It's time for the kind woman
on the warmth of your flowered bed covers
to put the joys of her blossoms in proper order one by one
and let the lamps rest from the jabs of sleepy eyes
under the cover of the night
on the sleepy journey. . .

I will tell them if they ever hear

Sad, my little one
got up shivering
in the breaking dawn of day
and in his eyes a fire blazed.
Out of his sky flew nightingale songs of dreams
                    a raving wound
When I asked him
about the secret of his tears
about who frightened the flowers
who stabbed the magnificent warblers
          at the snatching away of dawn
he responded, "the war oh dad
a night that's mangling the light
a ghoul that's hunting for children
          and birds
          and poets
a fire that puts out tempests
so tell them
Oh dad . . . tell them
to play the strings
so their tunes rise to the sky
          green
          enchanting
Maybe they'll hedge us
from the spark of an ember smoldering in the horizon . . ."
. . .
I wiped
the hot tears on his cheeks
whose fire strikes the match of fright
And I kissed the trembling words on his lips
I told him,
"I will tell them if ever they hear!"

El Khassar, Abderrahim

Abderrahim El Khassar, born in 1975 in Safi, is a writer, a teacher, and a poet. He was selected as one of the best forty poets in the Arab world by the British High Festival held in Beirut in 2010. He served as a writer in the cultural section at the Lebanese daily newspaper النهار (*The Daily*). He participated in various international poetry venues in Europe and America. He received a prize from the Festival of Asilah in 2011. He received three literary scholarships in Virginia, California, and Illinois. His major publications include: أخيرا وصل الشتاء (*Winter has Finally Arrived* 2004); أنظر و أكتفي بالنظر (*I See and Am Content with Seeing* 2007); نيران صديقة (*Friendly Fires* 2009); بيت بعيد (*A Distant House* 2013); خريف فيرجينيا: رحلات إلى أمريكا و أروبا (*Virginia's Autumn: Trips to America and Europe* 2017); عودة آدم (*Adam's Return* 2018).

A Faraway Home

The hand that came out of the book and caressed my cheek is the hand of the old woman whose breath used to fill the corners of the house. I long for the sound of bracelets on her wrists, her Indian hair, her toothless laugh. I yearn for the water urn in her room, for her Amazigh red scarf, the dust that used to fly off the doom-palm tray as she sieved wheat, the din she made at the end of the night heating water for her ablutions. I yearn for her, lonely and forgotten there, in a house far away at the graveyard.

Life

I see her with her toothless mouth, her wretched eyes scouring the broom as it hangs in the air by her legs, remains of straw on her shoulders, a herd of blackbirds under her rough black skirt, her gray eyebrows at my face make me tremble. Why are you afraid old woman, when death is timidly kneeling down behind you like a towering mountain? For five hundred years I've been drinking tea and listening to the opera and nothing has changed. Take it easy. We will keep on wearing jeans, going to cafes and writing poetry even when we are dead.

The City of Safi

On the outskirts of the old Portuguese quarter, as I sit alone at Café as-Safina, looking at the ocean and the mausoleum where one of my ancestors lies, a lute player passes with his red tarboosh and behind him a line of memories stream by: music at the church, poems I read at the pottery museum, a girl I loved who may perhaps still live in this neighborhood, old friends who were with me on the railway, songs of Enrico Macias and the smell of fish, morning tea and poems published in trashy newspapers, the blue shops and the French women in their short dresses on the corniche, the English literature girl fascinated by Byron, a novelist tracing back the history of the Jews, a poet from Holland looking for his shadow in the popular quarter, comrades fishing for words sailing in the air at the bar . . . the lute player gets tired and sits down on a cement bench. He looks at the ocean and the mausoleum where a long line of memories pass before him as they did before me.

El Khayat, Rita

Rita El Khayat (born in 1944 in Rabat) is a psychiatrist, anthropologist, and a writer. She has written more than 350 articles and 30 novels. Her works include: Le Monde Arabe au Féminin (*The Arab World in the Feminine* 1985); Les Septs Jardins (*The Seven Gardens* 1995); Le Maghreb des Femmes (*The Morocco of Women* 2001); and Métissages Culturels (*Cultural Mixings*, co-authored by Alain Goussot 2002).

The Raped Flower

I learned of your death this morning
Amina
while drinking my cold coffee

The judge married you
to the man who raped you
Your sex ripped apart like a crushed flower
bled yet again
on the day your nuptials were ordered
by legal advisors
their heads filled with feces and detritus . . .
it bled
the flame of hatred in the heart of your rapist-become-husband
by insane laws!

You saw death
the deliverance from horror
the sex of the man you didn't want
bitter as hemlock
hard as a falling pylon that kills a passerby
foul as the cadaver of a dog
who has never been happy !

The judge, Amina, here in these parts
is an eager and perverse coward
bribery a manure in his stomach
an egg of old age, filled with diverse depravities . . .

I looked on appalled
Just six years ago
a five year-old child was raped like you
. . . by a twenty-seven year old adult.
The judge decreed that she would wait until she was older to marry her rapist!

My soul trembled, sick with revulsion
Your mother and grandmother were peasants
looking for a non-existent justice
in places under the dominion of men satisfied with their impotence . . .
In Larache, northern Morocco,
from where your soul took flight in a white ship
in Larache, northern Morocco,
land of scrub, thyme and rosemary
the bushes cry in unison
with jasmine, pink roses
and buds of peacock flower devastated: Amina is dead!

She drank the poison, yellow flower, deadly bile
She left this spring morning
while all around Larache
orange blossoms embalm the flaneur to the point of intoxication . . .
eucalyptus shake their incredulous heads!

Amina is dead
in the snares of the Middle -Ages
she agonized in the turpitude of the virility
that has raped all women!
Amina is dead
on the anniversary of
the Arab Spring
we celebrate as well
the wedding of blood and rape!

Amina, beautiful fairy of our gardens
flower of our nation
rose of Morocco
red hibiscus
wild white hyacinth of the prairies !

Your torn virginity
gives my pen its brilliant blood
bursting with revolt
so that my poem rises to the glory
of all those that men have martyred
in the lands of men
lands abject and deprived of sense
blooming in all the infamies and offerings
torrid in the infernal summer
When a backward and blind justice renders
girls and women its victims
orphans and the poor
the destitute, the lacking, the lonely !
The Arab Spring is stained with the blood of virgins
the blood of frustrated men,
with rapacious desire, aggressive and overflowing with hate !

Amina, your smile fixed until the end of time shows
that the sex of a girl, the sex of a woman
belong only to her.
She is a splendid flower in a crystal vase
From a pink vagina the life
of generations emerges in the world
the treasure of only the girl or woman
for whom it is the center, heart, pleasure and joy !

Amina,
Rest in peace in my poet's heart.
You did well to kill yourself
No one understood the savagery you were made to endure
neither your parents, your judges, nor your neighborhood or country:
Like you we have suffered the rapes.
We have been murdered by villainy
one more yellow and demented flower that ravages our breast
by the one that brought you death
we are all dead
in a secret part of our hearts !

Amina, you gave us back glory and pride
You did not die in vain
I sing you today
I will sing you forever . . .
And when I die
this poem will survive
your parents, your judges, and the rapist
offered to you as a supreme punishment
It will survive the nameless stupidity that roots up the flowers we are
having not even dawned, having known neither perfume nor beauty
bunches of white Casablanca lilies
roses of Kelaat M'gouna,
orange blossoms pulled from the crown of brides!
(Casablanca, 16 mars 2012)
Amina Filali, sixteen, killed herself on March 10, 2012, having swallowed rat
poison in Larache (on the North Atlantic coast of Morocco), after the court of
Larache ruled that she had to marry her rapist.

El Maïmouni, Mohamed

Mohamed El Maïmouni was born in 1936 in Chefchaoun and died in October 2017. He attended primary school in Chefchaoun and high school in Tetouan. He obtained his bachelor's degree in Arabic Literature from the Faculty of Arts and Humanities in 1966, and then a master's degree from the same institution. He worked as a high school teacher in Tangier from 1966 to 1972 then he was a high school principal in Tetouan. His publications include: آخر أعوام العقم (*The Last Years of Infertility* 1974); طريق النهر (*The River's Path* 1995); and الحلم في زمن الوهم (*Dream in a Time of Illusion* 1992).

Return

Today I return to the gilded past
to forgetfulness
to shadows that weave night to night
stretching out to recover their height
seizing a moon
that converses with genies.
I return to late afternoons just
before the Feast
processions of spirits at sunset
on their way to a star with a strange light
that wipes out the hues of things
veiling the crescent moon
when it appears in the festival sky
on the shoulders of a minaret
that butts against the blueness of heaven.

I return to the winding steps
on the cobblestone street
to paths
that travel in the thoughts of
passersby
to ancient doors
and walls conversing with their shadows
on the edge of the lunatic sanctuary
where sane people stop
their pain disguised with forgetfulness
on their way to Chefchaouen.

Seaweed

The air has no trees
the birds hang from the clouds
in a corner of light
exiled from their songs
the letters have lost their language
the sea has folded its clothes
and the wind has reneged
withdrawing into a cave
Morning and evening
walk together
in equal pace
carrying the mortal remains of the city
seaweed left in puddles
that maps have forgotten
neither a sea
shaken by waves
nor dry land
where threshing floors find their home.

The Nightmares of the Harbor

Under the chill cover of night
light slithers over concrete
stagnant water
falls from a dim lantern
touching the still face of the rock.
The nightmare of the mute graveyard
floats on barren ground
a slippery sweat on the harbor
it screams like a flaming silence
a bird dreams with open eyes
its dreams fall off the dusty branches
and frozen pylons
stretch the rusty cable
to men tied to the choking
noose, they come when the bird shakes itself
from dream before the arrival of light
* * *

The caravan of worn-out men
seek shelter in their corner of forgetfulness
The rusty cable
stretches to all the huts
hangs down from the victory archways
sneaks through the cracks in the neighbors' walls
The forests of whispers on the harbor floor
arrive from a breach in the sullen night
a wound that proliferates in the womb of time to
come

from Eulogy for a Meteor

1

We went to the heights of Granada
on a wing of the falconers' soul
the doorway to heaven
and landfall of expectations and certitude
land of the martyr's death
springs of maternal water
the scene of one who met his end
without tomb or funeral
the living witness
of those who arrive at the appointed time of prayer
and leave
He alone is now the memory
But can the mention of remembrance take place
without the ones who remember?

2

From the rim where sky and sand meet
from faraway
they came
they got off at the flat plains
at a familiar place
from a fertile seed
and stretches of fabric the true color of creation
they fashioned the essence of civilization
and settled there
where they were the witnesses
of order and events
such as wind and labor

3

Like big birds
they landed on the brow of this hill
their shadow spreading its whiteness
on the back of day
streams of the unsaid
flowed in gardens of revelation

4

They planted a fig tree
and on it raised a sky bejeweled with imagination
bridges and sails
seas forested with longing
and tales enigmatic with questioning

5

The loyalty that seeds the womb of water
stretched its canals in the air
it flowed in the maze of tree sap
rose up the ladder steps
from earth
to trees
then clouds
to gold in the shade

6

When they arrived they lit the minarets
white clouds were filled with nightingales
they climbed the stairways of yearning
leaning upon a pen and stones
they built a bridge and waterways
with the ashes of a short life
and disappeared behind allusions and veils

they left their tears behind in the neighboring time
an eye wet with light longing
and ascended a rock with seven girls
who planted jewels in branches
and anklets in a basket of silk
they fashioned the face of the lady of time
with silver and copper
and spoke the secret of femininity
in earth and water
a sky parallel to the expanse of light
then they named it Granada.

(Granada, August 2002)

Meandering Poems

Every morning you are a waiting port
for the sweetheart's face to peck on your door
or break in without asking
You look for a sign of good news on every
arriving face
When darkness spreads you are a passage
to all distant shores
But the ship is of foam
breaking like a wave on the obstinate rocks
* * *
This earth is forever round
and time migrates
embezzling the sleep of dawn
Yet my fascinating lady spurts with beauty
Will you ask the ones standing in the snow
or those abandoning caravans
if the wind will howl in my lady's eye
and ships disappear?
No death will come after our encounter
Will you demolish the shore

so that the sea submerges all lack?
When a sea stretches between us
she herself is the sea
When a forest thickens between us
she herself is the sun
inhabiting the heart of every wind
* * *

The face of the city commutes between sleep and
waking
And the fire wakes pining for love
The road to you is burning embers
Now the time of dream is fleeing from me
And you seek refuge in the heart
Go back to your sky if you're not from the earth
Grow a palm tree
If you're a shell in the darkness of the ocean
light up my way to you
Wherever I go I meet your footsteps
on the killing fields
while the beloved's face
repeats like a song
in the corridors of a prison
and in the raucous laughter of childhood.

Elmannani, Abdellah

Abdellah Elmannani (born March 30, 1976) is a prize-winning poet writing in Tamazight. He has published books of poetry including Sawl S'ighd (*Talking to Ash* 2003); Ouwrawn oumeTa (*Handful of Tears* 2008); Timqa N'fad (*Drops of Thirst* 2010), and Ya Toudmt S'izlalayn Innou (*A Face out of my Splinters* 2015). He is also a film scriptwriter. He wrote the film script of Sguit (*Skeleton*) in 2007, and participated in the scriptwriting of the movies Aghrabo (*The Boat*), and Adriz (*Impact* 2014), a short documentary.

Here I am

Genuine coasts, here I am
Batting my wings
So they whistle while I wait
Here I am, among the naked
The stars scratching
Swallowing lunar insults
When I bend down, the lights go out
When I look, the earth dissolves
Once standing, I hardly recognize myself

Here I am among the footsteps of nights
The darkness pursuing
the folds and furrows of life
My orientation lost
I lean against the low wall to regain it
In the middle of the story morning saw me
Me who no longer recognizes myself

Here I am in the tomb of placid waves
The sorrow of the sea spraying
In boots the fleet gathers
The birds land to glean on fish scraps
The sun penetrates the clouds to fly away
From what quenches their thirst
It has noticed me
In the dream set sail
Twin of kings
It wove for me the canvas of Dihya
And the blanket of Juba

(Translated from Tamazight into French by Mohamed Farid Zalhoud)

Why are you tired?

Why are you tired?
Even the deep path
knows of our wandering

Why do you go back?
Don't you know that my feet are skinned
By the thorn of your silence!

Why did you turn off the glow of questioning
That washes my shy face?

Kill me
In the shadow of the moon
So that I scatter like the stars
Born of darkness!

Tell me the story of the cemetery ghost mare
Even if it is not yet dawn
No one will believe you if not me!

Why are you tired?
Your springtime has gone out like a flame
And I'm a bee abstaining from flowers

In dreams
I feed the honey of your word
To the future!

Evoking only tears
In the dazzle that clothes the flowers
With your memory!
Why are you tired?
Why are you tired?

And you want me to be tired too?
Verses tell the story of our love
The story where we were born
The sun typed
The foliage of our hearts in it
Here they are all in flower
Here are the days of our life of happiness
The minutes are the songs
Of our jousts
When I utter: get up, you say: bedtime
Here comes the darkness
Why are you tired?
And you want me to be tired too?

(Translated from Tamazight into French by Mohamed Farid Zalhoud)

El Ouadie, Salah

Salah El Ouadie is a Moroccan former political prisoner and civil society activist who is now a poet, writer, and diplomat. He was born in 1952. He obtained a bachelor's degree in philosophy in Morocco and a Diplome des Etudes Approfondie in political science from the University of Montpellier in France in 1987. He was professor at the Higher School of Business Administration in Casablanca and was a founder of the Moroccan Organization of Human Rights in 1988. He was also the television host of لحظة شعر (*Moment of Poetry*) on the Moroccan television channel 2M from 2000 until 2002. His major poetry publications include: جراح الصدر العاري (*Bare Chest Wounds* 1985); ما زال شيء في القلب يستحق الانتباه (*There is Still Something Worthwhile in the Heart* 1988); قصيدة تازمامارت (*The Poem of Tazmamart* 2003). Salah El Ouadie also published a novel العريس (*The Groom* 1998).

You . . .

You
who will love
leave
a corner in your heart
for evildoers

You
who will hate
leave
a corner in your heart
for the kind

You
who will anger
leave
a corner in your heart
for forbearance

You
who will die
leave
a corner in your heart
for remembrance

You
who will listen
leave
a corner in your heart
for silence

You
who will plan
leave
a mark of your pencil
for the subtle mind

You
who will welcome the newborn
from its mother's womb
pray
with all your substance for the miracle

You
who will be delivered of your pregnancy
remember
your womb being filled
with the universe's secrets

You
who will breastfeed
leave
some affection in your breasts
for the street urchin

You
who will fly out in space
take a look
down on us
the wayfarers

You
who will depart
leave
a glimmer
of your conscience for those bidding you farewell

You
who will decide
leave
a quiver
from your heart for doubt

You
who will pronounce the sentence
leave
a phrase in your consideration
for God's clemency

You
who will hand over trust
leave
a glimpse of your imagination
for secrets

You
who will rule over people
leave
an instant of affection
for your heart

You
who will bury the dead
leave
inside the tomb
an inch for memories

Goodbye Mohamed (Extract)
(To the memory of Mohamed al-Foulous, who left us after ten years of imprisonment.)

Goodbye Mohamed
Goodbye my friend
You came from the sea and to the sea you depart
alone to die as a martyr
Goodbye ten years gone by
Do they thaw out or does the soul become a vagrant?

Goodbye
The country's jails invested you with distress
while you invested them with pride
And here you are going away accompanied by crowds and memories
Are we sending off the friend that you were or are the barbaric times
sending us all to disarray?

The burning memory of friendship conflicts with our joy
So journey across the expanse of the country that denied you
Today don't be sad. The wilderness was enriched
as you stretched within it
Be graceful, now you have the bunch of flowers that desired you
and that you so much desired

The universe has declared you free
confirming that I lost and regained you now
How wonderful the moment you rest so as to rise

Goodbye Mohamed
Goodbye my little companion
Goodbye my companion prince

Goodbye the universe is all yours. Does anyone attain awe
from its vastness but the captive?
Goodbye, my heart grieves. Is it your leaving
Or is it my longing for the sea's blueness or the perfumed breeze?

Goodbye now my little companion
Your mother waits for your face
to break open the city's gloom
Your mother awaits your voice filled
with beatitude
your mother waits for your first gasp
Her nightmares have so often tempted her mind—you know—
May your heart, mother, be praised, you have loved him so much!

And here you are moved by the heavens
confused by the flap of the wings
that fluttered on your arms
Here you are escaping gravity and containment
So don't forget me oh my friend
and don't forget the face in my yearning glass
Don't forget me but forget the earth that covered us up
and the metal that brought us together and enclosed us
and those keys used to lock us up against our will
Praise be my love for you and your love for me
Praise be to this challenge
Praise to a heart that engraved in limestone
bunches of flowers.

The Poem of Tazmamart

Incessant rain
Earth's arid branches
like dried up knots around me
old pictures come in succession

and darkness

Space consumes the earth
Here I am going to it
You carried two stone tools
and forgot that stone is immersed in silence
Nothing is left in my heart but a flapping flag far away

How many tears were shed there?

How many shudders did your hands know?

How many painful sighs rose to the highest sky
falling down to the ground to overwhelm
my ears wet with moaning?

Oh you who has slipped over my song a quiver of
jasmine

Rain will fall down as the road draws more towards
my feet

I walk unhurriedly
The sun sets behind us and casts light over a building
a graveyard. The earth's surface swelled with pointed configurations stubbornly
     opposing
my lowering feet. I haven't yet had a sight of the village of
Tazmamart
I don't feel the paces of my heart on the pebbles
The sun does not feel the shadows either
As here there are no trees no birds and no clearwater springs

This
  is

    the

      sanctuary

        of fright

          bearing its dark night

This
is it
then

A herd of blackbirds resting their haunches above its passageways
is pushing its howls to extremes. Where does **the wolf** come from when
  darkness looks down from the haze of dusk?

I walk unhurriedly
Oh terrifying night of Tazmamart

This
is it
then

Terror covers up all the paths, a corridor of fear over here
a tunnel of death over there, settling like sediment in the hollows of the
  mountains

This
is it
then

Trenches of the dead whose blood has not yet dried
vomit still on their mouth
and the forgotten Morocco is a giant graveyard

Oh God the Glorious and the Compassionate!
Oh you the Eternal Forbearing Lord!

Shall I wake the dead that have gathered around me
and wipe away a pair of tears on the cheeks

of pain?

Shall I wake the dead and put on their coats
as they were before they left

I walk unhurriedly and enter their fears

This is it then

And here I am entering Tazmamart.

El Ouazzani, Hassan

Hassan El Ouazzani was born in 1970 in Safi, Morocco. He has a diploma in documentation and information science from l'Ecole des Science de l'Information in Rabat. Former secretary-general of the Moroccan House of Poetry, El Ouazzani is now a professor at the School of Information Science in Rabat and the director of the department of book publishing at the Ministry of Culture. His poems have been translated into several languages. His publications include: ما هدنة (*A Certain Truce* 1997) and أحلام ماكلوهان (*Mac Lohan's Dreams* 2016). He is also the author of documentation studies such as الأدب المغربي الحديث (*Contemporary Moroccan Literature: 1929–1999*, 2002), قطاع الكتاب بالمغرب (*Book Publishing in Morocco* 2010) as well as *A Socio-Bibliometric Study of Moroccan Literature in the Twentieth Century.*

Seedling of Wind-Born Dust

Over there
In the refuge. Near the river. Beside the tree.
In the dark corners of the house. In the basement. Under the stairs.
At the door steps. On the boat. On the harbor's dock.
Beside the stream. In the courtyard. In the wide café.
In the middle of the square.

No
lover found refuge in his sweetheart.
No companion played the chords of love.
No hand stretched to a woman's hair.
No lady dreamt of her knight.
And no one danced to the night.

And the heavens
the heavens didn't do anything
but outrun my footsteps
to take me to hollow graves.

The heavens didn't murder anyone
but weaved of my childhood
a homeland of hell.

The heavens
keep the clouds of the land close
filling my heart with barrenness.

It's all right
I'll win the next round. I'll go to
the frontlines determined. I'll keep my heartbeat
close to emptiness.
I'll lay ambush to the heavens.
I'll fill my chest with its night. I'll strip it
of all these stars. I'll hide them behind my door.
By the grapevine's greenhouse. Over there
where the anthem is the head's dizziness
and the echo
    is an abode
       for poets.
I'll tell
the night
Oh my friend, we'll stay up together today.
We'll open wells of blackness
for the sun and
for the earth
domes
of wind-born dust.

I'll tell
Death
Oh my friend, we'll lay a thousand
traps for life.

I'll say
to the wind-born dust
I don't have a homeland where I can hang my heart amid the moons.
There is no sky to hide my sorrows.
I don't have a sea
to moor myself at its shores. I have
so many of the earth's mirages
so many deserts of love
so much of the heart's disaffection.

Okay
The war will come to an end. It won't be over. Love
will run out. It won't run out.
The moons will vanish. They won't vanish.

Slowly
I tear the flower.
Perhaps the world will lie down and die, perhaps
Leila will leave her tower. Perhaps her voice will abandon my heart.

Let's share
the world then.

The world's bosom
is for Leila. Its oppression, for me. For her, its warmth. For me its nakedness.
For Leila its pastures. For me its barrenness. For her its flowers. Its losses
    for me.
For her its land. For her its seas.
For her the world.
For her its lament.

Farid, Mohamed (Zalhoud)

Mohamed Farid (nicknamed Zalhoud) was born in 1959 in Aday near Tafraout, Morocco. He is a teacher of French and a poet, novelist, translator, painter and sculptor. The recipient of four literary prizes of Amazigh poetry, he is also the author of many works in the Amazigh and French languages including the trilogy Imrruyn, Takat, Ighd (*Sparks, Fire, Ash*) that appeared in Brussels under the title afgan zund argan (*Similar to the Argan Tree* 2004). His first poem collection in French, Parole de Paria (*Word of Paria* 2001), was followed by Ultime Poème (*Ultimate Poem* 2007; Mots Dits Vains (*Words Said in Vain* 2012); and Passe-relle (2013). More recently, he has published Imriri n Umdlfaw (*Breaking Dawn* 2010); Izlan i Tayri (*Verses for Love*), a collection of Amazigh poetry translated into French; Tilag (*Breathtaking* 2014); Tayri d Waman Zuzwanin (*Love and Fresh Water* 2015); and Imula Imrwaln (*Shadows Running Away* 2017). He has a personal blog: http://amedyazamazigh.blog2b.net.

The Tree of Words
(for Omar Bihmidine and Driss Amri)

the tree of words
is not the south
or the west
not picked by hand
this ancestor
not written with a sapling
nor with the pain of a club
it is barely anchored in the earth

its foliage is hope
its fruit joy
the tree of life
doesn't grow in a wasteland

rain does not water it
irrigated by blood
sheltered from the harsh sun
it is sweet fresh salvation
its seed the remedy
for all evil

happy the wordsmith
happier than the water smith
if he finds you oh tree
he leaves his pedant knowledge
and hurries towards you
to heal his soul.

Desert
(for Mostafa Houmir)

my faith, will you find water there?
speak to the sea without salt without fish
dunes at the mercy of the wind moving drops of sand
the furnace of the Levant heat-wave sun

my faith, will you find men there?
speak to the brambles with thorns in the branches
reason moving its woven scattered threads to the heart
blood mixed with worry wandering in poems

my faith, will you find joy there?
speak to the cicada singing long life
bread a make-shift walking stick
valiant hope embracing the world

there you will find water
there you will find men
there you will find joy

Guennouni, Mohamed-Khammar

Mohamed-Khammar Guennouni (1941–1991) was born in Ksar El-Kebir but grew up in the neighboring town, Larache, Morocco. He worked for the Moroccan National Radio in 1961 and as a teacher at secondary schools. He received his Diplome des Etudes Supérieures from Mohammed V University in Rabat in 1974. He is regarded as a pioneer in modern Moroccan poetry. His poems were first published in the French anthology of Moroccan poetry La Memoire Future (*Future Memory* 1976, edited by Tahar Ben Jelloun) and then were regularly published in the cultural supplement of the daily newspaper العلم (*The Flag*). Some of his poems were translated by Abdellatif Laâbi and published in *La Poesía Marroquí: de la Independencia a Nuestros Días*, Santa Cruz de Tenerife:Idea, 2006. His works include: رماد هيسبريس (*The Ash of Hesperis* 1987).

The Marble Dragon

Hesperis* is calling you by your name: stand up oh marble body
Every stranger has knocked at its door until it has swelled with blood
Move your wings, strike at the ships of strangers on the river's edge

Tomorrow Hesperis will decline
Its doors opened to thieves, dying, disappearing
The swaggerers coming in
The thieves going out
The deceivers rising
The liars going down
Stand up on the river bank. Your bone, your skin, your flesh is still tender,
You are alive, you are so alive . . .

Hesperis and what it bore of ash, water, and lightning
the wind of wide lands that has moved the river trees
is calling you by your name

The face of dust that writing has filled
The ocean sun that has colored slopes and forests
The hand of leaves falling on you following the evening, is calling you by
     your name . . .

Hesperis is calling you by your name for every year its sons were slaughtered
     and it says:
Through the ash I saw you were fire, your fire is in you, your fire is you . . .

---

* Mythical gardens supposed to have existed on the North African Atlantic coasts.

The Changes of Golden Apples

All the fields, from the boundaries of the ocean to the river, bore their fruits
As one language ascended the others declined
When first they blossomed the language of trade and fraud had not yet begun
The words of brokers had not risen
But a language transited between singing and confusion . . .

They arrived, color had no hue, nor had perfume any odor!
Is the river green, did snow fall on western summits, did the wind blow?
It did not matter to the passing brokers!

Did they observe these things, or were they eclipsed from their consideration?
They kept silent, and only the language of haughty tone talked:
This is yours, and this is ours, this is ours
We kept silent and even our days would not utter a word!

(From hand to hand these fields transformed: earth, air, and water
And in between an old thief and a new thief the golden apples ripened
Was that God's decree and providential appointment?)

With whole fields the ships set out to sea
To where? Eyes could not tell
Had these fields answered: eat my body and drink my blood,
It would not have been right . . .
Had they been without owners—sleepy or ignorant—
It would not have been right . . .

(They are the ransacked trees for passersby
They are the impossible fruit for those who seed the land)

And it was not right, as they landed—in harbors and on dining tables—
on men who saw them and their flag of the impossible nation, they cried . . .
It's them: Moroccan Export

Hamrouch, Abdeddine

Abdeddine Hamrouch was born on December 27, 1964 in Casablanca and he is a professor of Arabic Literature at the Faculty of Arts and Humanities in El Jadida, Morocco. His poetry publications include: وردة النار (*The Flower of Fire* 1992); فقط (*Only* 2002); كفوهة البندقية (*Like the Nozzle of a Gun* 2010). He also published critical essays such as: تجلي العين (*Manifestation of the Eye* 2008); المثقف المغربي: من العضوي إلى الإفتراضي (*The Moroccan Intellectual: From the Organic to the Virtual* 2012); المعتمد بن عباد: ضيفا على المغرب (*Al Mutamid Ibn Abbad: A Guest in Morocco* 2014), that was re-edited under a different title in 2015, المعتمد بن عباد في سنواته الأخيرة بالأسر (*Al Mutamid Ibn Abbad in his Last Years of Captivity*).

Stones

From his mouth
The words roll down stone . . . after stone:
The fugitive hides behind them.
The believer lifts his Kaaba with them.
The desperate throws himself from their peak.
The old man gives his life a rest on them.
The lover carves a bleeding heart on them.
The child marks them with drawings of humans and animals.
The revolutionary hurls them into a popular riot.
The flower bursts forth from them with light and life.
The dead make them a gravestone.
The vagrant ignites the desert night with them.
Water drags them to close the mouth of a cavern.
The sea throws away the wrecks of its ships and drowned ones on them.

The sculptor fashions with them wings and waving hands.
The farmer fences with them fields of grapes and figs.
The woman bejewels her wrists and ears with the precious ones.
The king raises fortresses from which he overlooks his subjects.
The prisoner with a life sentence counts on them his remaining days.
The entrepreneur plants them into buildings in every green space.
. . . .
The poet retrieves them
to throw them in a still pond.

Peace, you say
To the poet Abdellah Rajie

Peace . . . you say
and the gathering whisks you away
from a hand that buds longing and jasmine
Not to the sea do you walk
but in your footsteps the waves are a boat
eaten by questioning
in the roar of the expansive waters

Peace . . . you say
Oh prince of seagulls
around whom horses gallop
How many times a day does the sun rise?
And the clouds?
And the shade?
When you walk like a star, a lion in the night
you are betrayed only by your coughing

Peace . . . you say
And the street cornered in glasses drinks you up
Set up by wine and tea
"He passed by just a while ago,"
the bridge said
"I saw him running beside me"

said the ocean
And you, as you are, distracted
drafting the intractable word
seducing the star that hugs the night at the corner

resembling the impossible

Peace . . .
you say: my words a traveling butterfly
in the tremor of borrowed logic
in the bolting of eloquence
stationed in short murmurs of longing
ignited by the journey

Peace . . . you say
But until when will you travel on metaphor
afflicted with
questioning

The Perfume of Love

When he handed it to her secretly
she wasn't careful
The glass bottle slipped out of her hand
It fell to the ground
where the perfume dispersed in all directions
When he handed it to her secretly
in the speed of light, the perfume of love spread
all over the house

Hmoudane, Mohamed

Mohamed Hmoudane was born in 1968 in El Maâzize, Morocco. He has lived in France since 1989. His poetry publications include: Poème d'au-delà de la Saison du Silence (*Poem from Beyond the Season of Silence* 1994); Attentat (*Attack* 2003); Incandescence (*Incandescence* 2004); Blanche Mécanique (*White Mechanic* 2005); Parole Prise, Parole Donnée (*Word Taken, Word Given* 2007); as well as two novels: French Dream (2005) and Le Ciel: Hassan II et Maman France (*The Sky: Hassan II and Mother France* 2010).

from *Word Taken, Word Given*

VII

On the terrace
a shroud that slaps in the wind—my childhood

My childhood
one thousand Quranic verses
that celebrated
and exalted my sex

My childhood
the table laid
clothed in night and my father
my father . . .

The milk and the melted
gold are going to spill

Light the candles
and light the heavens

Blood
blood is going to spill:

Sacrifice my sex
and the golden calf

Already
the sky wasn't the sky
and the azure
was mixed
with blood
The sky was an inflamed
sea
and the stars
a floating apocalyptic
alphabet
hieroglyphic skiffs
crossing the night
to the other shore

———————

VIII

Every moment
fleeing the hourglass of the body
only to come back grafted to it
even more frail

Every moment

dying
where is he going
nebulous

fiery
luminous

Where is he going
in order to mature

Where is he going
like magma
to excavate gorges
erecting himself there
like untenable
epileptic
sand

What burns in the veins
oozing black from pores
fuming with your
own putrefaction?

What rolls alive
stinging your body
with blue splinters
feverish
like your breath
that you straddle
neighing like never before
neighing blood
as if you snapped up
death by the horns
when in fact mirrors
block your steps and paths
in reflections that you anticipate
all around you
one after another rising up
and disintegrating

Every moment
dying
in the center
where only ghosts
collide
a devoted being—you
in the middle of the ruins

Every moment
dying
your impure tumescent
hand continues
to infect
the world to come
as much as the one that's gone

It's the end of the world
by the very world that never
ceases to end
the world that never
ceases to become

Houmir, Mostafa

Mostafa Houmir is a Moroccan poet, novelist, director and actor, and teacher of French in Agadir. He was born on September 5, 1959, in Oujda, Morocco. He has been recognized several times by the Moroccan Association of French Teachers and received the Atlas Prize in 1998. His work is included in Jean-Pierre Koffel's Anthologie de la Poésie de Langue Française au Maroc (*Anthology of Moroccan Poetry in French* 2005). More recently, he published a poetry collection: Les Quatre Saisons (*The Four Seasons* 2017).

The Wall
(dedicated to Hassan Idkaroum, political prisoner during the years of lead in Morocco)

I remember with pain
Alone at night I cried
Only the sea to soothe me
To calm my nerves
And extinguish my embers
I remember with bitterness
Alone at night I smoked
Consumed in silence
My flame going out
I remember with bitterness
Alone at night and scared
My tears flowing
Like torrents
Seeing demons

Suffering terror
Deep in my depths
My entire being burning
Fever, nightmares, hallucinations
Alone I desert the present
And the cacophony of the living
Only the sea understands me
Only the sea welcomes me warmly
Cradles me tenderly
Sings me its song
Slowly!
Alone I walk
Breathe in the sea
Deeply
I smile
I pray
I implore the Almighty
To pardon
My torturers
And all the monsters of the earth
No hate in my heart
No resentment
But I have not forgotten
I cannot forget
Will never forget
The body does not forget
Oh if I could forget!
The tearing
Rape of the flesh
Soul and heart
The burning
That spring night
The weather was so good
The crickets were singing
The stars of the firmament
Twinkled happily
Beings and things

Slept peacefully
Suddenly
They burst in
Like demons
Suspended time
And confiscated space
Vultures, hyenas, raptors
They raged on for years
Misery years
Terror years
Years of dictatorship
Operation years
Years of repression
Treason years
Years of denial
Deportation years
Years of detention
Execution years
Years of lead!
Lovers of freedom
Justice and peace
Young activists
Insurgents and rebels
Who believed deeply
In change
Were imprisoned
Without charge
Without trial, without trial
Or simply disappeared
I remember with affliction
The monsters searched carefully
Every corner of the house
Took my books and documents
Made my mother cry
Frightened my little brothers
Screaming, crying, wailing
Complaints, prayers, supplications

I beseech you, please leave me my child!
The monsters had no heart
They dragged me violently
Did not even give me time
To clothe myself decently
Barely dressed in underwear
They handcuffed me
Crushed me with their boots
Like a common delinquent
Bandaged my eyes
Threw me into a military truck
That rolled onto an infinite road
An unknown destination
I knew then
Everything was finished!
I still remember
Like it was yesterday
They left me naked
All night long
In an austere jail
Sinister, cold, obscure
At dawn
Two gorillas entered
They did not bring the morning
They brought death
They began the interrogation
With all the arts of torture
At which they excelled
My torturers overwhelmed me
Mysterious questions
Dangerous accusations
Requiring precise answers
Names, places, dates
I had no answer
Enraged by my silence
Irritated by my insolence
They went into a trance

Becoming carnivorous animals
They devoured me
Spitting, intimidation, swearing
Blood, pain, injuries
Sweat, bites, burns
Urine, stench, torture
Choking, spreading
Stunning, numbness
Vomiting, fainting
Cold, thirsty, hungry
Isolation, seclusion
For ten years!
Ten years of silence
Ten years of absence
Ten years of endurance
Ten years of suffering
Ten years!
To stay alive
I talked with the wall
Told it my life
Writing on the wall
With my blood
With my cum
With my excrement
With my sweat
With my tears
With my urine
Carving the wall
With my nails
With my flesh
Drawing on the wall
Eyes, smiles
Breasts, vaginas
Thighs, rears
Hands, figures
Rivers, seas
Dreams, chimeras

Questions, open doors
Access through windows
To sun and pure air
The sky, the light
Ear to the wall
Listening to its heartbeat
Marrying the wall
Making love to it
Disappearing in the wall
Seeing beyond it
To go someplace else
To never come back
Emerging from the shadows
Spying on any noise
To surprise life
Waiting
Defying time
Dreaming
On the lookout
Braving madness
Brushing with death
Seeing another day
Revive
Revive
Revive

Dignity violated
Humanity stolen
Youth ravaged
Mutilated for life
I will never forget
The body does not forget
I will never heal
Crippled I remain
Marked for life!
Surviving only
No hate in my heart

No resentment
I implore the Almighty
To grant his absolution
To my torturers
And to all the monsters of the earth

(Agadir 1/5/2011)

Ikbal, Touria

Born in Marrakech, Touria Ikbal is a poetess, a translator, and a researcher on Sufism. She is a a secondary school teacher and a former member of the Culture, Communication, and Education Commission in the Parliament. Her major publications are: Propos Précoces (*Precocious Proposals* 2004); L'Épître du Désire (*Epistle of Desire* 2005); *Fulgurations*, 2007; Jusqu'au Petit Matin (*Until Early Morning* 2010); Oasis (2012); Les Noms Divins (*The Divine Names* 2015); and La Burda* du Désert (*The Burda of the Desert* 2015), with Faïza Tidjani and Muhammad Vâlsan.

And He Tells Me

And he tells me:
    Submit yourself to me
    I will be your master
    the guide to all you need
    I will lead you
    on the path of truth

And he tells me:
    Take off your sandals
    Divest yourself
    of all that is not you
    Give yourself over to my wisdom
    and walk in my footsteps

---

*"Burda" refers to the Prophet's cloak and is the title of a well-known *qasida*, a praise poem by al-Busiri dating from the 13th century AD.

And he tells me:
    My gaze will always be on you
    You will not sink down
    Your eyes will be closed
    as from now on mine will be on you

And he tells me:
    The moment has arrived
    Your master is here
    He who has no master
    strays from the path

And then he disappeared just at the moment
    I was preparing to follow him

Without . . . Noise / War . . . Zat*

Ouarzazat without . . . noise
You prepare to welcome your guests
beings of projection and reception
offering a moment of serenity
to the soul thirsty for the absolute
and eternity
disillusioned wisdom
incurable grasping

Ouarzazat without . . . noise
your frescoes in pieces
rocks from elsewhere
your starry eyes
lie in wait for harmony
to embroider a string of hope
in hearts

---

   *The title is inspired by the name of the village Ouarzazat in the south of Morocco that, in Tamazight, is composed of *ouar* et *zat*:that is, "without" and "noise."

built and rebuilt
not dying in death
born again in the folds of your nights

Ouarzazat without . . . noise
water bubbles up from your depths
your oven
the athenor*
and its alchemy
sacrificing its dregs—*tha*
to become light—*nor*
purifying rancor
softening the sting

Ouarzazat without . . . noise
you dance in the waves of dream
breath
vibration
breathlessness
ahwash†
your divine ballerinas
sashay
to the drunk rhythm of lovers
your notes of light
tremble into ecstasy

Your blind company drinks
mouthfuls of your rhythm
the trance circle
wanders in a whirlwind of drunkeness
one step, two
then one, and two

---

   * Athanor is the furnace used for alchemy that makes water mount to the sky through an alembic still. In Arabic it is called a "tanour." Alchemy consists of getting rid of the "ta" so that it becomes "nour"—"light" in Arabic.
   † *Ahwash*: a genre of folk music and dance in the region of Ouarzazat.

extreme euphony
dizziness
the universe as symphony

Ouarzazat without . . . noise
sultan of the humble
frugal and sumptuous
your invisible horseman
prince of ambiguities
leads you
to the elder rays of dawn
elegantly
on colored butterfly wings
to the banks of a poem.

Vertigo

In the matrix of immensity
I bring you eternity
I bring you a meaning
ripening in my entrails
until old age
sometimes approaching me
sometimes breaking away
growing restless
according to my vicissitudes
growing
    growing
       growing
Dizziness and distractions
taper me
and the hurricanes of passion

Suddenly
a call to your existence seizes me
and the desire to appear floods out of your being
My body refuses to disunite
My senses anxiously cry and shudder
You persist in taking form
I acquiesce
You burst from the recesses of my being
a meaning that moves all the letters
You burst forth from the clay of my destitution
a light piercing the veil of ignorance
You root yourself up outside of me
to the last end of the universe
taking my quintessential meaning
bequeathing me the perpetual quest for your essence
and nostalgia the secret of my existence
Body mutilated
heart supplicated
I am henceforth but the reflection of your reflection
the shadow effaced at the bottom of your mirror
the desire in me burning with desire to see you
My powers weaken

States of terrifying complexity
take hold of me
                    uprooting
        tearing
    sentiments
        contemplation
    intoxication
        sobering
            solitude
relaxation
        nostalgia
    irony
            anxiety
        melancholy
weariness
        folly

Apart from you
is there truth ?

You are the truth of truths
the substance of unicity
In my innermost being
all is confusion
power is weakness
doubt is certitude
joy a borrowing from sadness
I no longer know who I am
if I would like to scream or whisper
what does it matter:
What does anything
that is not you matter?

Jouahri, Abderrafi

Abderrafi Jouahri was born in Fes in 1944 and graduated from law school in Marrakesh where he was a lawyer. He has been a columnist, songwriter and politician. He was also president of the Moroccan Writers' Union in 1996 and in 2002 he was elected to the Moroccan Parliament representing the USFP party (The Socialist Union of Popular Forces). As a journalist, he is known as the author of نافذة (*Window*), his weekly column on the back page of the daily الاتحاد الاشتراكي (*The Socialist Union*). As a songwriter, he is the author of some of the most famous Moroccan classical songs: راحلة (*She is Leaving*), القمر الأحمر (*The Red Moon*), يا جار وادينا (*Our Valley's Neighbor*). His poetry includes: وشم في الكف (*A Tattoo on the Palm of the Hand* 1981); شيء كالظل (*Something Like Shade* 1994); كأني أفيق (*As If I'm Waking Up* 2010); الرابسوديا الزرقاء (*Blue Rhapsody* 2010).

A Head of Rock

Laughter in the night . . . and sobs in the heart
The ashes of the Koutoubia in my right eye
And the stones of Notre Dame cover my left
Cross-eyed
I close my lids and open my heart
onto the street in the Latin Quarter
where I had my first drink.
The first draft is to your health
And the second to the memory of the ruins of
Imintanout
Give your head permission to turn
If a head doesn't turn, it is a rock.

217

The Ancient Wall

For the wall whose face we wounded
With a piece of broken glass
Whose chest we blackened
With the coal of braziers
We wrote on its stones what cannot be said
For the wall that does not weary of the misery of
Childhood
And its impudence
For the wall that has tempted the fingers of
Innocence
To draw and write
I lift this glass
And declare my love.

Kadiri, Mourad

Mourad Kadiri was born in 1965 in Salé. He is a poet and a researcher. He obtained his doctorate degree in Contemporary Moroccan Literature from Sidi Mohamed Ben Abdellah University, Fès. He is an active member of the Moroccan Writers' Union. In July 2017, he was elected president of the House of Poetry in Morocco. His publications include حروف الكف (*Features of the Hand Palm* 1995); غزيل البنات (*Girls Weaving* 2005); طرامواي (*Tramway* 2015), which was translated into French by the poet and translator Mounir Serhani in 2016; and طير الله (*God's Bird* 2007). Two of his anthologies were translated into Spanish as well: غزيل البنات (*Girls Weaving*) and طير الله (*God's Bird*).

Salé

1.

Sister my little sister by God
Why has your knife grown blunt
Why has your ember died out
    Yesterday it used to blaze
    Why have your blossoms turned yellow . . . and wilted
    You were known for waterwheels and grasslands
    You were known for acorn trees in Maamora:
A lady . . . a bride
A beauty mark and eyelashes
eyebrows, hair plaits
and tresses
dreaming of henna and maidservants

a bride's palanquin
that turns around
and around her father's house
dreaming of a bridegroom
who arrives through Bab al-Khmis gate
and on the pier
out there
what's to be done will be done

2.

Sister my little sister by God
He was a little child
who went to Koranic school
bread in his hood . . . with no meat
and for a weekly fee
he learned to recite . . . and read the slate
He would get excited
when the fqih was on leave
and run with a radiant laugh
up and down the steps and slopes
to Bouregreg River
Oh Bouregreg
your sight was a delight
your taste, rapture . . . and a cure
and your water sweet as sugar
He was a rabble-rouser from home to home
from Lamrissa Gate
to Khiyar quarter
and in Znata
you showered the plowmen's little kids
who chanted to the baker Bouzekri
to get their bread done early
I went out to ramble . . . to walk around
to put on the light in the lighthouse
to shake off the ash
from the children's hands

to keep the promise of a visit
to al-Amaoui*
the scar-cheeked prisoner . . . . They thought him a Gnawi magician
He dreamt of a bird . . . in the house
of the sun . . . of the daylight
    the color of the sky
    Thus was the dream of this man

3.

Sister my little sister by God
Doves no longer
bring peace
Food no longer
lasts the year
The well has dried up
No wheat . . . no beans . . . no barley
but
    the little child
    who went to the mosque, the masjid,
    bread in his hood . . . but no meat
    He had you on his mind
    and made a promise to the slate
the clay-washed slate
    that he would erase all the letters
    but your letters
    he swore he would spell them
    Salé
        Long life . . . . long life
        my lady
        all your gates lead to one
        City of Salé

---

* The leader of a workers' union who was imprisoned in Salé.

The Stake

I let go of one stake . . . I take up another
The stake in front of me, the stake behind me
    Wherever I turn my gaze . . . there's a stake
    Under me, above me, and beside me . . . .
    A stake in my head
        And in my heart
    The stake makes things go from sour
To sweet, poor to possible*
Implanted in my veins and deeply rooted
It threatened,
Watch out, be careful . . . if you untie your ropes
Your insanity will increase
You'll get tired . . . you'll be lost
Be careful
Move . . . sniff
I said: I will pull out the stake with my teeth
Let me take a sip from my glass
What is in the stakes's mind is in my mind†
I realized . . . me and the stake are brothers
    The lock and the key
    It scratches my back . . . I scratch its back
    The stake makes doughnuts . . . .and I sweeten them with honey
        And without it
        I die . . .

---

* *T-maskin u t-makin*, to change from maskin to mutamakin, to manage to have in one's power.

† *Lli fi ras lutid fi-ras-i*, like *lli fi ras jamal, fi ras jamala*, what is in the mind of the camel is in the mind of its mate (literally, "she camel").

Khatibi, Abdelkébir

Abdelkébir Khatibi was born on February 11, 1938, in El Jadida, Morocco, and died on March 16, 2009. He was a Moroccan sociologist, writer and a specialist on Francophone Maghrebi literature. He joined the French Lycée Lyautey in Casablanca and went to the Sorbonne University in Paris. He started writing poems at the age of twelve. His major literary works include: La Mémoire Tatouée (*Tattooed Memory* 1971); La Blessure du Nom Propre (*The Wound of the Proper Name* 1974); Le Livre du Sang (*The Book of Blood* 1979); Le Prophète Voilé (*The Veiled Prophet* 1979); Amour Bilingue (*Bilingual Love* 1983); Maghreb Pluriel (*Plural Maghreb* 1983); Un Été à Stockholm (*A Summer in Stockholm* 1990). Khatibi is also the author of numerous other books and essays. These poems were taken from his book Aimance (*Loving*).

Unexpected moments, an encounter with the rhythm of desire. A meeting opposed by its own powers: already nostalgic, in the midst of an offering a loss, a procession of whims and fantasies. I dream of being your stranger—in the crystal of your heart. Am I, without knowing?

****

The sex of a voice is like the threshold of a meeting. Sometimes, he only needed a telephone call to decide to take a car or a plane, to approach this voice, accompanying it into its mouth, its breath, its country and language of tenderness.

****

Nostalgia would only be depression, melancholy, vertigo on a radiant emptiness. I see it becoming a memory, at the crossroads, the powers of desire and destiny.

****

Mixed marriages: crossroads of beings, languages, signatures, ancestral memories. Does this woman think she has made a mistake in changing continents for her partner? Even still 'continental drift' remains a poetic metaphor, he says to himself. A mysterious sentence: to keep as is, like an incomprehensible word, slightly insane.

****

La menthe, l'amante: mint, love: words to pronounce between the voice of the Orient and that of the Occident. The cry explodes and disappears in one language or another. Yes, but imagine what an Eskimo woman murmurs to her lover when she wants to go back to the Midnight Sun or the Polar Star. In her country, one says: "You are beautiful like a little seal." A metaphor which is hardly preposterous: each language of love inspired by its own animal kingdom and clothing of vegetation. Why did I suddenly think of locks of Swedish hair? Do they not resemble a field of burnt wheat that a wind disperses above the festive islands? Or am I dreaming again?

****

Each gaze has its own aesthetic form, coded for centuries by poets and painters: the gaze of captivity, or of ecstasy, that of adornment, and more indiscreetly, that of ostentation. What mythic scene are we playing when the interface is with the theater but without the stage? Where is beauty when I am dead with desire?

****

Over the shoulder of a woman, what do you see?—another woman, she responds. Loving, an interval between vision and audition, between a single thought and the form of a song. The body inscribes itself with this constraint without losing the perspective of its pleasure, the horizon of a private life in retreat, given to successive couplings: bracelets fly off to the four corners of the room. Windows open onto each morning.

****

An evening of music. The dialogue that takes place between the piano and the violin wakes his spirit to an idea: thanks to this dialogue, he better understands bilingualism, a double voice in the same composition, from the same translation of sensibility. Her language of Loving, a vocal score in the clarity of thought.

****

death
and so alive
invoking new gods

do you remember
so many fugitive eternities

dressed in silence
the prodigious word
invents a life
a pain
where madness exults

to give asylum, you say
to the right to name
is that enough?

Khaïr-Eddine, Mohammed

Mohammed Khaïr-Eddine was born in 1941 in Tafraout and died in 1995 in Rabat. He was one the most eminent Moroccan writers of Moroccan Literature in French. With Mostafa Nissabouri, he founded the Poésie Toute (*All Poetry*) movement in 1964. In 1965 he migrated to France and settled in a Parisian suburb. He returned to Morocco in 1979 and died in 1995 on Independence Day. Most of his books were published by Seuil Editions: Nausée Noire (*Black Nausea* 1964); Le Roi (*The King* 1966); Agadir 1967; Histoire d'un Bon Dieu (*The History of a Beatific God* 1968); Résurrection des Fleurs Sauvages (*The Resurrection of Wild Flowers* 1981); and Légende et Vie d'Agoun'chich (*The Legend and Life of Agoun'chich* 1984). The following poems are excerpts from his book Quasars: Poésie 2006. Rabat: Editions Racine.

The Emanation

They stink, they have nothing left—naked,
eaten by the perennial river,
enlarged with the blood
of innocents;—their skin sails
bacterial
to Lake Kivu where the scythe stands
and the bones
of children float, oars broken, murdered
in the glimmers of Twilight.

"They have been eviscerated, a notorious
and mass murder. A genocide!"

There is Famine, Hatred,
a Scavenger that sharpens its beak, its
talons, its gaze . . .

The red clay lights up
with blood
in the sunset . . .

Here, we kill each other:
frenzy of skins, masks,
massacres!

Here, everything is permitted, rape,
assassination of clerics
in their convent; we are
what remains
of the demons of the jungle.

In Kalach, we go
with the machete to subdivide
the living! . . .
It's the dance of the witches . . .
caught in the trap of sorcery . . .
It's the unbridled escape
of cantankerous ethnicities! . . .
They kill, they wander.
walking painfully!
These wretches
are blind, spiteful, spineless.

Fear is a passionate Law.
Where are the old quivers, the spears
and bows, the poison arrows?

All the dead rise up,
crying in unison
over miserable hatreds . . .

Lake, oh Lake, your voice
pure tomb
of the Rwandan earth!

While they decompose at the bottom of the putrid
creek
a little girl limps along, followed close behind
by a vulture.

(Rabat, October 27, 1994)

To Aimé Césaire

It's not the earth that languishes,
it's the Lamp of Dreams that has gone out
in an ulcerative Laugh . . .

It's not yellow-fever mosquitos that
put venom in the sulfurous smile
of our chemistries, it's the outbreak
of entire populations . . .

It's the crunching of recurrent grey
sand, in the middle of a flight
without wings, Mantis!
a flight of neutrinos among
the unattainable ethnicity of the hacking
machete . . .
"here is my faraway island, daughter of Dorsal,
Oh lonely Country!
lonely for savannahs and for Hagar
who peals Africa
under the clarity of lights
in the rooting of meteors,
black frost of the Sun.

Night cracks and comes to an end; cracks,
a dry biscuit
of gamma rays linking the Circle
to the Square of burial mounds, to the Baobab,
to the flail of arms under forgotten nopal cactus,
peripatetic raptors . . .

A comedy this bush where the
sizzling fires produce
crickets;
the slow progression of unicorns baffled
by a wild Childhood . . .

Elsewhere, it's You blue as a lagoon:
black turquoise,
assailed by the wheels
of the poem and rhythm

Cacti

How examine this circle of cacti?
Will it take all summer?
How come to terms with these circles of
steam stacks
unnatural plants
concocted in the factory?
Tell me, how
forbid them from excluding magnolias
from Nothingness?

The dawn is boreal, the navy blue sky
reddened
by the alluvium river where your addictions
flow. Mercury!

The shad that came up from Canada
will never return.
Navigators, manufacturers, spitters
of lead, of sulphur.
the fish your ancestors ate
will never return
to the poem's interior
without a curse..

(Rabat, October 27, 1994)

Khaless, Rachid

Rachid Khaless is a professor of French language at Mohammed V University in Rabat. He is a poet and a novelist. He published two anthologies with L'Harmattan: Cantiques du Désert (*The Desert's Canticle* 2004); and *Dissidences* (2009). His third work, Dans le Désir de Durer (*In the Desire to Persist*) was published in 2014 by the House of Poetry in Morocco. In addition to his many other works, Rachid Khaless has also published translations of Hassan Najmi and others.

from *Dissidences*

Dressed in vigor, I hear a thought of disaster climb up the left side of a poem: like twilight! It is rimmed on both sides with crests of a poisonous light, it itches.

At first only sinister moving shadows register on my retina, scattering in hot wounds: I say to myself: let my dark suns burst like pustules and splash your faces so eager for the eternal.

Nothing will harmonize the dream with your earthen eyes. I hate you my fellow-men, I hate your being cut off like a chipped sole on its path of fatigue; I hate your clicking prayer beads titillated by a feeble voice.

My hand ejaculates venom and ashes, daughter of sonic ignition. A kindled fire restores my greed; I only appear to be clay; in me nothing is a matter of controversy, I am an exacerbated fire, a lecherous fire, a fire of regenerating groans, a fire driving brilliant fermentations to create shards.

And here I am threatening you oh putrid logs! And I rage; I want to strike the most fragile part of your villainy: dead star who thinks itself a moon.

In my hand cascades of fire, hardened germs, budding and sharp; my vigor gives me cedar, distills in me its poisons, its toxins: I want to rage, I feel as hard as a reef, as vast as a thousand liquid suns

Here I am tormented by a dark thought. I model the wind, I woo fire and deceive illusion; I sculpt the water and bite into nothingness, I nourish life with igneous sap dying every moment to be there where peaks and valleys agree. And I come to splash your virgin pride with my corpse sacralizing sublime carrion:

My hand returns from afar . . .

From an ancient wound. In it converge the cardinal features of the crime

It seems I've hatched the same plan for a billion moons: I am Jugurtha, Nero and the leader of the People of Hashish

I come back from so far—that I doubt my race—my skin is covered with mud and it pushes me under pits of appendages that amaze even me

I am the beast: in my eyes rise sparks that seem steeped in eternal fire

And I walk on the edge of the human; Rather I crawl—I am a snake that moults . . . Violently, I apply my bite and then I let myself die

As I gather under my skin all creatures of the night; I am my mask, a vast bestiary

Extracts from *Guerre Totale*

Text I.

How it spread its leprosy in my veins this century of crusaders and troubadors

I hold fast to my place—too bad for the glory—I'd die every moment not to abdicate my utopias

I labor in silence and own myself every time I approach my death
I go down
to the middle of the ruins
probing the essence of fire
that festers under rusty
skin constantly
tearing me apart

I am all absence all omnipresence. I easily pierce the hearts of my enemies:

"Out of the way carrion! exclaims one of them
And the other: "You have to grow up! "

I confirm. I am of the race of the faithless. I drank a dense wine whose bubbles were made with thunder ; your jeers mean nothing to me

Wars I've known them all. And virgin arenas . . .

As a child, I started all the fights:
The warning came from the peaks
From the buildings: terrible demons we committed our daring acts with armor formed from our hands—stolen broom handles and pieces of zinc—we were the tribe of Antar and our rivals the Dhobyane—we were ready to extend Dahis and Al-Ghabra for another century.

My voice became hoarse under my mask, I commanded guerrillas no taller than dwarf trees. We had frontiers to conquer, audacity to punish. How many fires lit up in our eyes when at the end of the alley the song of the rival gang rose up—a real trembling of rattles. The arena held infinite traps and as far as the eye could see the columns were ready for the assault. Barricades, torches, scimitars . . . We raised tattered shirts as banners

And suddenly the gang was on guard
The tenor—a chubby guy with a clear throat—sang the song of our Republic

Battles. Endless battles . . .
It was the blood that sanctified our loneliness

Texte II.

I usurp the entire carnal expanse of words—mummies of tubercular lineages and Mothers of books—I corner them into ruin—I am amnesic—and catapult ephemeral but glittering notes into the night of crime—let's say the night was charged with waterlilies of gold and dead stars—I stand up like the führer on the empty theater of my childhood—the past obliterates me more than any other drug—and like a music that might have surged from a dead moment architectural murmurs rise up—dissonant breaths—the madness of my always and inevitable brawls given over to nothingness—ah! I masturbate to the approach of an orgasm a sustained flow in my brain—and I come I come—for me by myself

ooo

I keep for myself the pus of my wound magnifying it with syntax and baroque eruptions—I erect this grammar while giving the finger to the world—my age-old sorrows are not for sale and despite my incontinence I remain standing: in this scene my footsteps sound here and resound afar—my shadow has been put up for sale: I was a certain March in custody in a prospectus and I had to sell as befits a monster—I was with other thieves exhibiting in the Majorelle gardens—I should have comforted myself with the beetles and slugs that sucked my wound without stopping—sanctifying even the flesh—I had to appear immaculate to avoid the dissonances of which I was guilty and ravish those soft shells that will certainly shake my ethereal approach—cute sounds and virginal singing—but I had committed only one crime—anthracite—I was surrounded by high-ignition gas—I must have drawn it from an underground deposit lashed to my heart nonetheless I was only the blood scribe—and the world was so horrified it was Shakespearian—that's when I chanted the night of the anti-poem

ooo

Now I make ferocious sounds so this bastard silhouette arises in my life so that I exhibit it in the public square put it on auction I am Orpheus and I flay my voice—in the call to my prayer of the absent—I am far from myself—elsewhere—I am a fake and a renegade I will erect my dagger and perform terrible crimes so that I am relegated to the margins of the pantheon and other ephemeris—what the hell can it do for me!—in the past I married this Christ sewn to my flesh and gave him the last kiss nevertheless I will kill all the others Christs and Buddhas and lacerate the parchments of the Hejaz that they parade in my minefield—I will destroy icons and books—from Babel to Byzantium—like I threaten you and I charge I choose war I choose escalation

Texte III.

Traffic...
Nothing enchants me except this abrupt music that rises from my fingers—
and tears them—and this amazing wound enchants me oh! yes I will transcribe
these wounds until I'm dizzy—whirling dervish I'll kiss nothingness and finger
my anus—I am male and female—I'll pleasure myself with myself—I will
dominate my astral mating season and my ruin :

I catapult symphonic
Gusts and fire
That gangrene the veins
And lacerate them from within:

I see emerge in me the worlds I have created and those
to come
There where I go masks and certainties will fall

Here is my *Republic*—I reign on my own chest
My carved stones and my trouble
Will belong to me for a long time to come

Come so I may bless you
With my tender
Poisonous
Kisses

I am the pity the castaway
the annihilation

Text IV.

A century ago I walked in a huge cemetery and the skulls that I was trampling
splintered with an incredible noise of crystal
But I picked up the fragments and made ephemeral stelae
And now I'm invading the world—the swollen chest of aggression the hand encircled
with rings of fire
I built an oeuvre stronger than bronze and more durable than your centuries-old
stones

Nothing excites me more than these mass graves where violently I throw my stiff corpses
What exults me is this love and its denial
Neither blood moves me nor the extinct bodies that find their resting place in the sky no
I am alone with my courage and soon will sound the anthem of my Republic
I display myself naked here in the middle of the arena

Just provoke me

Text V.

I will speak I will break the silence I will deflower the virginity of Orphic lyres . . .

In the gutters—my temple my tower of Babel—time dilated like a clitoris vibrating with choir-like shocks—I edify republics—rising from my childhood by acneic eruptions exceeding the hardened surface of the skin—it is to an instinctive arithmetic that I owe my breath and my muscles. I magnify these utopias—I encode in them a secret alphabet for a season to come—I mix so many antithetic materials that unheard and baroque shrapnel appear—As in a ceaseless disaster I drink without blinking my cup of poison keeping the heavy presence of my fellowmen in mind

In the gutters—I am drunk with ink and blood—I go down to survey my manhood and the pure gold that I flaunt and then evanescent I go back up the ascending corridors toward the falls of my death. Like a nocturnal insect, I commit suicide by brushing against the light. At the flush of an eyelid a frantic race of words and deaths. To distract me I contemplate the temple that I erected with steles of flesh—and with nuggets of myth:

Go world with your padlocks and your forms go taste and go decency
I'm hungry and nothing that already exists satisfies or fills me
I shape stones extracted from volcanos rooted in my heart
I crash
I forge
I deepen
I offer to this new century an unpublished word

So blessed be my hand a thousand times:
Another alphabet lights on the ruins of the West I shape
the modulations of a new breath
Unleashed torrents of the Sebou river will flow in the Euphrates and with
water I will write ash
I will offer a profusion of diamond syllables and mysteries of suspicion:

I ran toward my panting heart
Losing my breath
I got lost in
Its narrow streets in the distance
A star shone and I quickened
The pace of my steps

I recognized
The black grasses
Of Hell

Khoudari, Najib

Najib Khoudari was born on December 19, 1959, in Kénitra. He is a poet and a journalist at the national daily newspaper العلم (*The Flag*). He obtained a certificate in international journalism from the Center for Foreign Journalists in Louisiana in 1985 and received a master's degree in philosophy and sociology from Mohammed V University in in 2003. He has served as an editor-in-chief of three magazines: المجلس (*The Council*), الجذوة (*The Firebrand*), and العطاء (*The Offering*). He has worked as a visiting professor of language and communication in the faculty of Rabat and was appointed a counsel to the Minister of Islamic Affairs and Endowments in September 2004. Najib Khoudari joined the Moroccan Writers' Union in 1978 and was elected member of its executive board in 1991. He was also president of the House of Poetry in Morocco in 2008. He now lives in Kénitra. His publications include: يبتل بالضوء (*He Gets Wet with Light* 2009); يد لا تسمعني (*A Hand that Does Not Hear Me* 2005).

Players

They buy the joys of life
        jumping in the air
        laughing loudly

They run
the ball of whiteness ahead of them

shoving each other
their shouts rising
while the seagull takes off
        lonely
        in a little sky.

The Kingdom of the Sun

Oh you, coming
from the hills of light
Don't fill our threshing floors
with the wind of dust
or scarecrows that frighten children.

Let your springs
dance in our celebrations
wash our dead
and flutter
      like flags of victory
          in the soul.
Let your trees
carry us far away
to the kingdom
of the sun.

Passage

Something I don't know
commits suicide inside me
      every day
and smiles
      to every morning's face

I didn't pay much attention
to this silence
that chatters on the outskirts of the soul

I didn't pay attention
to what the tree sheds
. . . .

Something passes through me.
   I pass through it.
      every death.
         every life.

Behind the Night

Over there
behind the tree
a naked body

Over there
under my tomb
a whisper of desire

And behind the night
a light I don't see

Was I insane
to have forgotten my shadow
    lonely
    shivering
       in the garden
         of childhood?

Tremor

I gasp
towards
the high wave
       while
       the boat
       alone
       plays
       with a bit of
       water

A sun
    turns pale
       on
         the rocks
and the flag is black
announcing a cold autumn
        a cold love

Why does my heart tremble
          everytime
          I see
          clouds?
And why does the tree dream
          alone
          like
          a lonely
          boat?

Hands of Air

I let two hands of air
slap me on the face

And I went down
on
my bottom
counting my losses.

Roar

Where does this roar of night come from?
I sharpened myself
And honed my tears, wondering:
Is it from the bend of the waves
the wrestling of rocks
the humming of the willow
     or the barking of a dog
     behind a wandering soul?

. . . .
. . . .
It's unclear
like my voice

like the moaning of desire
like a suppressed cry
like a dive into the open air

. . . .
. . . .

It's clear
like the hiss of the sand in the desert
like the leaping of a bird
in the beginning of the evening

. . . .
. . . .

Where is the roar from,
resembling all this silence
chirping all this death?

Laâlej, Ahmed Tayeb

Ahmed Tayeb Laâlej was born in Fes in 1928 and died 2012. He worked as a woodworker in his early childhood and he learned to read and write in a Coranic school at a later age. He soon became a very popular writer of song lyrics, poetry and drama. He is now considered one of the cornerstones of contemporary Moroccan theater. He received several prizes and decorations for his service to Moroccan Arabic language theater. In 1973 he was awarded the Literature Award of Morocco, and in 1975, the Medal of Intellectual Merit of Syria. He composed more than forty plays and adapted more than thirty. According to writer and scholar Salim Jay, the theater of Laâlej is a "treasure of the culture of humanity." He has rewritten, in Moroccan Arabic, works by Molière, Shakespeare and Brecht and has had a great influence on Moroccan popular culture. This poem is *zajal*, written in Moroccan Arabic. He plays on the feminine noun "beard."

My Lady,* My Beard

Oh my beard. My lady beard
gently . . . walk on . . . only slowly
Just yesterday you were black
turning my face into a feast
but today, my lady, in the blink of an eye,
you and I turned suddenly white

---

*Lady is the usual equivalent of "lalla" in Moroccan Arabic but this word may also be used for inanimate objects that are particularly "dear" to a person. The word "beard" is feminine in Arabic.

You were a sign of youth on my face
a beloved who wasn't lacking for lovers
a key that opens all doors
a present time . . . thinking . . . of what's to come

A black beard. A rounded face
and a brightness lit up in the eye
How describe it? How depict
fresh and tender youth?

My beard was black. A flow of black
a coal of God's dye
a sun on my face lighting up my way
making me the paragon of my ancestors

The truth of whiteness: high esteem
and days bound to overawe days
a chain with no escape
as stalwart time sweeps us away

Time takes us by surprise and fools with us
It lowers our heads and bends us down
It wipes out and turns over our pages
aided by surprise, oh my friends

Doesn't the stranger lament by placing all his fingers on his cheeks?
Between black and white: there's only a wink
Time is the blade of a scythe
that reaps what has been and what's to come

Oh my beard just yesterday
you were still of coal, a crow of flat watered lands
and I was flying up in your sky
sailing away and unaware of the numbered days

Our ship is on a brink of a slope
between black and white
Oh mother, the distance is surely short
whether we hasten the walk or slow down

(Meknes 2001)

Laâbi, Abdellatif

Abdellatif Laâbi was born in Fez in 1942. He is a poet, a novelist, and a translator. He was a founder and editor of the very influential literary journal, *Souffles* (1966–1972). After publishing 22 issues, the journal was banned by the Moroccan authorities and Abdellatif Laâbi was arrested. While in prison, he went on writing poetry and was awarded several poetry prizes until he was released in 1980. With Mohammed Bennis and Rachida Madani, he is one of the most widely translated poets in English. He has edited and contributed to La Poésie Marocaine de L'Indépendance à Nos Jours (*Moroccan Poetry from Independence to the Present* 2005). His most recent works in English translation are *The World's Embrace* (2003) and *In Praise of Defeat* (2017). Laâbi was awarded the Goncourt Prize of French Literature in 2009 and the Prize of Francophone Literature awarded by the French Academy in 2011. Below are poems from his volume, *Ouevres Poétique I*. Paris: La Différance.

To My Son Yassine

My beloved son
I received your letter
You already talk to me like an adult
You stress your efforts at school
and I feel your passion to understand
to chase away obscurity, ugliness
to penetrate the secrets of the big book of life
You are sure of yourself
You count your riches for me
without doing it deliberately
You assure me of your power

as if you were telling me, "don't worry about me
look at me walking
look where my steps are going
the horizon over there that immense horizon
holds no secrets for me"
and I imagine you
your beautiful forehead held high
and straight
I imagine your great pride

My beloved son
I received your letter
You tell me:
"I think of you
and I give you my life"
without suspecting
what that simple phrase does to me
my crazy Heart
my head in the stars
and with these words from you
I have no doubt believing
that the big Festival will happen
the one where children like you
having become men
will walk with giant steps
far from the misery of the shantytowns
far from hunger, ignorance and sadness

My beloved son
I received your letter
You wrote the address yourself
You wrote it with confidence
saying to yourself if I address it myself
papa will receive my letter
and perhaps I'll get a response
and you began imagining the prison
a large house where people are shut in
how many and why?
Why can't they see the sea

the forest
why can't they work
so that their children have something to eat
You imagine something bad
something not pretty
something that makes no sense
and makes one sad
or very very angry

You also think
that those who built the prisons
are certainly crazy
that and so many other things
Yes my beloved son
that's the way you begin to think
to understand men
to love life
and detest the tyrants
it's like that
that I love you
that I like to think of you
from the depths of my prison

Poem for Hind

You will perhaps not understand
all the words of this poem
but listen to me
a poem isn't difficult
at least not the one I write for you
It's like when at night I squeeze you tight
and kiss you
before putting you to bed
Poems, even the ones
big people read
are a little like that
what you feel, what I feel

in such moments
You see
I've already made a poem for you
I kiss you
I hold you tight
I feel that I am next to you
my darling
I have abandoned simple words for so long
sound-the-alarm words
I made a vow today
How explain it to you:
I was so tangled up inside
it was a labyrinth
so many hells to exorcise
so many atavisms to expel
the words were flowing out from my chest
encased in a double armour
Very few mirages
in this esoterism
in search of neither glory nor scandal
believe me
it's like this
because having lived
in the entanglement of this bewitched cave
I neither flagellate
nor justify myself
with public confidence
because I know that what matters above all
is this permanence of
inner mobilization
I explain it simply
unfold the itinerary map
and begin again
strong with what my people have taught me
strong in my pain
strong in our love
I've only just been born
to the word

This human experience

I like this human experience
When I think of our history
since the appearance of life
in its most elementary forms
to the controversial being that is man
his staggering deployment of intelligence
yes this experience was worth it
and I say it openly
I am a fanatic when it comes to our species

A martyr

A martyr
then another then another
Death has taken its place in our ranks
She chooses at will
the best among us, it's sure
She has her own canons of beauty
the whore

Lahbabi, Mohammed Aziz

Mohammed Lahbabi was born on December 25, 1922, in Fes and died on August 23, 1993, in Rabat. He was a Moroccan philosopher, novelist and poet writing in Arabic and French. His work has been translated into more than 30 languages. Lahbabi studied at the Sorbonne in Paris and received a doctorate of philosophy. He was professor of philosophy and Dean of the Faculty of Letters at the Mohammed V University in Rabat. Lahbabi was one of the founders of the Moroccan Writers' Union and the review آفاق (*Horizons*). He was nominated for the 1987 Nobel Prize for Literature. His poetry includes: Les Chants d'Espérances (*Songs of Hope* 1952); Misères et Lumières (*Lights and Miseries* 1958); Ivre d'Innocence (*Drunk with Innocence* 1980), in addition to many other poem collections, novels, short stories and essays.

Sovereign Wounds

Assailed by insomnia
he composes verse to kill the night
The sky filters through the window
Gradually
an indecisive light
against a soft horizon exchanges
its pale morning white

another crazy night, empty,
angry white sleeplessness
gives the poet over to a doubtful
and heavy black day
where already giant space is losing its thickness

January grey with my sadness
how many wishes have I dispensed
to hundreds of indifferent friends!
No one else assumes sovereign
wounds
so full of fissures

everyone carries his own cemetery
where the ashes of days are buried

I'm Still Hungry

to live in song
the hymn without rhythm
becoming a fresh trembling bird

to open oneself to virgin love
on a clever earth
that offers up its salty lips

the lute sows tenderness
the bow comes to life and moans
music shares our passions

I am still hungry
in fact the word is
Appetizing passion.

Daily Ransom

every day pays its ransom
every medina consumes its part of blood
every neighborhood carries its grief, its ration

every family has its wall
its deep lamentation
ripping apart hearts and remaining

in the breast of conspiratorial silence
tears rebelling
alone, hearts stand up, accusing.

Lamrani, Wafaa

Wafaa Lamrani was born on April 15, 1960, in Ksar Al-Kbir, Morocco. She is an active poetess and has been a Moroccan Attaché of Culture in the foreign service in Damascus, Istanbul and the United Arab Emirates. She has also worked at the Faculty of Arts and Humanities in Mohammedia. Wafaa joined the Moroccan Writers' Union in 1984 and was elected vice-president of the House of Poetry in Morocco in 2001. She was also awarded the Moroccan Booker Prize in 2002. Among her publications are: الأنخاب (*Toasts* 1991); أنين الأعالي (*Moaning Heights* 1992); فتنة الأقاصي (*Utmost Chaos* 1996); and هيأت لك (*Ready for You* 2002).

Ready for You

For the stranger inhabiting the depths of my vows
his oboes resounding in ferocious heartbeats
his earth cleansed with the seduction of murder
for his wound   his feasts
for the language of his things
once in a poem
                         I consigned a jasmine to the loneliness of his forests

For the salt of his desires in my blood
for my old wine dream
for our night that wasn't
                         the affection in my heart pulsing
Let my sweetheart come to me
whispered an iris slumbering in the fading
                         dawn

I will make ready my tomorrow and yesterday
make ready my visions, my orbits, my magic
my lofty loneliness
my breath, the fragrance of the meadows
my beauty and desires
the celebration of words, my henna
my gusts and breezes

Let the harvest come
I will ready my wheat for it
His absence, like his presence, is peopled and ripe
Time, the senses, conscience overflow with him
the copper coffee pot
my desk, my balcony, its flower
the desolate pillow, the mirror, the cloth
the thyme of his country and the splintered sky of the heart
                              as if I had whispered him
Like my shadow
I slowly return to him

Like light, like surprise, like sound
He casts his fragrance on me

              Let the comer come to me
              I will ready my earth for him
blended with parts of me
He will scatter like wild pigeons on the bed of my day
the sea, his temperament
and my secrets, his promise

Be the wilderness and sweep me away
Be the wave and renew me
Be form and adorn me
Be green and make me verdant
Be water

Let the magnificent one come to me
I will ready all of me for him

A door flies open for us neighing
The thirst of fields on his lips sets me ablaze
His words are a bed for my yearning
I fill him and his flame fills me
I follow his wings
and take care not to blow on him
From the beginning of violets
    my cells have recognized him
    have experienced him
    have known him for certain
    I am addicted to him
    addicted to his starts
My trunk desires his branches
and the night longs for his abundance

If the distant one comes to me
I have readied my lifetime for him. . . .

Fidelity's Hymn*

With the eye of your wise heart, shelter me
delight my soul
fill my sacred time
under the tree of knowledge
    the generous tree
ready me
drench me
soak me with the advancing flame—
    I am your parched desire
enflame my thirst
make me your garden and your water
they are my horizon and my heart's paradise
encircle me with depth
flood my meadow
make it sparkle with your eternal tenderness

---

* Wafaa means "fidelity," which is the poet's name.

For you I ignited the candles of my desires
lit up the corridors of words
I am the poem of your youth
your fiery dream
your stormy vision
and the old wine of your wisdom
oh pillow of my vows
oh exaltation of my life
     the prophecy of what is to come in memory
the odor of its shores pervades me
its perfume blends with metaphor
inside my effervescent soul
supporting your footsteps
I wander where you are
dwelling in the ember of equanimity . . .

At the door to questionings' desire
the forests of journeys opened me wide to you
and the dawn of the word drew me, willingly, near
          to you
I am pregnant with your fruits
the wind opening its arms
to the fertilities of your orbits
longing weaves me
so I give birth to stars in the heavens
of your thoughts
          a sign of your heartbeat
I am your most magnificent wandering
I am your resting place and your flood
     make me your shelter
Seed the threads of your water in the bed of my worries
they will yield a wet blaze
strange as a shooting star
pure and rebellious
seeking the most beautiful and the furthest contours of the body
. . . that is the road buttons up its light for us
oh how sweet the raisins of your earth
oh honey of the soul
and the body's fill . . .

Outside the daily quiescence
we journey in the pregnancy of things
we chase the lightning of meaning
we sculpt ourselves into fugitive music

transforming spaces into brothers

visions that change closed alleys
    into waves
and renew the palm-trees of writing . . .

(Casablanca, June 12, 2000)

Footsteps of Embers

Between a sky that I desired
and another that seduced me
I wear the swelling burden of my youth
    between two points
The chains of time weigh
    upon my wings
keeping me from my longing
And a cloud of wisdom rains down
    on the banks of my table

Above the spider's house
I live today
like the lulling of heartbeats
I envision myself part of the future
leaving my roots behind for the river
    I breeze over you, my most beautiful paths
    I am inspired by you
    I come into you
    I seed you
and I plant in you, in the name of light,
my progeny

I root
I go deep
I stir the remote marshes
   I transform
   I discharge
before turning in the direction of the sign's orbits

I cover the walls of the soul's grass
   —I am the rebel plant—
and ascend to the heights of the hymn . . .

I have my other spring now
not the one in which I was born
with hardly any thorns
full of promise
I have sparkles
     a sea of clarity is my calling
     and my language is the distance of lightning

Peace on the desert of the alphabet that I tamed
   with a footstep of embers
Peace on the wings of love
   that gather together my dispersions
Peace on my abyss, the planet
Peace on what is coming to me, I see it now, and my yesterday
Peace on my visions and my gusts
Peace on the blaze of the journey
   peace . . . peace

I take you out of the gasp of things
I set you free
I recreate you, my remains
so you are nearer
     more invincible
   more profound more magnificent

Oh city in the heart that glitters
The sun consigns its secret to us
   every morning
and dresses us with what the dawn wears

   spaces open their arms
   bitterness lights its candles
This is "Arwa"
emerging from the fragrance of her ripe childhood
a sweet song
She stays up at night near my name
She wipes away my weariness
She glorifies my blood in her every move
   The waves are some of her psalms
   and the glitter of question in her eyes
   is my journey . . .

With her, I forget my wound
               on the verge of leaving
And when my bleeding burst into leaf
         I set off
I left my features to the passionate earth
         and set off
I built a kingdom of words
         and set off
My bodily remains yielded thrones
from treasures
         and summits
         and stars
But I desired distance
         and set off
As if I were the wind that doesn't wish to settle down,
       I set off . . .

(August 29, 2000, Casablanca)

Lemsyeh, Ahmed

Ahmed Lemsyeh was born in 1950 in El Jadida, Morocco. He is a poet who rose to prominence after publishing the first poetry collection in Moroccan Arabic in 1976. All his subsequent poetry has been zajal, that is, poetry in colloquial Arabic. Among his numerous publications are: شكون اطرز الما؟ (*Who Embroidered the Water?* 1994); توحشت راسي (*I Miss Myself* 1999); حال و أحوال (translated into Spanish as *Estado y Estados, Changing Moods* 2007); قتلتني القصيدة (*The Poem Killed Me* 2014). The following poem, "A Fool's Scribbles" (تحناش البوهالي) is from his 2005 book, خيال الما (*Water's Shadow*). The subsequent poem, "Watching the Soul," (حاضي الروح) is from ظل الروح (*The Soul's Shadow* 1998).

A Fool's Scribbles
(*to my friend* out there.*)

1.

I wrote a book
and pruned its sides
I rejoiced just a bit
planted a tree
embellished its leaves
It became used to me
When once I dug a ditch
and stumbled over it
they named it after me

---

*My "friend" is the artist Said Saddiqi

2.

My hand is in your hand
and the road twists and turns
If I become silent
the word will be seared

3.

Go away and let me be
Drink the tears of love
and when the glass is empty
I'll melt the soul and pour from it

4.

The train arrived
The train left
The one I'm waiting for hasn't shown up
nor has his shadow
. . . .
. . . They said he was here.

5.

The party all gathered around
together as brothers
the drinks spared no one
the table is set
but the chairs are empty
. . .
the leaves of paper wilted
the pens refused to go on
the joke was orphaned
. . .
perhaps my friend has died.

6.

The letter is at a loss for where to land
The only thing it finds is its place
If it is not happy, if it is revolted
it kicks its neighbor and goes away

7.

The letter asked its brother
who found us?
He replied: the one who read us
before we were found

8.

Your words came first
My silence came later
It is drowning in the bottom of the glass
The color of the inkwell is dark
and the pen is unyielding
Who can be trusted?

9.

The look threw obstacles in my way
and my words were disheveled
The paper is a shroud
and the pen is fevered

10.

I held you
and caressed you
I was in tears
as you lay down
I buried you
and didn't sleep until I wailed

11.

He cloaks you like sleep
You become a drop in the bottom of the glass
You become a bust without a head
You evaporate and say it doesn't matter
His words are a pitcher and you are the washing bowl
He erases your ink
Your words become a pickaxe
to dig your own grave
knowing your exact measures

12.

My eyes saw you
Your eyes saw me
I put on sunglasses
They saw me for you

13.

I bent down to lace my shoes
A lone match appeared
It could possibly . . .
. . . could . . .
. . . possibly set fire to something

14.

He meant the letter to unburden him
and sketched in it everything he saw
but time was in fact the letter
and a shroud was the envelope

15.

One word brings about another
and silence is an art
The fence wasn't pulled down

They raised it above the minaret
They paralyzed the light, they disfigured it
And sent it to a place of no return
The beard entwined with its likeness
They shaved the mountain up along the steep
They dug in the clouds
a bald head for the sea
The mirror disavowed them
Seeing them it was filled with fright

16.

His father was a waiter
Promised him new shoes
He was overtaken by boundless joy
He saw his father on television
drowning in his blood
and the shoes thrown down by his side

17.

My companion is a smile of light
Tearing away the veil of darkness
He gathered plains, mountains and seas
embracing the dove of peace
making you disclose every secret
that talks without words
There is no way without him even if you turn around and around
the interpretation of all dreams
I concealed his name inside my eyes
He is the ink of every pen
and light encircles him
He is a flag raised up in the sky
He is a tattoo in a book, on a wall
He is a stem for every word
When he embraced me I told sorrow to go to hell
My imagination woke from its sleep
To you my companions I will confess without falseness
He is my country and that's all

18.

Forget about me and sorrow will forget about you
pull down
what we have weaved throughout our days
wipe it off the mind
and if it disperses
your word is first
roll it, chop it up and savor it
they say you harvest what you plant
obey and serve the one you love
don't ever refuse him
see your shadow in the water and talk to it

19.

With braided words the body melts
flows out
infatuation drives the mind insane
it inhabits and nests in the joints
it heats up
a flame thrust in-between the ribs
if it is not evenly dosed it becomes
a nightmare
a word that stifles the throat
a wind that blows in the head
nothing is left to be licked out of the brain

20.

A word brings about others
If it flies away from your mouth how then make it return?
I gave my word to my own mind
Your word has denuded you
And your secrets have stretched out in the sun
There's no way out
Water is buried inside the rock
How then to draw it out?

Death is roaming around
Watch your mouth
Wall it and shut it up
Don't blame anything said on me
I said what I had to say
And you keep what you have to yourself

(Finished on 11/18/2004 at dawn)

from *Who Embroidered the Water**

Time sneezed
And space was seized
A ray of sun sniffed
And sleep came and went
The skein got tangled and I couldn't find the tip of the string
I want to weave words of yarn out of images
And the poem is the loom
I saw a voice in the soul turning around
It wrote to me:

"Give me your attention
And listen carefully to my words
I want to listen to my bones
I ate too much guinea fowl and now I'm sick
I want to reconcile with my days
I want a cave where I can sequester myself
I'm sick of crowds
I want to be a letter and its envelope
A burning coal that's wrapped in darkness

---

*"Tarz" means "to embroider" in Standard as well as Moroccan Arabic but is also used in Moroccan Arabic in combination with "talk" or "words/language" (طرز الهضرة/الكلام) to mean resorting to all kinds of figures of speech to say something indirectly. In standard Arabic it may mean to employ prosodic devices to say things elaborately or to put in a hidden message.

There are things hiding in my head
Entanglements that won't be resolved except by death
Life is a flower with a worm

The pen wandered in its inkwell

A cavalry with its flags
And plenty of ammunition
It's like this that injustice spoke to my brain
And the tyranny born of blood that can't be swallowed
Spare me your gifts and presents charged on credit."

My side tickled
And worry raised its eyebrows
The secret's corpse is washed and now I will make its shroud

I mumbled:
"Let go, oh my mind, and be generous
This is the time of monkeys
Make a difference between the slaughterer and those who just bark
Silence has become their weapon.

Oh you there, your weakness is evident
All you have left is what's behind you
Once there was horsemanship, manhood, and pride
Today it's become the visa for beggars
Your weakness is clear
    Your weakness is evident oh you there
All you have left is what's behind you

Make the difference, I said to myself, between the slaughterer
and those that just bark
Go forward without rest
The city's night is a false bride
One drink follows another
And death is always watching
Among the horses of desire, the bitter are indomitable
Injustice rules over the mind

longing for its ancestors.
If you want to get there, let go of the reigns
Life relentlessly bears children
Everyone is born into it
And our offspring will be ready the day we leave.

Don't retaliate O mind of mine
And don't build yourself a nest in which to dive.
Stay on the path
Keep after the goal
But don't reach it."
Words are the foundations of their ink
Dust off the paper's coat and get the words back
They tell us: find the door to blankness, and fill it up
Find the words sneaking under their skin
There's so much foolish talk
Yet people are silent
Present but denying it
Who will reconcile us?!
The one who chose water and embroidered it

We will say it doesn't suit us.
Lie in wait, take care of yourself.
As you give out so it comes back.
Scarf your head and tighten your pants
You who's stretching forth your shadow.
Sharpen your worry and file it smooth
Try to see what it's worth to you.

In a flock each bird talks to its own
But your bird has flown away.

When I saw what was going on
I was furious, and my spirits flowed over the brim
Since ammunition is lacking
I said I'd tell it all with naked words.
The word is an obligation
And the one we sought is still tarrying
The solution for them is not gentleness

Your side applauds
And we command.
The government agent rules as a president, and gives orders
The woman who spoiled the minister's ablutions gives orders
The Quran-reciter licks his finger of the officer's food
and fills his bags
Someone gave him some sustenance
And sharpened a vein for him
He will host him for the night in a narrow cave
The corks go popping, bang, bang
The blows on the skin go tak, tak
And the one who utters a word will get a sharp slap

Watching the Soul

The spirits are veins in the glass
A shackled wave
And the song of a flute in the head
The guardian of the soul converses with all the senses
A sea where people hide
A pillow on which the head rests
A cane and some clothes
A gate in the water without a guard
A key that opens the unyielding lock
And I slither, fleeing
Undecided between a body that drips in a glass
And a glass that beats with feeling
It has its own die
It decorates the soul
Paints its walls with obscurity
Pregnant with a shadow of glass
Stabbed with a dagger of light
Sleepy
Veiled by the air
Its charms spin words
That conceal a secret
A long silenced outcry like the night

is planted in the skin
The eye reads the talking look
And the pen begins to stretch
Worry leaned on the heart
covered itself and lay down
I saw the hidden become visible*
I fear its madness will reappear
If it wakes up, where will I shelter it?
If it comes back to life, where will I bury it?
If it balks where will I keep it?
If it goes into a trance, how will I calm it?
I saw death covering its face
mounting a black stallion
It tied its horse to a palm tree
and it became a swarm of ants
that started to move in my ribs
I became a bee
My breath is a sea
My mouth amber
The guardian of the soul drank
and snacked on an ant
It kneaded the body and put it on the bread board
My voice is an oven
Compared to it, life is worth an onion
And we, to death, are fated†
We wait for it to turn its back on the qibla
He who said life will come back in a piece of wood
planted on the top of the mountain
and the whole world a sea
He who said that the thread of death is in a bamboo pole
He will reach life
Every death renews age
The wind is soap that sings
and the trees are mute town criers

---

   * *al-ghabir dhahir*, « the absent became visible »
   † *al-mut haqq ʿali-na*. Death is our destiny.

Light rays have become a crooked finger
And speech has not yet gone to sleep
The morning yawns
The labor of birth is hot and about to lay its egg*
And death is chaste, it does not take more than its due
Time turns around
Life has not had its menses
Those who abandoned it in fact so . . . desired it
Everyone forgets death in diversion
And I live day to day
He who denies and wants to live forever
Will see his face in the clouds
The axis is not the dynamo of life†
The mill is not the battery of life
The secret is fearing death
Oil that ignites the candle of life.

Hamiya fi-ha al-bayda, warm and has to lay an egg; making a noise like a chicken about to lay.
† In French in the original.

Loakira, Mohamed

Mohamed Loakira was born in 1945 in Marrakech. He studied at the Faculty of Arts and Humanities in Rabat. He published his first poems, L'Horizon est d'Argile (*The Horizon Is of Clay*), in the journal *Souffles* with a preface by Abdellatif Laâbi in 1971. Since then Loakira has contributed to several journals like *Intégral, Lamalif, Al Asas, Liaisons,* and many others. Loakira is the author of several collections, including Marrakech-Poème 1975; Chants Superposés (*Superimposed Songs* 1977); L'Oeil Ebréché (*The Chipped Eye* 1980); Moments (1981); Marrakech: l'Île Mirage (*Marrakech: The Mirage Island* 2008); as well as many other poem collections, novels, essays and articles. Loakira was awarded the Grand Atlas Prize in 1995 for his poem collection Grain de Nul Désert (*Grain of no Desert* 1994), and again in 2010 for his novel L'Inavouable (*The Unavowable* 2009).

Born from the desert's retreat
from footprints rising through the sand
upon impact

Born from the wound of wandering
from the sober rocks of the Atlas
from the source

Born from the aquatic fugue
with its intransigent markings
from pebbles
from the gesture of a thousand virginities
from the fascination with eternity

Nourished with poetic promise
And the pliancy of the echo

My city

Geological amalgam

Where my roots fit together

Trained up

As a pure-blood stallion

On the day of the feast

. . . born also from the glacial worry
          of porters
from the insomnia of horses
the drought of the trough
from headquarters
Born from tomblike memories
evoked during spirited theatrical asides
intrigues
ransoms
blood
born also from morning's
          submission
from outraged sweat
the crushing of blossoms
          of clay
          of thistles
yes, born from blood
and from locks of hair suspended
          and ricocheting down

Sedentary are my caravans
and their thirst flows
dense abundant
Cartel of blood
Cartel of tears

Touched by grace
at the threshold of the millennium
halo of light
shimmering insular reflections
you were given to the warrior as an offering
native of the desert
Eagle
eager for freedom and space
svelte
long hair
with a piercing gaze
to bless the sword that slays
thick dust
a piercing eye
the frenzy of confluent springs
flowing
mute

on the expanse of this rebellious plain
appearing
                arid
                extravagant
Remember also the abnegation and endurance
of the horses
under the joyous flight of birds of prey
when the rest of the burned boats
                once
stood up
as ramparts
with nothing but the folly of the seas before them
and hardly anyone left to inherit
Faithful to the movement of their entrails
these mounts served
other men
other dynasties

have carried the word so far
the flag
the arabesque
the canopy of thrones
and the movement of letters undulating
from right to left
What does it matter covetousness subtle biddings
subterfuge unpunished treachery what does it matter
the copy and the original
the fear of memories
the murmur of mass graves
a name dies
while someone else has a foot in the stirrup
alliances the gyrating emigration of the core
What does it matter
the horses advance

subjugated by the reign of stars
proud from the beginning of time
they advance
going beyond the cunning edges
beyond the shadow of the warrior's
           finger
pointing to unveil the extreme mystery
sleeping only to tread on the confines
whose existence no book describes
Neither frost
nor the shell-clogged mist
not the sour and impudent winds
or the sun
         rising setting
as it likes
nothing manages to slacken their pace

The horses advance in columns
raking the horizon in large sweeps
gripping its joints
above the unleashed waves

Wide open if the departure is
like destiny
washed up
a tatty line on its forehead
at the apex of rage
A flood of fire of flames
crash of boots and arms
Blood blurring dividing lines and wakes of ships
the horses advance

———————————————————————————————————

————————————————————————————

The farther away the sea
the more high tide leads to intoxication

. . . yet you are always there
chiseled in age-old understanding
soothing the fury of your surroundings
going forward
though crumbled by the stubbornness of the surf
and the helplessness of the fig tree vainly
seeking
the shade of its own solitude
Translucent
you sway your hips
covering with humility and constancy
the dissidence
of the cross-roads

. . . and I belong to you
carry the stigma of the stutterings
of the first stones
        of your foundations
the first roots
        of your wandering
the first fibers
        of your mixing
run up through rocks dunes and big widths

to be one body with your unity composed
of the first cry
of your birth
abundant the rhythms the tones the nuances
of a blink of an eye
igniting the clacking of hands and feet
arriving on pilgrimage
from all over

the body feigns the swerves of notes
scattered along trances
where cohabit
waists gazes braids
fleshy or heart-shaped lips
finely drawn
. . . and the nonchalance of the accent
the sharp verb
that turns brightness to derision
you protect them
with your carefree restraint
since cleansed in the rivers
below your ramparts

the unwoven branches
it would seem
are missing flavor

You are always there
Beloved

opening the door to the extreme
you welcome
beggars saints orphans
and repentant criminals
You nourish them
with the breath of the desert
with the constant call of the ocean

You are the Kingdom of convergence
the cardinal points
the pattern of all the senses

You are the Marvel
that no marvel across the ages
will know how to equal
where the distraught paths of passion
bitterly haughty
discuss grace
before the sacred fire

Maadaoui, Mostafa

Mostafa Maadaoui was born in Casablanca (1937–1961) and died in a plane crash near Rabat. He was a founding member of the Moroccan Writers' Union. After his death, his poetry was collected and published in an anthology ديوان المعداوي مصطفى (*The Anthology of Mostafa Maadaoui* 1963), edited by Ahmed Mejjati, Mohamed Adib Slaoui, and Mohamed Ibrahim Al Jamal. Much of Maadaoui's poetry is characterized by nationalist and political themes, written in a highly formal classical Arabic.

Oh, You . . . Oh . . . .

And then you appeared to me
In that luxurious dress
Pampered and desirous
Swaying then turning away
What has come over you, what induced you into madness
Weren't you aspiring to
That beautiful neighborhood? Yet by the gate of the destitute
You stuck to my side, playful and repeating unceasing
Whispers of yearning and deep love
My love, wetted with desire
I asked you, my abundant dream,
About my poems streaming out on the great shore.
Haven't you read other poems on 'small' love
My love, wetted with perfume
Did you forget; can't you remember?
That sad boy from Tangier

And the dance giddy with love and the necklace of jasmine
All of it swaying coquettishly
Blissfully pushed by a longing
To silence, the silence of lovers
To whispers and the rubbings of chests
On a bed of silk
Do you remember?
A phantom enfolded by memories
A perfume harbored by evenings
In that awesome silence
In that melancholic night
Or are you unaware
Oh you. . . my deep love

Return from the Plateaus of the Impossible

Here we are, back to the fireplace
both small, hating the horror of departure
the echo of the impossible
Once upon a time of our yesterdays
and all the years before
light froze in clouds
without even a hint of longing
as if we had ended and beauty died
and all the sacrifices
the hearts worshiped
and all the smiles
the lips built
had become shadows
whose beauty was deadened by departure
My beautiful dream has turned out to be
impossible
Is it true that the call has shrunken within us
and the fragrance died
in our dreaming eyelashes
the wellspring dried up

the flowers and the hills denied us
and even the rays
of the moon
looked down on us with what remained of their brilliance
and their longing
and their odor died
in our dreaming melodies?
Is it true that spring is sick of us
that we surrendered to the pale shadows
of our illusions?
Is it true that light has become something impossible?

A Song for Peace

Oh flock of doves
Peace upon you
Star of a bright song
That emerged there, behind the horizon
Shining like fluttering banners
Souls long for you, flooding over
In the water-spring of yearning
The eyes that gaze at you have been thirsty
For hundreds of years
Greeting the flock of doves in your melody
The emblem of peace
* * *

Oh flock of doves
you are the live ember of eternity's light
Existence welcomes you
The existence of souls thirsty
For the light in every hand's measure
For liberty
For a tune that daisies embraced
In the garden of sacrifice, immortalized by
The blood of martyrs
* * *

Oh flock of doves
I am where a wounded nation lies in wait
It is a deep wound
I am calling you from the highest peak
And on my lips, oh dove,
Remnants of the leaves of an olive branch
A metaphor on the bleeding lip
Of the banner of peace
For the flock of peace
* * *

Oh flock of doves
Oh repository of the sweetest tunes
The brightest hopes
I sang you in the festival of youth
Songs of torture
And I kissed in your infatuated feathers
The truth of a bright song
That nurtures my existence and inflames my longing
For liberty
And sends to me a thousand new meanings
Profuse with light
* * *

Oh flock of doves
If you ever pass through my beloved land
Don't forget to spread the good news
On Algerian soil as well
Because I have brothers and sisters there
Who all went to the guillotine
* * *

Oh flock of doves
I stand where prayer ascends
Repeating the call
The call of peace
To the flock of doves

(08/02/1959)

Madani, Rachida

Rachida Madani is a retired high school teacher, a novelist, a poet and a painter. Her publications include: Femme Je Suis (*Woman, I Am* 1981); Tales of a Severed Head, translated by Marilyn Hacker 2001); Blessures au Vent (*Wounds in the Wind* 2006); and Ce qui Aurait Pu Demeurer Silence (*What Could Have Remained Silence* 2017). Rachida Madani lives in Tangier. The poems here are excerpted from Blessures Au Vent (*Wounds in the Wind*), Paris: La Différence.

The sun was in my hand
in the days I had a sky
but I was walking in the shadows
and my childhood had the freshness
of a broken pane of glass
harpooning the afternoons of plague
since then I remain
        poet of bad days
            and
        bad poet.

                ****

I leave them the period
the comma
all the punctuation
and know-how
for a while now I've no longer surprised myself
no longer questioned myself
no longer stopped myself
        I am no longer a poet

just the oasis and the doe
that you dream of
Pilgrim my old brother

My words have become livid
on the milky way of your fantasies
insomniac city
where I lose my name.
I hug your walls
my delirium conjugated with your fountains
my mouth on the mouths of your sewers
where I vomit the detritus
of an aborted poem
From where can it climb to the sky
this cry decomposing in my entrails
the one spontaneous cry
of a destroyed woman
emptied of herself
                    agonizing.

Woman
I haven't finished dreaming of my childhood
haven't finished lifting each star
on the path of expectation
sentinels watching over my cemeteries
where I sit without counting
the tombs
without saying anything
watching for your return
Pilgrim my old brother
                              ****

In a burst of sun
    O Vincent
I lose more than one ear
emptied of my visions
of fresh water and mother of pearl
ruined to the point of chanting an old refrain

where it's no longer a question of being
I prophesy nude
neck digging in the dryness
in the capital lack of a cry.

****

To leave like that disarmed
when the wind lifts!
We are two oh Don Quixote
to be nothing but torn
    and like you
      poor defender of justice
    I always have
    fewer arms
    than the windmill.

****

Only a bad poet appeals to me
I have neither sun in my eyes
nor waves in my hair
not even an exotic
perfume high under my arms,
I go about pale and old
I go about hugging the walls
where it is grey
In the solitude of rock and moss
I have unlearned the language of the city
      of emeralds
I am Scheherazade
half crazy on a minaret level with the ground
recounting my last tale
to the rubble
before the scarlet dawn
that burdens my chest.

****

When you were born my siren
the sun stood on the edge

of my window.
I love you for being so beautiful
                              having neither my eyes
                              nor my hands
I love you
citizen of the evening oceans
        who brings me back from afar.
                                   ****

You didn't come into the world
to see your bones whiten
in the white waters
of a Bou-reg-reg river
nor to contemplate your waning shadow
on the roads of distress.
Catch fire from my voice, brother
I have the happy privilege
of planting the storm.
Get up and scream your night
                              if you dare
raise it above your shaky head
and throw it on the ground
                              if you dare
the night breaks like glass!
then let your cannabis speak
you have a prophetic bouquet
when you sing catastrophes . . .
Get up brother
each sunset
is a dead man.
                                   ****

Come hide yourself here
just behind my heart
from there you will see
life with its long teeth.

Why is the sun so little
you say with your child words
why isn't there enough
          for all the world?
why is the sky so low
that my toys hang from it?

Why this rain of mud, fetuses
and distraught lovers in the city?
These women who no longer veil
anything but their number
lying down next to the other
for a glass, a dream,
                    a cigarette?

Why a woman so young
on a path so naked
towards this house without windows?
Why these corridors, these curtains
these bars
this solitude
this parlor?

But patience you say, Patience
it's already so late you say,
that water is unweaving
that men on the street corner
stamp and blow on their fingers
keeping watch you say
for the first star
          to defuse the dawn.
                              ****

I am there
in your cell
there sitting in the corner
for five years there, dear brother
                    pale and taciturn
                    I look at you

and in my eyes pass
the hearses you couldn't follow.

We were thirty
in a class of history
we were poets, artists
we were already men
      already women
      and we had dreams
      for the men
      for the women
that's why on the blackboard
we hung Mussolini
   Hitler
   Von Hindenburg
   and the old history professor
And we sang
   we sang
   we sang
      Victory.

In my eyes pass
the hearses you couldn't follow.
Mimoun the comedian
at the end-of-year parties
became a cop
saluting Mussolini
   saluting Hitler
   saluting Von Hindenburg
   and the old history professor.
Don't cry dear brother
for the hearses you couldn't follow.

We are no longer thirty.
Hazlim our poet
threw his poor blind head in the fire
surrounding himself with little dogs and screaming to men
and the full moon

a big song of love and
                         bitterness.
Don't cry dear brother
for the hearses you couldn't follow.

We are no longer thirty.
Fatima the big bitter clown
wasn't pretty, do you remember?
Her husband realized it
and at the feet of a judge
she killed herself
with big bursts of laughter.
Don't cry dear brother
for the hearses you couldn't follow.

We are no longer thirty,
the other one
our sister of the shantytowns
our living water
the fresh spring of our thirsts
closed her long black eyelashes
on the world
dead of hunger in her cell.
Hold back your tears dear brother
for the hearses you couldn't follow.

But we are many more
than thirty
And I am there,
there sitting in the corner of your cell
for five years now,
                   dear brother

pale and taciturn
you look at me
and in your eyes pass
the burning men of the hearses

burning Mussolini
burning Hitler
burning Von Hindenburg
    to remake
       History.

              ****

Even if you weren't one of those
who sing
You were my brother in despair.
Dusty, nomadic and ageless
you drank from the same bitter goat
And told me:
      "Your voice is too naked woman
      your song too frail
      to chant my despair
      take your anger with two hands
      and strike."
The wind pushes the dunes
And time passes
oh, these morning songs
between the green and pink almond trees
the goats and the laughter
how soft was the sand
and the world malleable!

But wind pushes the dunes
And time passes
You are more than ever my brother
              in despair
still demolished, trapped and without a
              password.
You drink from an even more bitter goat
And you write me:

    "The wind pushes the dunes
    and time passes

like our camel
my despair is patient,
sing oh woman.
Sing our anger
To the almond trees without flowers,
that your voice reach the stars.
Sing on the stone edge
of every well where
orphan goats die.
The wind pushes the dunes
And I pass by
                    Sing oh woman."

Majdouline, Touria

Touria Majdouline was born on June 7, 1960, in Settat, Morocco. She is a poet, a writer, and a civil society militant. She obtained her master's degree in 1988 from Mohammed V University in Rabat. She is a professor at the Faculty of Arts and Humanities, Rabat. Her major publications contain: أوراق الرماد (*Leaves of Ash* 1993); المتعبون (*The Tired* 2000); سماء تشبهني قليلا (*A Sky that Resembles Me* 2005); أي ذاكرة تكفيك (*What Memory Would Satisfy You* 2008).

Inscriptions of the Soul

A blind body
Surprises its reflection
Shattering
On the mirrors of the night
A shadow cast on its shoulders
Weary of its silence
It retains the wonder of fire
Then melts

* * *

The wind comes to it
Washed with dew
Warm it comes
Adorned with its sacred names
It writes them again
With the ink of fire
Sketching nets of seduction

292

On its whiteness
Then withdraws
* * *

And before
Its blindness fades
It writes its name in the air
To remember
Pouring its features on the wall of the night
To remember
Touching the edges of the wind
To ignite
Then it is finished
* * *

Peace is upon it
And darkness upon it
Upon it lean the heavens
They go
And come back
Shake the side of the heart
Follow the traces of its perfume
Then spread out
* * *

A blind body
Languidly
Opening its eyes
Seeing nobody . . .
A body that does not resemble me
Walks far away
From the seething fire
With no desire
It wears its nakedness
Comes to a halt behind the soul
Then vanishes

No Time to Steal Sighs

Oh woman
Inhabiting my body
Filling it with secrets
Embroidering its rims
With threads of silence
Leave my body
And live outside me
You are not of this time!
* * *

Take your clay
Your silence
The reddening shame in you
Inside and out
Hurry up
Hoist your clouds
On the edge of the rocks
Out there
And abandon the
Abayas of the body
* * *

Oh woman
Flow out
Scatter your spikes of grain
Far away
Write yourself
On the edges of the night
And dream
Of drowning
In the waters of yearning and wandering
Expose yourself
On the face of basil
Take the color of ether
And leave
On the fast train
Towards the springs of passion

There is no time
To embezzle sighs
And wait for the far off evening . . .
* * *
Oh woman
Leave the cradle of life
And dance
Upon the wings of the wind
Leave your desolate field
And mount the horse of forgetfulness
You are not
Of
This time . . .
Your face does not fit
This veil
Your water does not accord with
This earth
Hurry up
One step
Two steps
Three
The time of illusion is over
So
Unfasten the buttons of the shade
On the face of the sky
Quickly wash with the water of the sun
And dance around the mirrors
Shout
With all your heart
With all the circles of silence in you
And declare
How much you are
A woman
When you so wish . . .

Mansouri, Zohra

Zohra Mansouri is a novelist and a poet. She is a professor of semiotics at Ibn Zohr University in Agadir, Morocco. She has a doctorate degree in the semiotics of cinema. She has many publications in poetry, novel writing and scriptwriting. Her publications include two prize-winning novels: البوار (*Perdition* 2006) and من يبكي النوارس (*Who Cries over Seagulls* 2006), and the poem collection تراتيل (*Incantations* 2000).

The Mirror

A table for talk
Drawings on the walls
As I fade in pale silence
I sketch my face on a broken mirror
And the splinters run away with my features
When my courage was wiped from the mirror's glow
I wept . . .
I drew my face on a myriad of pieces
Yet it wasn't my face
But a burnt butterfly
* * *

How do I climb up the sky's dusk
Without being burned by the clouds
Without its expanse slipping away from me.
* * *

I gather stars from the sky's belly
Design a little girl with wings of roses

And a dream that flows like the wind
When she flutters
She makes me shiver
A little girl of haze.
* * *
I will plant the stars in my bones
And raise bridges of absence in my heart.
Clouds offer me their tents
Death is a lily covering the body's fountains
What memory is large enough for your dream
Oh grass wet with thorns
And exile.

Van Gogh's Evening

In his room the evening falls in beads
misty flowers
undulations of cruel yellowness
the evening's complaint
the paper pants
the body's moisture on the vases
he fears the grass will be swept away so draws it
he guards his flowers
and his fresh vision that always slips away in fleeting depths
as I draw the color of shadow on the grapevine's pulse
and listen to its hues:
delicate as I step
I whisper to the clay
I sip the dew from the morning grasses
and sketch the memory of the bridge
and I speak . . .
of the iris on the overpass that traverses me
of the small dreams that grow old before me
of the bird that flapped its wings
as a slow wind passed by
and made me flutter

as drops of thick mist fell . . .
sunflowers bow down to my steps at evening
I tend to the garden of vines
to the heartbeat of the evening bridge
I revive the past, conversing with stars that pass by
and old enlightened footsteps
I reach for the water's murmur when the clouds brighten
and my sky dissolves into seas held close by all my stars
damp, I am the grapevine of youth
letting down my fresh spray
on the drawing board where I live
the inkwell inebriates me
and the pulse of dew at dusk
here my daisies have languished into suns
here my drizzle has ripped me open
so that swallows smell my walls.

Mejjati, Ahmed

Ahmed Mejjati was born in 1936 in Casablanca. He received his bachelor's degree from the Faculty of Arts in Damascus then a Diplôme des Etudes Supérieures from Mohammed V University in Rabat in 1971. He obtained his doctorate in 1992 and died in 1995. He joined the Moroccan Writers' Union in 1968. He published two critical essays, ظاهرة الشعر الحديث (*The Phenomenon of Modern Poetry*), and أزمة الحداثة في الشعر العربي المعاصر (*The Modernism Crisis in Contemporary Arabic Poetry* 1983). His poetic work includes الفروسية (*Chivalry* 1987). Majjati was awarded the prize of the Spanish-Arab Culture Institute in Madrid for poetry in 1985 and is considered a founder of Moroccan modern poetry and literary criticism.

Jerusalem

I saw you burying the wind
under the arbors of darkness
shrouding yourself in silence
       behind the slats of shutters
pouring graves
        and drinking
        decades thirsting
        and all that I fermented
        from clouds and cups thirsting
        we, too, thirsting
        while in you is only extinction
So where do we die my dear aunt?

* * *

The daggers of the snake
  nick the gray-haired
   light of your eyes

The bite of the scorpion towers up
  from the cracks of the desert

and I rise greater than my sky
  greater than the clear hatred in my eyes
   I rise

Your desolate face
Oh gateway to God
  has fallen down
how can I reach you
  when you are death, you are death
  you are the
  most difficult aspiration

* * *

I stretched to you the dawn of my longing
for death and sunk my plough

in the belly of the whale
so that what darkness pulsed in my heart
  and in the blood of the desert
  what hope
dissolved in the purity of death
illuminated the darkness of the coffin
  in my eyes
so that I came to you buried
weighed down with the corsair's laughter
and the misery of dawn
  in Oran
and the Lord's silence sailed in the ruins of Mecca
  or in the mountains of Sinai

* * *

And you turn your face aside
nothing remains with the blood
but the dawn on your forehead
but an ashen-colored ostrich
and a night that cut off the wings of the tent
      croaking with death

You pour the graves
               and drink
          and the desert thirsts
          we too thirsted
          while in you is only extinction
          So where do we die
                  my dear aunt?

Casablanca

Why do letters that spell out your name
               whirl like a hat in the grips of
                         the wind?
When I recall the loved ones of my heart
               I scatter their names
                    one by
                        one
When I recall the loved ones of my heart
Are you a tourist?
The sand imprisons your Parisian dreams
Here I am as I catch the wind
I weave a flag out of the rusty chain
And from the rusty chain
               a graveyard for letters
               an inkwell for swords
               a guitar for sadness
And you, abiding by the law of silence,
                    stretched
               between my chain and me
                   between the borders of my country

in you I entertain the winds of loved ones
I entertain their rains
                    in exile
their body parts strewn in the bellies of the wastelands

And you, abiding by the law of silence:
                    I closed your eyes
              before prayer
                    before proceeding to burial
        Then we met on the river bank:
        your face a banner in the streets
your voice a sign

I faced my death for a second time
Your silence was between me and the snipers
                              firing calamity
        When I discovered a barroom
              I was dizzied by the wineglass
                          I sailed
                          I sailed
                    Until I missed you

The train was crumbling my face
                    sketching in each crack
                          an identity
I wondered:
        Are you my lover?
              Why didn't you seed me in the womb of eternity
                          or seed me between earth
                                    and rocks?
Your eyes remained fixed
              You were pregnant
                    Prison cells contained me
                    I saw the loved ones of my heart
                    I saw the loved ones of my heart
                                    killed

And here came the summer knocking with sun and blood
                          on your closed doors

And here came the summer
        the funerals revived in your caves
        And the cloth of the burning flag
           joined the funerals

So what do the daggers say?
        Did the head fall?
        Or did the columns of the guillotine
           fall in gloom . . . ?

Your houses move out of my memory
I stretch the black of my eyes as a bridge
And you are on the thousandth bank
        sailing in coughs
           and in the stumbling of men
     sailing
        The river falls in you
and all the rifles fall
        killed

And all the poems enter the age of silence
        and the salty teardrop
           So you sister of hungry Granada
           Tear my shirt
               Wipe it on the Rif mountains
           And extract something
        from my remains
     other than wine
   and barking desire

Posters on "Dahr al-Mehraz"*

First poster:

When he used to visit the city
      he'd knock on my door
I made him afternoon coffee
      he stifled his cough
I scaled his gigantic size
      with distrustful looks
He'd offer me a smile
      and stare at the bend in the road
      through the window left ajar

I'd leave the key of my house
      under the flowerpot
      for him
and advise him when the glass of wine
      matured
      between us
though he preferred
      cold beer

He came back one day
      just before the call to prayer
      and one time
      he disappeared behind the vases
before surprising the door
      then he vanished
      once and for all

What might he be doing now:
      sealing his dreams with red wax
      recalling
            how the women in Al Qasr†
            wrap themselves in cloaks

---

* The area where the university college of arts is located in Fes.
† The city of Lqsar L-kbiir.

Or reading what he can
from chapter al-Maida of the Qur'an

Second Poster:

And here you are now
drunk with resolution
drunk with the day's defeat of students
drunk . . .
                    Good
But I chose the line of dissent
Here are our jeers
                    filling the public square
So go on eavesdropping
                    if you want
Or else tell your military circle
                    on the university campus
                          to take a rest

One moment
they started to march
            They were on foot
            their hands aloft
            They fired at them
            and a gap opened in the dissidents' lines
O newcomer wrapped
            with a bleeding tear
Stand at the entrance to the dormitory
            where the heads of the rebels rallied
            that's my blood
                and let Fez be your glass
For Rabat, the whore,
            remakes its virginity
                    to become a little girl
peace, let there be peace

            If one day there could only be a decision
            to return the heads to their necks

and the blood
        to where it used to bleed
a decision to stop time
to remove Zalagh*
        from its impossible love
a decision to furnish the proof for heresies
                peace, let there be peace

Third Poster:

When I caught sight of your eyes
        fully charged
the hair on the head on the alter-cloth
        had turned white
and the way to the university restaurant
        was abandoned
The tree branches were falling
    burdened with spies . . .
Does the new little girl know
that ten years have passed
ten years
have brought to light
    a language threatening even the hope
        still in us
Does she know that yesterday's lecture was
      canned
        cold
This is the new form of notebooks
and bodies of reference
    The rate of those who passed the year provisionally
    and those who passed the year without provision
      is like the color of report cards
    a foul color
This is why my face looks as
I don't want it to.
Does the little lark know

---

* Zalagh is the mountain overlooking Fes.

when her beak carries
the Rif Mountains to me
and the vast plains between Rabat and Tangiers
that the ignition of poetry
takes place in a time between two sides
On one side I sit behind a glass
On the other in a cell
as the tip of chalk draws
a qibla, a direction
for me
between the end of the lecture
and the graveyard.

Reading in the Mirror of the Frozen River

In his nausea he carries trees
yellowed books
and tables
silence and poems
the world
its ruins
and walled cities
When he came to the happy domed chambers
he scattered red anger
became a thread of water
the wall of the palace laughing
in its stubborn mirror
But I come out of old stakes
mixing spices, fishes and bricks
I knock on the prison door
in Marrakech
I escape from the grip
of the executioner
I draw the sign of revolution
on the pirate's head
Then I bend myself tirelessly
I dive in the depth of the waves
crucified

I dive I don't see anything except
the boots of the horsemen
and the rust of steel on the weapons
                          of the battlefield
as if when water flowed
those passionate Atlas mountains
cried blood and dug a desert
in the desert
* * *

And here I am on the path of rude seaweed
          weaving
          a line of ink
          a hungry rain
          a banner that walks in the streets
          from my way of being, my name
          and my qualities
Oh you, remnants of lost time:
          my blood on the dead heroes is a flower
          a mark on the wrist
          the bracelet's noose
a fine wine comes out of old barrels
and here I am on the path of victory and defeat
holding the blade of the sword
the water of the river
the decapitated head of the country
          the color of the raised flag
                    that I hold . . .
          You got bigger oh river, the branches have grown around you
          and your black stones have come out
                    from their names
                    Time has come out
Who says that this chain
          doesn't come out of its own names
                    as dew
                    and red wine?
Who says that this passionate Atlas
                    when water flowed
                    cried blood

     and dug a desert
        in the desert

The Stumbling of the Wind

snow and silence
    are resting on the ocean,
the waves nailed to the sand
     And the wind is an unmanned
       rowboat
    with a crumbling oar
        and cobwebs
Who will ignite the joy
    in my eyes?
Who will awaken the giant?
Who will die?
     The smell of death is on the garden
mocking the seasons
and you, my girlfriend,
    a rattle in your throat
    a virgin's teardrop
    And the sound of your footsteps
      on the ruins
searching for
       truth
       a dagger
       and a forceful arm
The eagle's feathers
    in our deep wounds
    were a mouth
    with a craving thirst
    for the beat of drums
for a generous gust of wind
    to moisten its throat
      and the battlefield
What gentle cloud
     will hang over the stumbling horses!

Take back my severed remains
                    My blood did not foresee its path
                    Whoever stretches a hand to dawn
                              will hasten the end
Who tied my thoughts to a rock
and stretched out a beak
to my eyes?
Oh thief of the torch
clamor is hidden in silence
So pick the flowers of light
from across the stubborn darkness
We resorted to silence
        in the cave
for the stench of salt
        will not be washed by words
Let us dive into the sea
        beneath the waves and rocks
there surely is a flicker of light
        that sails through the depths
Take back its spark
shake the wind's yearning
from the chains of silence
and teach humans
        how to die

Writing on the Beach of Tangiers

The Riff mountains
stumbled
over the haunches of dawn
The wind blew from the east
Pine forests flourished
                    On the western horizon

Don't tell the wineglass:
                    This is the land of God
But in Tangier God remains
                    Thirsty

In his back prayer niche
Making Caesar into a lion

* * *

Have you had tea
In its downtown marketplaces

Dipping the year
    In the instant
    And the instant
In seventy years' time
Or did you plow a river in its bowels

    You said:
        It is like Yarmouk*
        Exquisite Zellaqa†
        Is one of its names

    You said:
        It is the letter
        On the tombstone's epitaph.
            It sings

And on the column of the palace
        It dies

You knew God in the inkwell of fright
        And the
            Lexicon of silence

---

* The Battle of Yarmouk was between the army of the Byzantine Empire and the Muslim Arab forces of the Rashidun Caliphate along what today are the borders of Syria–Jordan and Syria–Israel, east of the Sea of Galilee. The result of the battle was a complete Muslim victory which ended Byzantine rule in Syria.

† The Battle of Sagrajas (23 October 1086), also called Zalaca or Zallaqa (Arabic: معركة الزلاقة, translit. *Ma'rakat az-Zallāqa*), was a battle between the Almoravid army led by the Almoravid king Yusuf ibn Tashfin and a Christian army led by the Castilian King Alfonso VI. The battleground was later called *az-Zallaqah* (in English "slippery ground") because the warriors were slipping all over the ground due to the tremendous amount of blood shed that day, which gave rise to its name in Arabic.

* * *

The shrouds will leave their tombs

                Someday

But obscurity remains here

With the crazy tourist

And the café where we used to die

              Each evening

Perhaps dawn veered us towards the house of the one we love

                    For a while:

"And we wrote on the clean sand and you didn't memorize it"*

         And the letter remains crucified on the pillar of the palace

* * *

As if God had not overcome

           A sword

           And a sun

           And hope with it

If only he had bent toward the gray-haired Marrakech

           Palm trees

     And on the dunes of Ouarzazate

           Water

* * *

Alas the Riff Mountains have turned into subterranean tunnels

And silence has become a pulpit

Don't tell the wineglass:

           This is the land of God

But in Tangier God remains

       Thirsty

       In his back prayer niche

       Making Caesar into a lion

---

* A line from a popular song.

Meliani, Driss

Driss Meliani was born in Fez in 1945. After his secondary education in Casablanca, Morocco, he went to the University of Damascus, Syria, and the University in Fez, Morocco, where he obtained a bachelor's degree in Arabic Literature and a degree in educational psychology in 1970. He also studied Russian literature in Moscow. He worked as a teacher and a teacher trainer in Casablanca until he retired. He was the vice-president of the Moroccan Writers' Union until 2019. He translated Alexander Pushkin's *The Little Tragedies* into Arabic: التراجيديات الصغيرة and Fyodor Dostoyevsky's *The House of the Dead*: مذكرات البيت الميت. His poetry includes: زهرة الثلج (*The Snow's Flower* 1998), and مغارة الريح (*The Cave of Wind* 2001) which won the Moroccan Booker Prize the same year. More recently, Meliani also published a novel, كازانفا (*Casanfa* 2016).

Profile

Why
are you overtaken by sadness
in the overflow of joy
gurgling in my arms
—like a small child—
you burst out laughing like a ghost?
You sing a mournful tune
an echoing bird
you call out for help
and swallow your tears
mixed with my blood in a wine glass
How do you stretch your arms far away

dancing in drunkenness
like a slaughtered rooster?
You close your eyes
until you see
the white northern
star
whose light travels to you by night
like a rainbow?
As if you abided here . . .
A body without soul!

Melissa's Last Words
(for Deborah Kapchan)

Melissa's last words
at the World Trade Center
during that dreadful grievous event
that defied belief
that had not been seen
Melissa said,
I love you!
to her father
She said, I love you!
to her mother
She said, I love you!
to her husband
Sean, the lover
She said, I love you!
to her brother Michael
And they were all happy to hear
Melissa's voice on the phone
And each replied,
I love you too, Melissa!
Even if Michael
couldn't
talk to her

He said, I was working
then got out.
I couldn't say anything
I cried
I didn't know anything
but was hoping
Melissa would be able to get out of the tower
(the northern tower)
perhaps the stairway
the elevator
the helicopters
I was following
what was going on
as my heart
was being ripped out of me
as it was being ripped
from her chest
and my father's
and mother's chests
Little Melissa used to worry about me
a lot,
her brother said.
He was older than her
the only one
stronger than her
the only one she wasn't stronger than
Her father
taught her
to hope for what she wanted
clothes, hair style,
It was long
but has become short
Her father, the only one who did not believe
her hair style
did not expect
her to buy
and drive a car

when she was still
in Massachusetts
and California
Little Melissa
from a love kiss
between a beautiful couple
Melissa and Sean,
the Hughes family knew
were like twins
the husband like the brother,
the father and mother said
Only a
year and a few months
had gone by
September had hardly begun
the eleventh
the beginning of love
Sean woke
from his sleep
Sean woke
from his dream
to Melissa's voice,
I love you, Sean!
And he, saying to her,
I love you too, Melissa!
But where are you now?
Melissa said,
I'm stuck here
above and below
a ball of fire
going up and down
the tower is falling
(the southern tower)
in front of me
over there
the flesh of the building moans
no way to escape
all I hear

is cries and wailing
this strange feeling
whose surface
expands like fire
through all the floors
(over a hundred!)
It's the end, there's no doubt.
And before my father
and mother arrived home
the northern tower had gone down
But on the phone
an echo or a smash
ringing
the last words of farewell
memories
and a single question
and answer:
The necessity of love!
One existence
Life is short!
I listen to that message
I will be all right
he often says
I will be all right
she says as well
I will be all right
I listen to that message
over the years
And tell myself
like all the family victims do
The message is a memory
a sad inheritance
I will leave it aside
I say this so often
I choose this
myself I say
Love is most important
A condolence to the families

of victims
Love is most important
The message will live with me
and I will listen to it
as long as I live.

May life be long.

The Cave of the Demoness

My grandfather's old house is over there
standing on a mountain
with towering views
overlooking the gorge
guarded by the demoness
with its kinsfolk the Ghoul*
holding in its arms a treasure
in
the depth of
the sky! . . .

The Oil Press

Where's the oil press . . . ?
I gambled it, my son . . .
And the she-ass
the balking she-ass
that threw me when I was young . . .
Do you still beat it
with the oak stick
whenever it stubbornly refuses
to go to market
overburdened with the years' firewood?

---

*The tribe of Ghiyata and the Cave of the She-Ghoul is a place in Taza, the poet's place of birth.

I sold it, my son
like worn out belongings
And I gambled, gambled, gambled
betting even things that can't be sold . . . !

The Narrow Path

Gueldaman!*
Oh Gueldaman!
Where is that narrow path that used
to lead to you?
The narrow path
on the side of the ravine
whose arms were covered with almond trees
and wormwood fragrant with
pervasive scents
The narrow path
on the side of the heart
bound by the songs of birds
winding green like the tattoo
on my mother's face
The narrow path
red-stained like the blood
in my father's gaze
and the veins in my hands
The narrow path
filling the eye and the heart
with tears from the pain of boxthorn
The narrow path
flooded by your blood
oh King of water
crowned son of the heavens
is now
covered by a forest of thorny shrubs! . . .

---

* Gueldaman means "King of Water" in Tamazight, from "Agueliid" (King) and "wa-man" (water); it is a name of a place in the eastern part of Ghiyatha in the region of Taza.

Mesnaoui, Driss Amghar

Idriss Amghar Mesnaoui was born near the town of Tifelt, Morocco, in 1947. He taught secondary school from 1966 to 2006. Mesnaoui writes poems and prose in Moroccan Arabic and has been in the forefront of the movement to make Moroccan Arabic a literary language. He started writing zajal (colloquial Arabic poetry) in the mid-sixties of the twentieth century and has published more than 30 prose and poetry collections in colloquial Moroccan Arabic so far. His books include الواو (*al-waw*); قوس النصر (*Arc of Triumph*); كناش المعاش (*Booklet of Retirement*); and تراب المعاني (*Soil of Meanings*). In addition, he has an essay: أسئلة السفر أو سفر الأسئلة (*Questions of Travel and the Traveling Questions*). He is also author of novels and plays written in colloquial Moroccan Arabic. Mesnaoui retired from work 12 years ago and now lives in the countryside where he is fully devoted to reading and writing.

The Earth's Nuptials

Over the sound of a wailing flute
the day
gets out of the bed of illness swaying
its broken-winged heart
throwing itself down amid waves of sighs.
Who will open an aperture in life
to hand in a little glass of hope to
those falling down—rising up
rising up—falling down?
*

In dreams my woman
said "I will"
Joseph's coat was her share
and what's new in treachery and defaming
scandals.
*

She was a bride
entering the home of worry
The wind showed its canine teeth of treason
My lady carved a smile
The son of blood got suspicious
Desire got furious
Rage bit to the bone
until blood gushed forth from the one in clutches
*

The land cracked
in the wretchedness of time
The earth moved its stakes
The ozone tent flew away over our heads
with no appointed time for return
The gap opened up
bringing with it the devastating dust storms of the age of Aad*
Oleander mourned the death of the river
The time of high heat awoke
searching in the crusts of earth
for what was left behind among the provisions of the past
from "Ram that al Imaad"†
*

The chest of the land tightened
The bottom of the sea widened
The cheeks of water

---

* Aad, thought to be the great grandson of Shem, son of Noah , and the sons of Aad
thought to be the earliest inhabitants of Arabia.

† Iram *the city of pillars (arabe* ذات العماد إرَم, Iram ḏāt al-ʿimād) is a lost city thought to be
situated in the Arab peninsula.

are they crying or
are they laughing
for the fate of youth!?
*

From the white hell
I gathered the splinters of life
I discovered my time is the time of myself
Sometimes it makes me remember my duties
Sometimes it makes me forget.
The new world is based on
"Don't do as I do
Do as I say"
See the needy getting more impoverished
and the rich getting even richer.
Will I, after this old disaster,
seek more riches?
*

Time is running away from the pharaoh of the day
blown away by the rocks of hell to the barren desert
a scrap of a ray
Poverty is an instinct in the history of blood
It gets out of dire straits
and sits at its door
The slave
is unmoved by a kick or a blow
The owl said to the crocodile
"who can lend me its eyes
to cry over the miseries of this world
that is dying unaware of where to go or turn?"
The moon read it with a stolen glance
found it sowing its worries on the hilltop
building houses of sand
for the wanderers
with ideas of wind.
*

Bounty looked down from the neck of the bottle
asking after its kinsfolk

while its kinsfolk were watching the boxes of illusions
The earth is constantly turning round itself
as if having lost its way
and the road is tied to its stones
bending over its neck like a chicken to a buyer
And the sons of blood
blind one after blind one
hold tight to the dust storm from the bottom up
*

This world
has abandoned its people
as if it owed them
nothing
*

A voice rose up from the marrow of the earth
It tore open the wing of darkness
recounting to future generations the story they missed
"every hour the land of dreams
will be on the throne of dreams
until the poor inherit the earth and what's on it
and the earth itself will inherit a wedding of peace."

Part of a Country Symphony

the crowd drank us before we entered the city
worry we wore it
and we wore the wounds of the swords of deceit
those who needed a boat became, themselves, a ship.
those who gave birth to us
hunger ate them before they could eat
those who raised us
the grave swallowed them before they could dig it

we found fasting the medicine for hunger
our thirst drank our tears
the tears sprouted wings

they flew away   with me
they wandered   with me
far away   from myself
and close to the sea
they brought me down
I drank a handful from a wave of chaos
drowning like the sun before it sets
in a sea of wars

the bands of forgetfulness swallowed me
the heels of the wind threw me in the mill
the days chewed me up
am I a person?
in my chest is an ember eaten by ashes
on my shoulder is a tree where crickets play
am I a person?
I'm the forgetful one . . . I am the drowned
I'm the inattentive one . . . I am the awakened
I put out my neck to help the drowning
hope, my eyes and arms.
I extend my hand to sew the patch of star
rising from the bottom of the dirty night
I sew my skin to the bones of the flayed day
with saliva I wash the face of cheated luck
hope, my eyes and arms
I said it just may be that the buried root with live again
I said it just might be that arms and tongues will sprout from the clay
I dug in my brain in my veins
I looked in the sea in my worries in my blood
for myself
for just a bit of myself
I found Abdelkrim Khatabi rising like a giant
from a circle of vicious
cares
he split the ground . . . he split the seed
and he came down on the notebooks
he opened his hands and said, "here's the qibla"

a new thirst inhabited me
like the flower's thirst for a drop of water
my thirst can be quenched only by that red star
I ran behind the dewdrops of night ... behind the star
I found Abdelkrim in the spring of water ... in the roots of the tree
I found him harvested ... yet planted
I found him in the vapors ... in the clouds ... in the waves ...
I found him ... ink ... paper ... feather ... wings ... bird

Mesnaoui, Nafiss

Naffis Mesnaoui was born in 1982 in Rabat. He received a bachelor's degree in French literature from the Faculty of Arts in Rabat and holds a doctorate degree in modern Lebanese poetry in Arabic and French from the University of Limoges in France.

Cinema

We'll meet by chance in the cinema that's behind the sea
sit next to each other to watch a comedy
about two selfish lovers who don't leave
a chance for us to take their places (you and me).
We'll set everything on fire: the sequence of desire, the warmth of touching,
    matches for the cigarette halves we
smoke equally, cigarettes of time.
And we'll intertwine like two palm trees until the wind of rapture
pulls out our roots.
We will laugh to the limit of crying over this mortal body.
And when the show is over and the public applauds, the public that came for
    entertainment, when the curtain falls,
we won't leave the theater of our bodies.

Morchid, Fatiha

Fatiha Morchid (born March 14, 1958, Benslimane) is a Moroccan pediatrician, a poet and writer. Her publications include: إيماءات (Gestures 2002); تعالى نمطر (Let us Rain 2006); مخالب المتعة (The Enjoyment Claws 2009); ما لم يقال بيننا (What is Not Spoken Between Us 2010). The poems here are from آخر الطريق أوله (The End of the Road . . . is the Beginning).

I haven't felt at ease in the surrounds
(To my Soumaya)

A quarter of a century has gone by
These surroundings
And still I haven't felt comfortable with the surrounds

Preferable
To draw the border
Though I continue to wait
For a touch to collapse
The wall
On the side of the heart

A quarter of a century has gone by
And still the dream is a kid
That tries to pick up the neighbor's daughter
Believing
She got pregnant
From a kiss on the lips

And the moon
Is the cake of God
Distributed among lovers

A quarter of a century has gone by
Inadvertently
And we still
Plan
Daily details
Postponing love
Until sometime . . .
How many sometimes have passed by?
How many of them are left?

A quarter of a century has gone by
While you've been looking at me
Yet don't see me
And I listen to you
And don't hear
The echo of my songs
Still I insist on singing
Hoping my soul can
Produce rapture
Out of the mouth of the earth

A quarter of a century has gone by
Seedlings
Have become trees
And the sap is still
Looking for a passage
And we are still preparing the birds
For rain
Afraid
That the shade will leave us

A quarter of a century has gone by
Days following days
And we flirt

With steady words
Polishing
The glass windows
Of couplehood
Intertwining our hands
In the darkness

A quarter of a century has gone by
And we're still
Sacred
Entertaining our isolation
For fear of solitude

If It Were Possible

If it were possible
I would have offered the clown
My ropes

And conspired
With spectators

To topple
"Forbidden for those
under forty"

If it were possible
I would have jumped to you
In one kiss

Instead of
Stammering
On damned paper

If it were possible
I would have spent a lifetime

In a dream
You were in

Instead of
This wakefulness
That makes the bed tight

If it were possible
I would ask the barber
To prune
The locks of my memory streaming
On the neck of time

Instead of
My bangs
That stir no one
But me

If it were possible
I would wipe
The maps of place
With a wandering towel

Instead of
Glass
Unable
To flirt with the sun.

If it were possible
I would have planted
The heart of a pelican

Instead of
The longing
Of a sailor on land

If it were possible
I would have targeted
The sky
With my hurricane

Instead of
Acquiring immunity
Against the rain

If it were possible
I would have cast my sins
On the roofs

Instead of
Hiding them
In filo dough

If it were possible
I would have disclosed
My screams
On the mirrors

Instead of
The wrinkles
Of chords of silence

If it were possible
I would have gathered all the coming years
In the moment
Now

Instead of
The tomorrow
That squirrels away like a cough
In my biography

Moumni, Rachid

Rachid Moumni was born in 1951 in Fès. He received a bachelor's degree in Arabic Literature in 1971, and later a master's degree. He worked as a teacher in a high school in Fès, and joined the Moroccan Writers' Union in 1974. Among his many publications are النزيف (*Bleeding* 1974); ثلج مريب على جبهة الحطاب (*Suspicious Snow on the Woodcutter's Forehead* 2008). He is translated in English, Spanish and French. He is also a painter. The first two poems as well as the fourth were translated into Spanish in Las Noches Azules del Alma (*Blue Nights of the Soul* 2001) translated by Enrique Villagrasa and Belen Juarez. The third one is found in مهود السلالة (*Cradles of Descent* 2002).

Blood

hauls its other
across eons
half of whose air
is a bitter mineral
such is the march of illusion
confused
it gleans the fruits of cosmic ruin
bound for
traps of blue.

Her call

was the earth's longing for water
It woke the dead
It woke the stones sleeping in their white slumber
In front of me
She said:
Over there, there are as many invisible faces
as the stars awaiting you
Be careful not to lose the way to me
The sign:
I am the palest idea
in the middle of a labyrinth of blue
Be careful not to stray from me.

The Ladder of Confusion

The ladder exhausted with leaning on
a wall exhausted with standing
thought of sleeping
on an earth exhausted with dreaming
so it tore off its clothes
revealing the ashes of its nakedness
to an observer
exhausted with confusion

With what's Left of Lightning

I sing with the night's ashes
glancing at the face of doubt
so that its eyes see only
the history of a light
taken with its own extinction
straying beyond the walls
that words have melted

Mourad, Khireddine

Khireddine Mourad (born 1950, Casablanca) writes in French. He is a retired professor from Cadi Ayad University in Marrakech. His works include: Pollen (2001); Nadir ou la Transhumance (*Nadir or Transhumance* 1992); Marrakech et la Mamounia (*Marrakech and the Mamounia* 1994); Arts et Traditions du Maroc (1998); Chant à L'Indien (*Song to the Native American* 2004), and a novel entitled Les Dunes Vives (*The Living Dunes* 1997).

from *Pollen*

Far! Far! Always far! Even when closest to us.

At the hour of song we were nowhere
Pollen
It follows its oblivion like one follows a path

deaf to the fruit of rhizomes, to rocky outcroppings,
always rushing in its law of new beginnings.

The aged wind shakes the stalks
toward other trips without maps and astrolabes

disintegrating departures and returns, cries and screams
agitating forest, rock and dust

towards the desert between asymmetrical dunes
towards the sea that taunts the immobile schooner

But what do the scattered grains tell our memory?
What do far-off eras murmur to our emotions?

Far! Far! Always far! Even when closest to us.
Only the ramparts of tumult accustom us . . .

Disembodied wind, you who in all of space fertilize
expectations adorned with flowers at the hour of expiration.

But who can tell you without making you separate from yourself?

Meandering water in all impenetrable places,
You roll, fertile, rare, dissolving

The waiting is for us,
supplicants of the sky for a happy downpour.

Crystalline turbulence between the folds of the earth
you wander the ravines you dig without sketching your reasons.

I seek your surrounds for a high communion.
But who can tell you without separating you from yourself?

Palpitating pollen you go awry,
accomplishing the vertical phrase in these places that absorb you.

It's the water, here, this leak of perpetual communion,
solitary water for the regard that stops or passes by

Water that gives you your streams of pollen—no water,
grain for an elusive survival.

Diatoms of arid earth, tumultuous waters, skies
You say nothing to my untreatable despair

Bodies tell another story . . .

Lustful undulations, flux and reflux of flesh, of salination, of wind.
Movement on the roads of secret disseminations.

Bodies repeat the word in the splashed air
Tell of the vast noise hidden from the stars.

In every place that welcomes euphoria
Parades call back the released spring-times.

Song to the Native American

> We are there where
> We receive no news even of ourselves.
> GHALIB (1793–1869)

> We die desiring death
> But death never comes
> GHALIB (1793–1869)

They are only a rumor

They are not more than a rumor of water and wind
A dream of a distant hum
A fugitive light of a denuded soul
The impossible instant of a torn regard

And that is forever

Sing water, Lover of the Island, you who remind places of the mass graves of men.
Sing water until the hour of beginning
Slow mating ceremony of flocks to the hollows of chaste wellsprings

They are only a memory
The tearing of a stone between the stones of Time

And that is forever

Until the farthest dawns of memory
They are the forgotten name of men

The earth.
The place of our existence, there where forgetfulness is,
There, the sojourn of mislaid lights.
And you meander like the rebellious mane of a tempest above sleeping waters.
You were the glimmer of a land. The promise of an East on the waters of the
Atlantic. A country of spices on the arid banks and the furtive islands of an ignored
India.
The glimmer of a dream for the heros of iron and fire.
Man dead from man.
Merchants of land, spices, men. What does the secret of places mean for charioteer
thirsts. The places and their gods will be erased.
I will leave the broken branch at the entrance of the port as a goodbye to the tree.

The Lover of the Island was multiple, like a song of steps and departures.
The sharp pain of human jubilation. She didn't have any North in her gaze. And
her body full of salt and the South, all the Souths of Time, gathering the painful suns
of life.
The Lover of the Island was from all the Norths also.
These lands always suspended on the edges of the eyes.
And the sandy boat without hope of a port. Happy grace of dawn
and dusk, the tenderness of sea foam, you carry the cardinal points of man until the
end of you.
Where was India?
Mirage of spices and silk on the steep slopes of days and nights.
Where was India, Lover of the Island, other than in you?
And all the Indias of man will not say your name.
And the East and the West are nothing but the eternal here of intoxication.
Give your name to the children to come pacify the anger of trees.
Deliver the rolling hills of your body to bodies in search of peace.
And leave the tragic joy of the Andes to shatter between the colors of death and
harvest festivals.

And the *Indian* has no place
And that is forever

And the earth is but an island.

Moussaoui, Abdesselem

Abdesselem Moussaoui (born January 1, 1958) is a poet and a teacher trainer at the Ecole Normale Supérieure in Fez. His publications include: خطاب إلى قريتي (*A Letter to my Village* 1986); إيقاعات ملونة (*Colorful Rhythms* 2006); لحن عسكري للأغنية عاطفية (*A Military Tune for an Emotional Song* 2011). Abdesselem Moussaoui won a number of poetry awards in Paris (1992), Fez (1999), Asilah (2000) and Beyrouth (2005). He has also published studies of the poetry of two major Arab poets, the Egyptian Amal Dunqul and the Palestinian Mahmoud Darwish, as well as other books.

A Forest of Letters

The shadowy ones surround me
blowing smoke from their pale faces
They approach the thresholds of their wine glasses
insolent and boisterous
But me, I am lucid as the day
My glass turns away . . .
The light recedes
And from the ornaments on the walls
new details emerge
I see the threshing floor . . . over there
And my father who died
jumps in the midst of dust and wheat
In his hands a mule groans from the anger of the whip
and a bird races stones straying
from my side

Feathers of all colors bounce in the evening
Over there is my hiding place in a tree inhabited by a woman
that I snatched from a novel
by Ihssan Abd El Qaddous
I embrace her whenever I seek shelter in my secrets
She offers me her flowers—as many as I want—
when she succeeds in deceiving the hero
Better for me to tend my garden
and make room for the orange tree
its suns stuffed with honey
As tomorrow is Sunday
I fear waking to the voice of the poet Assayab*
And to the apocalypse of poets in Al Maari's† large tree
I fear falling asleep
before deflowering the page
before I pull smoke from the last cigarette
Coward I be
if I don't fence my field with words:
         C for the child lost in the jungle
         W for a woman I ran into at the street bend
         I inundated with similes of her features
And she went away with a shake of perfume followed by butterflies
I will disappear in the forest of letters
searching for my father
to direct him to the labyrinth . . . to meander . . .
to tell him:
I walked so long in your shouts
and I saw your palms cracked with a labor
more eloquent than the hills of books I read
but the question that—in my childhood—irritated you
cuts its teeth in my chest, oh father
like the scythe in your fields!
Coward I be
if I don't wake my friends sleeping

---

    * Badr Chakir Assayab (Iraqi poet).
    † Abu Aalaa Al Maari (Classical Arab poet).

in my memory
to tell them:
You orphans
who lost the way to paradise
and slept crowded in the barroom of dreams . . .
perhaps it's better to sleep
Detestable Sunday rings in the morning alarm
and the milkman is at the door
Oh God! . . . It's life anew
and the obituaries
in the paper as everyday!

(2001)

Incantations for the Opening of the Great Gate

I sipped my sorrow and listened attentively to the oakwood door. I counted
ninety pieces from the black coins my
grandfather forged into a clove of metal, welcoming the metal's heart to the
house . . . I counted the knockings of the
boy I was and the yearning . . . and heard beards uttering the sacred names of
God in the bending of old men spinning
wool:

> Jellabas for the wind
> For the night of prayer
> For the sun of harvest
> For the sea of journey
> For the impenitent holy day . . .

I counted the bullet holes penetrating the nation's history, and the smoke of
memory that still fills the nose of a
woman time has not killed, mixing with the smell of oil in the combatant's food
so the words hang down like heavy grapes:

Here is where Abdelkrim dined
Here is where the greatest of men slept

　　　Here is where the virgins of the house wedded
　　　Here is where I took the flesh of your circumcision and kneaded it
　　　with rose water and grains of gunpowder tea
The gate was lofty like the horned centuries and its color was ashen
You gigantic oak
From which mythical forest did they bring you
to lift you up with columns and call you the great gate?
In the age of wonder:
　　　black jellabas . . .
　　　silk shawls . . . honey jars . . . milk jugs and fig and pomegranate baskets
　　　. . . recent laments and the sighing refrain for past abundance, and
　　　another lament for the man killed once upon a shot in the saint's forest
　　　. . . Your tears oh bereaved mother do not lessen the loss, and the horse
　　　returning without the horseman will no longer carry a man the size of
　　　loftiness . . . You woman with dug-out eyes set the rhythms of sobs aright
　　　fix the date and time of disasters and velvety blood
To the slaughtered doorstep under the feet of the great gate the place of
entering and exit:
　　　They used to stand in the courtyard
　　　their tattoos raised in splendid song
　　　and majestically pour down the flanks of goats
　　　cooked for the Quranic reciters,
　　　spilling glances over the black darkness of rough
　　　moustaches:
　　　Oh gardener pondering the green
　　　little leaf . . . by little leaf you used to fall
　　　And there you remained
　　　He who chooses passion as his path
　　　can only know pain
Oh grave of mine dug beside the oleander
Oh guardian who follows me like ill-fate
Tell me: how many drops of blood will my embalmed body
spill on the wedding dress
so my spouse won't kill me?!
I will remember oh great gate my knockings
a little girl will draw them on the notebook of prophecy and color them with
the nectar of daisies

streaming away here and there . . . I will remember the incense
of spirits, remember their offspring's history from the first sacred grandfather
who threw
his walls around a perimeter of earth, closing you off on the secrets of
intercourse,
who nailed on the walls the delirium of an unknown painter recounting the
story of genesis with the color of shouts:

> Two spouses hiding fertility in the ink
> of nature and courting the roar of deprivation
> and of Satan . . .
> A mythical sheep before the rising light
> From the blood of Ishmael
> my lord saddles up a yellow lion and leaves
> the country's prison
> a horseman freeing his color from the handcuffs of ideology
> driving Ablah on the desert's canopy . . .
> Green blood . . . red grass . . . the town palm trees . . .
> I will remember, oh gate, the faces of people who were . . . and those
> who left the morning aloe for the horses of those coming from Fes . . .
> and almonds
> The heart for those whom the heart loves . . . and the face of God on my
> slate.

Oh roar of the great gate
Awakened by the comings and goings, by the stink of nature
Shape for me a talisman for a baby to sleep
The moaning of the millstone over grains of sweat and barley
I counted the old coins
and with my palm . . . I pushed
the great gate open on a sea of wasteland
and my hand also stretched wide open

The Tamer of Satan

With all her features
and all she kept in her bag
from last night's party
she swore she would offer him
some space
and a promise of love on parole
** ** **

When the time for their meeting came
the thread of her perfume
made up for the anxiety of waiting
And the lisp in her mouth
was an outburst of distorted expression
She wanted to make him poetry
                   without rhyme . . .
From meter to meter
she jumped
and in the lines of the wind . . .
After she saved all the trochees
in the bank
she went on weaving
a night of explanations from prose
and a lover mounting the back of the word . . .
Who exhorted her not to leave the garden door open
in case Adam walked by exhausted
looking for a peddler of apples
Temptation is here . . . and there
on trees
where the snake lies in wait
or in the telephone booth
She said to him:
—Don't worry
I appointed you a tamer of Satan!

Moussaoui, Jamal

Jamal Moussaoui was born on September 28, 1970. He graduated in Economics from Mohammed V University in Rabat in 1995. He has served as a board member of the Moroccan Writers' Union and is also a member of the House of Poetry in Morocco. Jamal Moussaoui works as a journalist for the Moroccan daily newspaper العلم (*The Flag*). His publications include: كتاب الظل (*The Book of Shadow* 2001), that won the prize of the House of Poetry in Morocco in 2002; مدين للصدفة (*Indebted to Chance* 2007); حدائق لم يشعلها أحد (*Gardens No One Ignited* 2011); أتعثر في (*I Stumble over the Cloud as it Cries* 2014); and على مرأى سحابة (*Before the Very Eyes of a Cloud* 2016).

One Such Boy

With deep vacillation he reads the book of creation
extinguishing all words that lead to God
in order to cross the sea behind the darkness towards the void:
there is no time for him to open his flower to the sun
the advancing dust tells tales about the desired paradise
and about
a frightened
seagull
There is no water for him to burn all the distances
or to argue with the shape of the sunset
journeying towards the distant morning, this dust
blows over the heart from the chosen flower of twilight
sketching a face on the lip of sorrow
and staring longingly
at extinguished towns.

Splinters of a Returning Dream

naked like the fleeting distance
I roll from one shroud to another
and perish spontaneously on paper.
the sea knows I have no boat
only rhyming
words that will kill me
if a letter passes into the body in my visions.
this is my wide-open tale
my language flies off in splinters—peacefully—like an effusion of sun
flirting with the loved one's face at the crack of dawn
so that I raise my eye
towards the distant sky to see
how a dream returns to its nest from my footsteps.

The Wind's Memory of a Misty Woman

Open a window for me. Open far and wide
a door for short dreams that crumble now in the broad arid light
For all words choose a snare
of sorrows
Because the wind I embraced has retreated into
an ascending prayer of
pain. A frightening memory: like the sea breaking
in the face of words.
Shall I say the sea?
What woman stops the waves
as the boat journeys along?

Beginnings have short details, so open a window for me . . .
Here's my longing for a twilight retreating from low-lying ages
stretching from a miserable polestar. Alone. Naked.
Here's my departing from psalms that have crumbled behind prayer calls
of terror: They were splendid. They entered
the hallways of noble phrases from the gates of sacredness and rested

upon the heart like time that books of pain have turned over
Because the wind that I held close has turned into the splinters of a prayer. An
upright horizon. An exasperated memory. A caravan of stones of wakefulness.
Sands.
Can the sand be a face of palm trees from the corners of the heart
sneaking into the light and opening the window for me?
How then
does it open a window for me while a woman inhabits the tower of the wind
Is she not frightened of the desert . . . !?

Najmi, Hassan

Hassan Najmi (born 1960, Ben Ahmed) is a poet, a novelist, and a journalist. He now serves as the director of the Commission on Books and Publications in the Moroccan Parliament. His publications include: in poetry, حياة صغيرة (*A Little Life* 1995); المستحمات (*Female Bathers* 2002), مفتاح غرناطة (*Granada's Key* 2003). In studies and criticism: الشاعر و التجربة (*The Poet and Experience* 1997), and غناء العيطة (*Aita Music* 2007). His 2013 novel, جرترود (*Gertrude*) was translated into English by Roger Allen.

Neighborhoods

A shadow on a wall.
A shadow is relieved from itself . . . and from light.
There is a thunderous outcry inside me and I am like
a drenched cat.
The sound of cascading submerges my words.
I exhausted my soul—
And I am no longer myself.
I don't want to see anybody.
I don't want to meet myself tonight.

. . . in the Streets of Casablanca

The usual mornings come and go
and the city in its marine shape like a tent that sleeps and wakes
pilfers its scent from the froth of beaches and perfume shops

takes its color from the pallor of streets and vagrants
its momentum from the railway lines and factories
from the complaints of those oppressed by colorful advertisements
from the chants in schools and the speeches in rallies
from a class conflict that rankles in the head
in between left and right
the eternal mornings slip away and come again
and the city abides in its religion like a saintly woman that wakes up and sleeps
illuminated and pouring forth like ingenuous waves . . .
white and beautiful like a dove
unshaken
it grew up in the secret rooms of martyrs
in the uproar of machines, the gurgle of brothels and the bullets of executions
it went beyond heaps of blueprints, the ink of governments
and remained tumultuous, reaping
the lying words, until the lovers of Andalusian towns crowned her
queen of the cherished beloveds
the word spread that today we are to worship in a loud voice
exercise our right against their oppression, infidelity and secrecy
against usurpation and violation and rape
we said: Yes, and were astounded by untimely death
by hunger frequenting the cheerless slums
the word spread that today is a strike
and we held back and the city held back its moans
buried them in the floor underground
sent them off with persecuted eyes
by the time the soldiers arrived with nerves scorching
like clouds tearing through the still sun
the city
an unforgettable
history
memorable celebrations of grief
. . .
Then came the promised strike
out there nothing remained but pigeons who lost their nests
nothing but the run into barbarian bullets
and mothers performing their intimate weeping

deceived by the hatred of distinguished bats
then the children's noise was no more
and they never came back
they embraced their dreams and lay in Derb al-Kabir
bathing in their blood like slaughtered sheep
shrouded by the leaflets of their frightening fears
carrying in their fingers morsels of hard bread
Oh, city of the autumn summer!
tainted with blood, the fires of smoke
the smoke of fires
wide-mouthed wounds, bullet holes
you who color the press reports
in speeches of ministers, postcards, and on advertising desks
in the songs exported to the north pole
to our oil brothers and the exalted American God
the twin born with low death
and the petrol dusk staining our miseries in hotel rooms
Oh, white one in pure red
as you took off your lower veil
out on the public way
uncovering your breasts and your resounding lips
uncovering your disheveled hair in the beautiful nights of peace
to the custodians of the Kaaba
those coming from the noble oil wells
Then came the promised strike
the city gave up its carnal pleasures
and immersed in the joy of grief
its strike has special rings that must surely sing
its strike has special ciphers that identify the people's enemies
its strike has the worth of a strike
Oh! City that sings as it weeps
and cries when it sings
even God's lanterns were on a strike in the sky
and human bombs ignited the earth
It doesn't matter
if the city resists or falls down!
It doesn't matter . . . if a child or an animal dies

Even the official papers were on a strike: gave up their silence
radio stations, ministries, police offices, television channels . . . were on strike:
left their daily work
and set out to the front
unloading
their lot
of frustrations
Hello, oh June!
Hello sorrows of distant mornings
Hello kingdom led by small grocers and school teachers,
sons of workers, and bands of the dispossessed
* * *

(Ben Ahmed, September 1981)

Anna Akhmatova's Grave

(Pray for me, Anna Akhmatova, 1938)

No winter is longer than this one.
Only the small gods know—
Why we stayed behind, until now, guarding the grave.
(even at night we never leave you)
Some have written, the Tatar woman will rise from her eternal sleep—
And you will come with us, with a green heart, returning to the palace of life.

We are here for that purpose, our poem praying for you.

The Last Elegy

Her lips on his. She was kissing him, her hand on her heart,
"If it were possible, I would have torn out this heart of mine to kiss yours."
She cleared her voice and sang for him. She embroidered her songs as though
they were white handkerchiefs! She raised her arms to shade him. And she gave
him her eyes so he could see his sun paling on the window glass.

———

His look was dying so she made some ink from her tears. And she wrote for
him the last elegy without need for words.

A Woman

Why didn't you leave your hand and a little bit of you for me to know?
They said you came
That you did not find a door to enter (the fluttering of my heart)
What if you had told the air
(so that I'd wait for you)?
What if you had left a finger pointing toward where you doze
(so that I'd see you)?
If you had wrapped my heart in a bandage of remembrance—
you would not have found the window closed to you
Let me then, share the defeat of my bed with this sleepless night
After you leave, I will prepare a cup of eternity for my screams
I know that you are thinking about me right now under some moon
that at this time of the night you are rubbing your thin flesh
But, I am not sure about anything anymore (I have forgotten metaphysics).

Nissabouri, Mostafa

Mostafa Nissabouri, born in 1943 in Casablanca, is a Moroccan poet and one of the founders of the Moroccan Journals Souffles (1966), an avant-garde bilingual quarterly that published essays, poetry, and fiction. (The magazine was banned in 1972.) He also helped found the journal Intégral (1971). He served as the director of the School of Fine Arts in Casablanca. Together with Mohammed Khaïr-Eddine, Mostafa Nissabouri wrote the manifesto Poésie Toute (*All Poetry*) in 1964, an important milestone in the history of Moroccan literature. His major poetic publications include: La Mille et Deuxième Nuit (*The One Thousandth and Second Night* 1975), Approche du Désertique (*Approaching the Desert* 1997) followed by L'Aube (*Dawn* 1999); and Manabboula. Nissabouri is also a translator.

from *L'Aube* (Dawn)

I

Dawn

nothing but a dawn
for the appearance of these poorly rhymed
dunes advancing
through the retina's blur
without my knowing
the liftoff of ultimate parables
sketching the fever of shrunken suns

it emerged from dreams that moved me here
the foliage and its writing
in ornament that exhausts itself
a retention of sparrows
on the walls of delirium
dead regions of other peripheries

nothing but a dawn
haphazard extension of myself
nudes
at the paroxysm of denied night
including the one I freed myself from
in order to measure its trace
my pale phalanxes
have captured places that by day
the body hallucinates

II

My desiring hyperbolic night
less in the apostrophe of these successive exteriors
with dividings and devourings
that alternate life death and rebirth
than in voyages from the confines of absence
an illumination that exhumes
revisited in the tenuousness of a dream
a habitat of wild roses
so much dissolving beauty
inheres in any place of recollection

retention to retention the poem loosely
dresses the silhouette of white cloud
like a shroud
which would be all of its materiality if it were not
silence on both sides
inexpressible mixture of eternity

of the idea of escape
submerging from a beyond of thought
if you were not pure shadow cloud
always ordered inside
with a reserve of receding lights

proximity blurs so much the path gets lost
if your waiting was but mingled with a feeling
of abandon among horsetail and coronilla with waking
comes the promise that dawn
was censored up there at the ceasura of time
that there is only an opening of universes
before the outbreak of this share of worry
that does not want to be consoled

if only the stranglehold of this country hadn't begun again
promising nothing of its spells
absent of combinations of the birthing light
which flows bathed in scents of angelica and rosemary
extending its veil on my face
and then paradoxical and almost over determined
seeking to share
ever pushing its limits
while in the meantime it's a country to never leave
one that gives credence outside to the passage of time that awaits me
the weave reddened with mud and granite
the education of bare stone

from *The Thousandth and Second Night*

street
knotted with every fetish
a young maelstrom
street
a handful of sand
for those who want to cure the warts of falsehood

I neither know you
nor your bones anymore
street
hyena tattoo
street of revolution bookstore street
where the history of blood sleeps like a baby
four-legged street
street
with dykes for posters

tidal wave street theft and hello misery
the souk in the hot hours of the morning
in a country of lavender and mafia
shit street massacre street what is its curfew name street
street of women who collect blood for
sex magic
street of
poets selling postcards
quacks and everywhere
French guys
suddenly I'm a brothel
you can remove these brooches
these timpani
this henna
monkey money street
greet the men of gutters with me
tell me behind the scenes my joy
at the shit market
street
I follow you with a laundry of abortion
crossing
a lynched crowd
my idioms
empty casbahs
and the city
the city because we were right there the city
laughed

the city pissed
the city bit its fingernails
the city asked my age and I answered with a
        tarantula
you know the street
this chancre
barfing at one o'clock in the morning
the weirdos of the moon and the lefties in parliament
with writers who quote frustrated pre-Islamic poetry
mu'allaqāt
it comes out of the tips of my nails
return to Baghdad
with your vases the heat waves of your navels
how amputate from me the weathervanes of water if
I allow the sediment to subside
subside convert
hands without fingers
hand of fatima
hand
my other citadel
hand of blood
rat tail wind-fly terror
I subside
the crowd subsides cuts their toenails
now I become the chergui wind
hand green moon-hand
        who's there
begonia hand
my hand that no longer knows how to travel
hands without fatal nails my hand I imitate the cry
        of the jackal between my legs

spider-monkey
hand
one hand
Semiramis
the other hand without a street

in a handful of sand
hand
the wind
swamp hand
my hand of torture sit down strip down shut up
hand in hand
signs of little fathers
she-wolf hand
and street hand
that says tyrant
that says everything's cool
that says the street is
fucked

oh wall if you knew
what hand taught me the terror of crowds
I go out bleeding almonds
rough mouth if you knew
how suddenly I was hurt
up to your eyes
my hand another street out of this shantytown
        trash
grub without grub
and there you go, Françoise is sick weed mixed with
the flesh of my days
and playing cards playing pack ice and me
she's killing me
I am a bachelor poet she kills me exterminates me
in the queue in front of police stations
in the bitterness of soldiers
in the civil state
I drool
concave
dr-drool
if you knew from what wall in what street I return
and how painful cannabis
if you knew into which street I threw myself where

I saw
a child afraid of beggars
his mother eating raisins while burning
magic herbs
if you knew the wall how the city crumbled
a punch in the belly and how they laughed
and I lost my glasses
becoming exile

Ouagrar, Mohamed

Mohamed Ouagrar is a leading figure of Modernism in Amazigh poetry. He is a founding member of the House of Poetry in Morocco. A native of Agadir, he was born in 1964 and he has published four poem collections: TINITIN (*Pica/ Pregnant Woman's Desires* 2004), TINU (*My Muse* 2010), Afnuz ns gr Iman d Tanga (*A Molecule between Soul and Matter* 2013), IsmDay (*Flavors* 2016). His poems have been translated into French, Arabic, German, and English. He has participated in several national and international events such as the Rabat International Festival invited by the Moroccan Writers' Union, the International Forum of Mediterranean Poets, Montpellier, France 2005 and the International Forum in Tizi Ouzou, Algeria. He has also produced several plays in the Amazigh language that won him several national prizes, including Samuel Beckett's *Waiting for Godot*.

Wave

I saw in you
The reflections of the moon
Are they caressing you?
Are they licking you?
Where are they leading you?
Where are you rushing Mistress Wave
When at at any moment
You'll be consumed on the shores?
Why the hurry?
Who forced you
To be hostile?

To be playful?
Tell me where are you precipitating?
I am a fisherman
I know all the labyrinths, the watery abysses
Above you
Below you
In front of you
I am your witness
Lucky you
So where indeed are you rushing?
It's better
In fact
that you leave
Recede behind us
For you will never be able
To appreciate my witness
When you mount your madness
Where in fact are you going?
With your quarrels
Your scum
Your delirium!
You don't even know
Where you're headed
You've tamed insomnia
Your legs do nothing but wander
Bravo!
But where in fact are they taking you?
How tall you are O wave!
When you rise up
Tell the truth
I want to know
For whom is your capriciousness destined
What is this abyss
To which you are so attached?
Where in fact are you hurrying?
You found me with my fishing pole
Its silence

Along with its bait
While your ambush
Bending over
Its dense height
Only waits
For its part
In your peregrinations
How sad for you!
Where in fact are you going so quickly?
O wave, you ran aground on the beach
As if it weren't the case
You and your slender waist stood up
Only to wither in the sand
Becoming foam
And crumbling on the rocks
Cursed daughter of the cursed
There's no reason
You are the size
Of the one who observes you
What a pity!
How sad!
Where are you rushing?
Where in fact are you rushing?

Thirst for Stings

the heart of my beloved tumbles
down
it oozes and follows its course
forming an entire waterfall
by surprise
but then meets a swarm of deaf bees
there where the water diverts
nested in the heart of the breeze
where I sequestered it
grass has already taken root

blackened with dung
and here I am
standing in the mud
of the river

the basket you shake
is of embers
I hold it in my hand
a dilemma
when water is lacking
and when it flows
even if I have tasted honey
and drank water
my liver will be strung up
with the flames of thirst

(translated from Tamazight into French by Mohamed Farid)

Ouassat, Embarek

Embarek Ouassat (born October 16, 1955, in Mzinda near Safi) is a poet, a translator and a former teacher of philosophy. He currently lives in Salé. His major works include على درج المياه العميقة (*On the Stairway to Deep Waters* 1990); فراشة من هيدروجين (*A Butterfly of Hydrogen* 2008); محفوفا بأرخبيلات (*Surrounded with Archipelagos* 2001); راية الهواء (*The Air's Flag* 2001); and عيون طالما سافرت (*Traveling Eyes* 2016). He has also translated Tahar Benjelloun, René Char, Frantz Kafka, André Breton, and many others into Arabic.

Places

On a side street
a familiar face multiplies while waiting for me
In a nearby suburb
a tribe performs the rituals of their regrets
In the battlefield
many victims fall under the sunset's hoofs
In my memory
cities are showered by rains and sorrows
In a forest
a woman kisses a crippled wolf
On the terrace of a café
a moon bleeds in the navel of a dead body
On the threshold of a forest
skeleton bones laugh with the stars
In an abandoned hut
I lie down to stifle my cry

A Dance

This paper infects me
with its fever
There is no way to be healed
from the ritual clatter of these teeth
I am left defenseless
A shooting star passed by my window
and left me nothing
but crumbs of advice
and the coat of its ancestors' armor
I will wear it against the warring winter
I will go deep into playing my music
on the fiddles
of desire
But what can I do now
as my bones
pull me
to the source
of shivering?

Details of Bewilderment

The lights are dim on the lilac stalks
The footsteps shattered on the street
The waves are still on the sides of the garden
Nothing has changed
since you left this window
where the bird laughs
This room where water lives and thinks
and pots and pans are weighed down with metal insomnia
Your shy look and the jingle of your bracelets
your shawl and your lisp of violet
are still scattered on the bed-sheets crowded with your
confusion
And on the desk spotted with ink
where the statue of the fat Buddha

laughs impudently
Sorry, I couldn't despair
like a dried-up song
like a senile old brook
The details of my bewilderment took place
outside of me
my breaths stuttering in the open
While the snow falls down from the ceiling
and plays in my arms like a child
Nothing has changed
The murmur of the shrubs spreads over the distant meadows
The sky puffs the drizzle of delirium
And you are getting rid of your blood and running away
among the sick larch trees
along the sidewalks that overflow
with the pain of music
The rainbow rolls down on slender haunches
and the foam repeats the ocean dreams
Your dreams were following you
And you were delighting in whispering and words
In the middle of the sentence you disappeared
leaving your small worries behind on hotel doorsteps
your image on the mirror
your face in the first stalks of wheat
and your blue seconds in the golden heart of the clock
Nothing has changed
Your trembling seeps through the holes of the lacework
Your fear drips down my forehead
as I invent an epic for dead flowers
Before I put my hand on the knob of the wardrobe
and my head outside the gallery of splendor
Before I dip my eyes in the saliva of the pillow
bejeweled with your sleep and your scent
and listen to the moss of the marshes
that grow between my ribs
in this sad room like the smile of the murdered
where time is forever midnight

Innocence

The man who spent long nights
engrossed in the garden's rapture
did not steal medals of lavender
and wasn't the one who uprooted the air's nose
Why did they chase him, then?
He is now hiding in a cave
guarded by
the ovations
of ants
He doesn't leave unless he must
for deserts
that dead men cover with
trembling shrouds
But he needn't be afraid
When he gets hungry, he can sit
at the breeze's dinner table
And if he is pursued by birds of prey
he mingles with the sea foam
He needn't be afraid
He's got a tent
where the disciples
of the wind
rest
when
they are tired

Oussous, Mohamed

Mohamed Oussous belongs to the young generation of writers in Amazigh language. A talented poet, researcher, and civil society activist, he studied at Ibn Zohr University. His publications include poetry: Ixfawen . . . D'isasan (*Heads . . . and Spiderwebs* 2006); Tagldit N'tiggas: Timdyazin (*Kingdom of Scars: Poetry* 2009); a collection of short stories Ayt Iqqjdr Di'uxsay (*People of the Gourd Lizard* 2009); and a novel, Inakufn (*The Uprooted* 2018).

To the Soul of my Deceased Father

Father
Father
All senses have failed
You have become like ragged hay
Dead leaves of dried herbs
For me nothing remains but the wick
At the end of the candle
Extinguished like a twig
At your side

Father
The desire of life adorned itself with kohl
And with your eyes so close
How you would have liked the stars
To be your blanket
Just to see them
You would have tried to straighten your posture

And climb
The mountain of ills
That made you grow old

Father
Here I am I see you
Inert
See the cold seeping
From icy drops
See the birds wake
And chirp
As you used to do
I would like to open the windows
To the whiteness of the sun
But you closed them
They are no longer open
You weren't able to reopen them

Father
You are a man
An angel
No resemblance to Satan
Yet you are common as all mortals
Like all that live
On the embers
Like all who suffer
And peddle their burden of loss

Father
You labored and harvested
In life you ran
As you could
As the seasons wove you
As the days envisioned you

Father
You hid your regret
So it could hardly be seen

As you hid yourself
I seized what you crushed underfoot
Even if you left no stone unturned
I read the hiccoughs of regret
That turned you bitter
You so wanted to speak
And yet you remained silent
Before winter tears
Spilled
Over your chapped skin
I read it in your face
A fear that tames
Horses

Father
At the end of my rope
I have nothing left of you
But the tip of a thorn
A skeletal face
That's what you've become
Just like your image

Father
You camouflaged your desire
You chose to keep your secrets
You wanted to bury
Your interior worlds
Words
Extinguished in your mouth

Father
Broken mirror
Wandering to leave hearts bare
As the sirocco wind dries
As the leaves of the trees crumble
You brought me to the essence of life
And to the way it falls apart

The Night and You

The night
Rids itself
Of embers and extinguished stars

Little by little
It spits out
The smoke of days
You're dreaming!
Dressed as a horseman
In a cursed tunic
And a spider web
You sew
Names to shadows

You lower yourself
To the half-lit faces

Are you dreaming?!
Your weary head has become
Drops . . . tears
A powder of leaves

Rabbaoui, Mohamed Ali

Mohamed Ali Rabbaoui (born January 1st, 1949) lives in Oujda where he worked as a professor at Mohamed I University. He is the editor-in-chief of *al-mishkaat* (*Lantern*) magazine. Major publications include: الكهف و الظل (*The Cave and the Shadow* 1975); البريد يصل غدا (*The Mail Arrives Tomorrow* 1975); الطائران والحلم الأبيض (*Two Birds and the White Dream* 1977). The poem below is taken from الرمانة الحجرية (*The Stone Pomegranate* 1988).

Sitting in the Company of the Hookah Smoker

For a long time my eyes wandered far away in the glass,
a face appeared at the bottom,
I ignored it, and I turned toward the sugar.
The wet spoon landed on the dry table
then a map of the copses of Ajdir was drawn in the coffee seas.

Oh flower . . . spattered in the snow of hell
How have you changed into a tattoo that abandoned the chin of a woman
        coming out of the valleys of the Atlas?
Secretly, I sat down with it in the woods of Oujda,
my eyes climbing the stalks of its loving visage,
the blooms of fear and the trees of love
encircling my cold throat,
—"Will you tell me, uncle fisherman:
who, my uncle, has restored the giant body of smoke to the mouth?"
—". . . . ."
He brought out his hookah

371

His eyes hanging loosely down from the branches of astonishment
He lifted the cup, my second face showed itself in his coffee
or my millionth face,
He let out a boisterous laugh that echoed behind the trees
and went on smoking the narghuile.

(Laayoun, Oujda 02/07/1977)

My Sweetheart

My sweetheart
Our peaceful love is growing amid the sand dunes
Its gardens suddenly invaded by the black darkness of the night
while we are outside time
embracing the close-distant harbors

My sweetheart
The wind courts the stones of my stream
Its mirror shattered this morning
My pillow split in cracks
My memory swollen with tumors
But you are all the time my sweetheart
You are forever the celebration of the sea
And you know that you are the princess of all seas

My sweetheart
When I saw the rooster planting flowers in the garden
the hills of my face bent down in a bow for two little whiles,
What have I seeded in you oh one who looks down from my head
embracing the sky,
embracing the thick sand
in my boat searching for sails
What? Will you not forgive me oh my sweetheart

My sweetheart
I fight wakefulness so that the trees laugh
I try to exit the water's eddies
but you my sweetheart do not know

(Laayoun, Oujda, November 5, 1975)

Rajie, Abdellah

Abdellah Rajie was born in Salé in 1948 and died on July 28, 1990. He received a bachelor's degree from the Faculty of Letters and Humanities, Dhar Mehraz, Fes, in 1972. He worked as a high school teacher and later joined the Faculty of Letters in Casablanca. Rajie published many poems and critical studies including: الهجرة إلى المدن السفلى (*Migration to the Low Cities* 1976), سلاما و ليشربوا البحار (*Peace on those that Drown at Sea* 1982); أياد كانت تسرق القمر (*Hands that Robbed the Moon* 1988); القصيدة المغربية المعاصرة: بنية الشهادة و الاستشهاد (*The Moroccan Modern Poem: The Structure of Faith and Martyrdom* 1988 and 1989) a critical study in two volumes. The poems here are excerpted from الهجرة إلى المدن السفلى (*Migration to the Low Cities*) Dar Al Kitab, Casablanca 1976.

from *The Verse of Pain*

For you oh homeland oppression is drawn on the walls of the heart
Here I am leaving the shadow of my sweetheart and the eyes of my sweetheart
to follow your shadow
Here I am changing you into a suitcase of love oh homeland
drawing for you
a map on the wall . . . and I mark places on it
in red: this is my beloved's home
My beloved doesn't know my address . . . doesn't know the date of return
Since when have I been the lone wanderer?

(I tell my friends about you, recounting to the wailing wind . . . to children
coming tomorrow or after tomorrow

I tell the story, on the gate of reptiles and illnesses as it closes in the face of Damascus, of Al Khalil* who, because his grammar books did not sell, opened a brothel and sat down on its lintel bartering with clients. About my country's eyes I tell my friends. About a poet rolling his moustache over a hookah as the sky of Damascus is in smoke with phantom war planes† About you I recount . . . the testimony of a man from the people of the heart . . . Have I delivered my message.

Have I delivered my message).‡

And so when I stretch my hand in order to touch your face oh sweetheart
my hand springs back to me
Or the longing takes me on the backs of sorrow to you and I am not
able to take a single step
Oh you lady carrying in her eyes the map of the homeland
spreading like a tattoo on the chin of the Mediterranean
Here I am. When I extend my sight: I see what eyes do not see
A homeland getting beyond the deadline of June 5th
As the frowning homeland steals me from your eyes
I am closer to you than yourself . . .

(Correction: Grammarians agreed not to use "won't" after "going to" a negation in the future is not allowed along with affirmation of it. As a result of this we use "not" instead of "won't" . . . will you give an example? A young pupil raises his finger and answers, "Israel is going to won't enter Damascus." The teacher jumps over his desk. And he falls on the boy with blows and insults.)

Do not cry my darling your face is more than tears can wash
more than news of casualties hanging on its smile
Do not cry my darling . . . your heart this spherical green
too feeble to house the torrential sorrow
or kill in it blossoms of oleander
high heat that thickens in the rosy deeps

---

   * Al Khalil Al Farahidi (died about the year 876 in Al Basrah) was the author of the first dictionary of the Arabic language. He was also author of the first comprehensive study of meter structure in Arabic poetry.
   † United States warplane.
   ‡ From the Prophet Muhammed's last speech before his death.

So pray for me
Since I so much prayed for you
And for your eyes I sing . . . to the homeland panting in your eyes I sing
When longing encamps in my chest and sorrow
the size of the Atlas Mountains sneaks in

(10/10/1973)

Migration to the Low Cities*

(1)

I was the closed head
carrying the world's sorrows on one side of the heart
And on the other side
the shape of a woman who repudiates my face
I cast myself aside in the yellow books
I stretch my hand to the palm reader
and fall prostrate to hunger
My days disintegrate but the tear remains . . . a tear
Forehead burnt I rise from the womb of history
My flags: sex—hunger—opium
I change into a body ravaged by plague
I know nothing but the challenge of he who steals the lover's face
from my eyes
But I am as yellow as the green and dry when they were burnt
by Maamun's calvary†
I was the closed head

---

*In this poem Rajie speaks of the Zanj Rebellion, ثورة الزنج, a major uprising against the Abbasid Caliphate, which took place from 869 until 883. It began near the city of Basra in present-day southern Iraq and was led by 'Ali Ibn Muhammad. The insurrection is believed to have involved enslaved Bantu-speaking people (Zanj) who had originally been captured from the coast of East Africa and transported to the Middle East. It grew to involve many slaves and free men from several regions of the Caliphate, and claimed tens of thousands of lives before it was finally defeated.

†The Caliph Ma'mun reigned over the Islamic empire (AD 813–833), also famous for having founded the first astronomical observatory in Baghdad about the year 830.

Summer breezes cross it and not a hair moves
—Where did we leave the story, grandfather?
—(Muatassim* said to the king of Rome: the taxes of the meanest region, run
    by my meanest slaves, are greater than the taxes of your land)
—Will you please tell me, grandfather:
Who dismembered Al Hallaj?

(2)

My grandfather is a heap of white hairs grown by self-denial
a boat of faith, my grandfather
a face the color of wheat
He lives on the highest mountain on earth . . . he built a retreat on the summit
that cannot be seen by the eyes of those at its feet
He taught me to hate the inhabitants of the earth . . . and to love
only God and the rulers of people!
He taught me that the creator is the essence
and the essence is the absolute
The creator's attributes are the conditions that reveal the self
And those conditions are not separate from the essence
Said Abu Hachem:
He who denies the conditions of the creator, in the wide sea he drowns

(As to the cause of the quarrel, it is a famous and well-known story.
My grandfather said: the attributes of God are four: omnipotence,
omniscience, prominence and omnipresence. And when I asked him about
man he said: a bag of excrement, he does not clean himself except through
the adoration of God. I said: his destiny. He said: No. I said: man has two
attributes: an oppressor or an oppressed. So my grandfather stood up angry
and stayed confined to his house. And he never talked to me again!!)

Will you tell me grandfather
Who took the bread away from the hungry?
Who burnt the face of our city when the blacks rebelled?

---

* An Abbassid Caliph who reigned over the Islamic empire in Baghdad.

(3)

I was nothing but a lump of sorrow exiled by the inquisition
the whip dug into my back and the horseshoe, the arrow, the pin
When my face brightened one autumn—I remember—
The wali's* horses were
clouds crouching in the chest of Al Basrah, looking for a poet
one of the ruler's innumerable mistakes
I said: land is an undulation, people are an undulation, land—people
So shall I close the door of the heart before the beloveds?
Shall I let the size of bread shrink
in one night's time?
The kinfolk's sorrows proliferate to the echo of the soldiers' steps
and the size of fear widens in the depths of the houses
Shall I let the smell of scattered corpses
suffocate the breathing of the universe?
Would I not live if one spent the night hungry in my country

(I was whipped in the year 270 hijri. Then my arms were cut off . . . one of those
who saw me being whipped said: the wali ordered that you should be beaten
and your arms be cut off because of your atheism, and for inciting people to
corruption, so that you be an example for others. Then he asked me if I feared
that. I said: no, and when he asked me for the reason I said: I have been beaten
since I was born—and when my members are cut off they quickly regenerate as
the falcon's wings regenerate.)

The face of Al Basrah is burned, the face of Al Basrah knows me
tears off my body
is the dark color in my eyes a festive premonition
heading from the eastern side on the back of the wind
and the beat of women's drums
and tomorrow . . . heading from all sides of the earth
one day it takes the form of the wind and another day
it takes the form of fire
that burns what is built of walls

---

* A "wali" is the governor of a province in the Islamic empire.

(4)

Correct is the wisdom of those who used to say:
this time of mine . . . in it the bread gets smaller, but the whip gets longer
Openly I procreate in all parts of the terrestrial sphere
I stretch my eyesight . . . it is covered by light
From my body I let go a child the size of anger aging
in the depths of darkness
He who does not know the sophistries of the paralyzed on the thresholds
    of bars
knows the secrets that restive cities have hidden
I get out of my skin
My members grow tall in a body like a palm tree
I am openly renewed in order to let my body fall from above
I breathe in the odor of earth and wheat . . . I become a palm tree
My roots extend—the tears of kinfolks water them—
Something like a knife itching in my head hurts
When I perceive the traces of the whip on bodies burnt under the sun
I see them coming with the wind: dear black folks
coming with a killer anger
I open in their faces the gates of the resting cities
Pour . . . pour . . . pour O clouds
the horses of the blacks have come back, nothing broke
but the chain rings of oppression
Pour . . . pour . . . pour O clouds

(Fquih ben Salah 1972)

Salhi, Mohammed

Mohammed Salhi is a Moroccan poet and critic. He was born in Iligh near Tiznit in 1963. He received his high school degree in 1981 in Agadir, and obtained his bachelor's degree from Mohammed V University in 1986. He works as a high school teacher in Témara. He has published: أحفر بئرا في سمائي (*I Dig a Well in My Sky* 2000); شيخوخة الخليل (*The Aging of Khalil* 2003); أتعثر بالذهب (*I Trip Over Gold* 2004); among others.

Water

Murmur
is not
the voice of Water.
Murmur
is the moan
of stone.

Alchemy

Only the night
reverses the evidence
It is born aged
and dies
young.

Bed

The horizon
is the pillow
of the sun.
The night
is its bed.

Dozing

As usual,
every midday
the day
dozes off.

Paradox

Oh this lightning
It lights up
the way
for the rain
and it is
blind.

Sebbagh, Mohammed

Mohammed Sebbagh was born in 1930 and died in 2013 in Rabat. He was a Moroccan poet and a founding member of the Moroccan Writers' Union. He received his master's degree in Madrid in 1957. He worked as an editor-in-chief for many magazines and as an attaché at the Ministry of Islamic Affairs in 1961. Among his major works are: العبير الملتهب (*The Kindled Perfume* 1953); شجرة النار (*The Tree of Fire* 1954); أنا و القمر (*Me and The Moon* 1956). The poems translated here are taken from the 1995 book دفقات (*Gusts*) and from the book, ديوان الشعر المغربي الرومانسي (*Anthology of Moroccan Romantic Poetry* 2003).

All That Happened Yesterday

In the end ...
What could I possibly tell you.
I called you with many names, and I called you a thousand calls.
When I speak out I feel my veins interlacing with my gasps,
And my bones and ribs rising to my throat, stifling my words,
How much I shouted ... ! How much I spoke out ... ! How much I called ... !
With sparks of my breath, I feel this air writhing in pain.
Don't you hear ... ?
Perhaps my volcano reaches you extinguished ... !
Perhaps my trumpeting leaves you cold ... !
Perhaps my thunderbolts and my hurricanes fall lifeless in your ocean ... !
On the anvil of my heart
I sharpened my daggers and my swords.
Don't you see ... ?

In the bitter whistling wind, I collected the splinters of the sun and shot them
    to you,
And in the hot desert winds, I rolled heaps of snow and moved forward on
    them to your homes.
Don't you understand . . . ?
All that happened yesterday!
And dawn was filling up my right hand.
But today,
How mute is my grief!
My dreams petrifying in my eyes,
My lips sewn with my words.
What else can I do?
I already dipped my pen in my heart this morning,
And I tore up my clothes in front of the mirror.
Here is the naked dumb mute walking in the streets:
Bewildered butterflies turning around him;
Tapping your doors with his stick
saying goodbye, surrendering.

(February 1954)

Absurdity

I am dust:
the offspring of excessive haze
the virtue of rising and settling
the whirr of obstinacy I am
I vanish in visibility
And appear in concealment:
I swagger. I deride
I laugh. I jest
Here and there
And everywhere—I am—
Humble or revered
Strong or soft
I am expelled from the prayer mat

So I jump on the chandelier
I am shaken off the sheet
So I turn towards the art object and the medallion
And the head of the great and dignified
I am dust
I am the fodder of mankind
And the ease of his misery.

Sleep my Angel

Sleep my angel
The moon is asleep
In your bed of moon:
A gazelle of marigold and water
Sleeping
A sail blown by the wind
A gift of heaven
Carrying the glow of roses
And a basket of presents

Sleep my angel
The moon is asleep
In your bed of moon:
A ball of slumber and joy
Tinsel and fascination.
Sleep my angel
The moon is asleep
In your bed of moon:
A dream is calling you
From a doll's song
From a kitten's bell
From melody and silver.

Sleep my angel
The moon is asleep
In your bed of moon:

A dream woke up to tell you a dream:
A camel riding on an ant
A giraffe sleeping on a wave
A snail combing the hair of a star
Sleep my angel
The moon is asleep
In your bed of moon
My angel.

The Summer

From the sneeze of the blazing heat
From the thirst of dry lands
It came
Rubbing
Grains of sweat between its fingers
A water-skin on its back
It desires: and we are full of blue
Of sands, of seashells
It came
A fan in its right hand
Every time he flirts with it
We feel a subtle breeze
We adorn ourselves with waves
We flap with water birds
And before it's over
It leaves us
A basket of grain, oysters
And a yellow seed

The Wind

It let loose its locks quickly
and slipped away
Roving recklessly in all directions:
shattered. scattered. dispersed
Carelessly
it mumbled: and the sands wrinkled
The stalk of grain and the branches prostrated themselves
It murmured: and the streams and the rivers chirped
It thundered: and the tall woods howled
The trees collapsed
The caves and caverns spoke
revealing the shallowness of the swamps.
Who on earth can grasp the wind
in his hand
and judge it
after it calmly gathers its locks of hair
and turns into
a breeze of blossom

Serghini, Mohamed

Mohamed Serghini (born in 1930, Fez) is the author of several poetry collections, a novel and numerous translations. In 2004 he was awarded the Argana International Poetry Prize. After studying at the University of Al-Karaouine, he continued his education in the field of language and literature in Baghdad in 1959 and later at the Faculty of Literature of Rabat and finally at the Sorbonne in Paris. He received a diploma in comparative literature in 1963, a PhD in 1970 and another PhD in 1985. Serghini taught at the Faculty of Literature and Social Sciences in Fes, where his first book of poetry من فعل هذا بجماجمكم (*What Have They Done to Your Skulls?*) was published in 1994. His major publications include: و يكون إحراق الأسماء الآتية (*This Way The Following Names are Burnt* 1987); بحار وجدتك في (*The Sailor of Mount Qaf* 1991); الكائن السبئي (*The Flayed Being* 1992); جبل قاف هذا الأرخبيل (*I Found You in this Archipelago* 1992), a novel; The poems here are excerpted from Fes de la Plus Haute Cime des Ruses (*Fez, from the Highest Peak of Cunning* 2003).

Assembly of Dreams

1.

Four neighborhoods recount the soul of the city. Utopian melody in four/ four time; the birth cry of the disadvantaged Being. The body wakes in an unattractive physique. Reaction of libinal chastity and the race of life's routine. Outside these four neighborhoods there are only nests of straw to shelter the old eagles at the summit of the mountains, only bramble reeds to nourish the stray goats in the plains. Evasion assures the survival of chaos. (No plenitude escapes emptiness.) What will the hanging gardens say when their rotations are paralyzed, when water no longer flows under the norias, and under the grindstones of the mills. Energy will be in a state of absolute grace. The wind yielding before the capricious pressure of the spheres. Blowing against the wishes of sailboats no longer.

Silent blood.
Mixed blood.
From the height of the disadvantaged Being.
From the depths of his fibrous cartilage.
We celebrate the birth of the inorganic.
We celebrate the mysterious extraterrestrials.
The fluid and robotic machine that forever nourishes the pendulums of time
    with moldy water.

II.

The taste of the city is strange. A mix of kif, tobacco and mint. Only these drugs can braid the strands of insomnia. Time passes inexplicably. Candles waste wax illuminating only their own circles. Logics crack under the weight of heretical slander. The militia of grammarians, of lawyers and illustrious engineers sharpen their theoretical arms. Ancestors in intensive care (revived we imagine with cooking gas mixed with fish manure).

Strange ironies that laugh while crying
We allocate salty tears to sweet eyes
When grief doesn't have the time
To pour itself on the shores of the impossible.
We allocate absence—that sees its emptiness
When menopause attacks—to time
When the big clocks on the wall
Ironically wink with their wings

III

At dawn the alleys and footpaths of the
Kingdom are deserted. The red of daybreak
No longer infects the ruins'

facades, receiving only a mute
Light from this red. (We fly over history
With red wings) Taken with fire, a thief
Has taught the phoenix to fill
The attics with onions, garlic, coconut,
Dry figs, black pepper
And raisins. (This dosage an
Effective remedy for unrequited
love) Reviving the burnt
ashes, the same thief demands
that the genealogical tree, blessed by the
City, only drug itself with its own
fruits gathered before their time.
Who dares hope for the withering of this
Tree? Who dares refute the crime
Of its secular age?

From closed to open,
The shutters of the door
Reaffirm the nostalgia of two beings separated.
Reaffirm that return is nothing but union.
Reaffirm that leaving is nothing but divorce.
We carry our dreams to the next sleep
Where the bed, inert and shivering with cold,
Hides its insomnia under the sheets.

IV

In the beginning, the Earth edified its throne
On a river with two floating bridges:
A place of passage for
Pedestrians, an archipelago for the
Strolls of unloved lovers.
The bamboo banks were ready
To receive the thirsty nostalgia
Of tender souls, souls
Clinging to an obscure tomorrow.

All of them rejecting any
Imprisonment that strangled the space
Around them. Complacency covering
Them with error and doubt. These souls
Foresaw that their deaths
Merited praises equal to the
Deceptions that they had
Lived. Death that issues from the
Evil eye stings more
Than the bite of the
Satyrs. (Is there a worse sting than the
Hedgehog?) Such elegies say
Nothing since they propose neither
Joy nor distress. They resemble
The ingratitude of the summer that
Lacking gallantry, passes without
Greeting the City jealously hiding
Her treasures.

The era of grey ashes
Doesn't endure red embers.
A face so felted and metaphorical
Erases the nature of her deaf traits
Tracing them on libidinal illusions.
We prostitute ourselves with the implicit order of piety.
We legalize the fetuses born of collective sperm,
Citizenship tolerates such genetic acrobatics.

V

The slave trade of whites was openly practiced
In the City. Sudanese,
Caucasians, Somalis,
Greeks, and Antilleans.
The world was there, from the Nile to the Caribbean,
From resinous corn to hard wheat, from
The wisdom of Aristotle to the madness of

Néron. There was thus a market for
Slaves. Where return is
formally forbidden. The sellers
and the buyers must have a
special derogation. No need
For Siamese cats, rodents,
Insects and hunting dogs.
Those who attended to the
Slave trade were pious
People given the task of setting a price on the heads.
The prices would not be enforced
Until after the return of the buyers
From the testing beds.

The sickly virility of the corsair
The suffocating speed of a yacht
The traces of the billowing waves
The virulent odor of fear
The pale shame of the imprisoned
The frequency of the rusty oars

Communicate better with sea sickness.
Charity collects in brass spittoons.

VI

From the narrow window with its thin
Iron grill, we dominate the universe. From this
Window covered with sanctity, women
And men implore God to
Preserve their life from all restitched
Virginity. Exemplary democrat,
A king, discharging his viziers
Of their duties, makes himself a
Prisoner of his throne. This king has
Only one thing in mind,
To vanquish the absurdity imposed by the

Repetition of actions.
Amused, the viziers take pity on him
Since he hides himself in the harem
There where Flesh is consumed marinated in the
Hamlets and stables. He dismisses himself.
(Everything marinated is appetizing.)
The wishes of each and every one are not
Enough to legalize the share of divine heritage.
No sin is erased with damp excuses. So many
Insomniac nights are necessary to correct mistakes.

There are only impasses.
Space put between parentheses.
Time on the chronometer.
Earliness guided by lateness.
Everything depends on the clocks.
A meticulously calculated report
Dries up the veins of the gourds.
Cliffs and earth live their inertia.
Speechlessness is still unexplored.
Who can compete with silence?
At Ras Jnane the birth of the disadvantaged Being.
At Sidi L'Aouad the discovery of repressed instincts
At Qettanine the maturity of one being in another.
At Zenjfor the essential burst of the habitual itinerary.

VII

Four neighborhoods of the City have written
Its soul posthumously. A soul that
Persecutes itself still on the dream of a
Poet, a whirling dervish who,
Nourished by dreams, tears the golden age
From reason. In these neighborhoods, the heads
Of fetuses ventured from their
Shells, giant tortoises
Peopled the wild beaches, the

Killers and the killed escaped their
Cadavers, babies cried to mothers
Without breasts,
And droughts, scorpions, gods,
Countries, lights, greenery, shadows, oil presses,
Cradles, stables, suburbs and fireworks,
Reappeared slowly every three centuries.
Gone the tales of grandmother. The hour of resurrection
Has rung.

Reassembling the Fragments

The sages of the City used to recount how
an apprentice potter broke a jar on
his hard head because he couldn't
perfect the trade so loved
by the first creator. This punishment
was enacted near the stones of a legendary
well. Thus do all failed encounters
of lovers merit such a violent sanction. (More
sorrow on the jar than on the skull.)
Concerning this, the apprentice had the
habit of identifying himself with the colors
and the shadows of the City reflected in the waters.
A professional historian who had no eyesight
made him a talisman on perforated paper
so that the jar would regain its original
virginity. Innumerable, the fragments
of the jar refused all manner
of reassemblage. Torn to pieces,
the body swears only false allegiance
to its future resurrection.

The City Recounts its Legends

Legendary and fetishistic, an Oriental
adventurer arrived in the City. He was
accompanied by a mythic disciple
and young and beautiful servant girls.
(Lyricism makes art and flesh.) The trips
between the Orient and the Occident followed
one upon another. The jokers flocked to
this new paradise. They put down their roots
there. (Distilled and filtered, the sap
of the vine served as lacquer) As ogresses we
we stone ourselves with rocks reserved for
sculptures. The empty doors close and
open. The cities fix up only their peripheral
roads. From names to crumbly syllables.
Fresh saints buried in the comfort
of Buddhist mausoleums. The offering boxes
moistened by the rust of coins. Volcanoes
with several craters. Palaces with doors and
windows that overlook prison cells and
the corridors of bordellos.

Celebrating the Kingdom's Ashes

1.

City of utopias, you who has in the "congregation of the state" founded a home
of straw for me, and a nest for aging eagles on the summit of Zalagh and a
wood of boxthorn for billy goats in Wislane. It is here on the thresholds of my
prison of stone that emptiness constrained the voice of poetry. (What is it that
fully formed preserves itself from its emptiness?) The sweep has not despaired
of raising river water to the mill, and the wind has not surrendered to the
pressure of sudden astral whims as it blows against the desires of ships courting
the love of the sea.

2.

Narrow streets lead one into the other, and old ruins overlook dust-colored
time from over the prayer calls of minarets. Tombs furnish their epitaphs with
the stones of caves and caverns. Prometheus taught embryonic youth to steal
fire whenever the storehouses were filled with onions and garlic, coconuts and
dried figs, black pepper and raisins. (Their combination a cure for blood clots).
On its pages genealogies have assembled (oh tree whose bark is an anesthetic
and its leaves a stimulant for tears) ever since Neolithic times built pyramids
for the burial of history.

3.

"Ras J-Jnan," since before Adam names have rolled across its surface. An
alphabet I have watered with the liquid of hemp, mint and wild rue's nectar
until it got drunk and never sobered again. My lamp and its holder worked
on enriched gas and the remains of my dim eyesight. What if I dismissed it
from light, what if I took on the task of pursuing brilliant grammarians and
engineers and brought into light its veiled treasures from the bottom of the
earth's ruse and silence?

Derb Sufli

He started between the two edges of a line and two points,
and went on walking on the bones of his knees.
He delayed his birth beyond its fated time,
and saw desire dripping from labor pains
the pain of afterbirth knotted on his eye sockets.
When a woman and a man brought him into life,
their blood was flaming between two births,
a white ray passed by his cradle
It went the way the incense of the four seasons passes.

(Note)

I don't want anything from what I recount but that it be carved on stone.
Constant places and moving times. The revolving sphere of heavenly bodies

stutters, and the course of events go against what I wish for. In Derb Sufli the names that Adam learned crash against the limitations of the numbers that Pythagoras developed. I was a being by name and a sign by number, and I wasn't able to disentangle the intertwining between the two with what Quranic school offered me of deceitful wiles. Courtyards before me and courtyards after me wherever I crossed the hunched streets plated with cobblestones. A paradise in front of me and hell behind me whenever my eyes stuck to what was written on the front of mausoleums and sanctuaries. Do the spirits play up their charms for me? Do they track my footsteps? I only know that my roots intersect with historic lineages, one numbed with chamomile powder, another anesthetized with herbs that make you cry, a third with organic pesticides, a fourth with insulin shots. I should have been born with a sign on my head to take me closer to the neighborhood of Derb Soufli and its inhabitants.

Serhane, Abdelhak

Abdelhak Serhane, born in 1950, is a French-speaking Moroccan academic and an award-winning writer. He holds a doctorate in Psychology from Toulouse-Jean-Jaurès University. Among his publications are the novels Messaouda (1983); Les Enfants des Rues Etroites (*Children of the Narrow Streets* 1986); Le Soleil des Obscurs (*The Sun of Obscurities* 1992); Le Deuil des Chiens (*Mourning Dogs* 1998). His poetry collections include: L'Ivre Poème (*Drunk Poem* 1989); Chant d'Ortie (*Song of Nettle* 1993); La Nuit du Secret (*Night of the Secret* 1992). He taught for a long time at Ibn Tofail University in Kenitra before going into exile in Canada. Since then, he divides his time between Morocco, Canada and the United States where he teaches French literature at Louisiana State University. The poems here are excerpted from his 2001 work, Les Dunes Paradoxales (*The Paradoxical Dunes*), Québec, from Ecrits des Hautes Terres, and particularly from the long poem, The Infinite Grain of Solitude. In 1993 he received the French Prize of the Arab world, then in 1999 the Francophonie Prize for Mediterranean Africa.

from *The Infinite Grain of Solitude*

To name the Desert more silent than the shores
to go far into the shadow of its fevers
ensuring the portrait of unfathomable parallel
flights to the deepest depths of the dunes
to the place it is said of the poem

Every night of marbled thirst
a salty taste among the stones

forged in pervasive crime
inflexible with drunkenness and bundles of dross
the khamsin wind trails fire from its entrails

Like no other Desert
of stone or skin
with furrows quarried by time
the quiet march of the dunes
runs in the veins of centuries
like the writing of mirages
saddled with red suns and aspics
immutable as the white book
that closes its pages
on the tomb of the marabouts

To write
in the wake of your voice
Desert of Mourning
where men erase the sand from their tracks
in silent crossings
a sign of bitterness
the verb in the basalt of impudent cries
on the slope of the catacombs
time
in the dust of the desert
that the freedom of dunes
takes towards unknown marshes
I received the signs
an offering of the Desert
like these dreams of youth
at the edge of trance
I received the song of stones
the reverse of my loneliness
when the jackal thirsty for wandering
screamed his gangrene into the hollow of the waves
I received the call of the sands
of freedom and sun

if words can heal our excesses
tell me again about this eternity
where the Desert advances
to repose in an hourglass

Among my winter nights
like dervishes
in the dunes' orphan sands
at the crossroads of mirages
the infinite grain of solitudes
this immutable chorus of inertia hidden in silence
when night settles its jaws
in the hollow of my nightmares
it's a black anthem of interference
of contradictions at the edge of trance
of thick delusions across centuries
of vertical breathlessness in the gut
moving intermittently
when the crossing of the Desert
begins again

Serhani, Mounir

Mounir Serhani was born in Ksar El Kébir in 1982 and is currently a professor at a teacher training college in Rabat. He received a master's degree in literature from the Ecole Normale Supérieure-LSH in Lyon and a doctorate degree from Chouaib Doukkali University in El Jadida, Morocco. His has published poetry collections: Je Vais au Noir Silencieux (*I Go to Silent Blackness* 2013); J'ai Vécu de T'Attendre (*I Lived to Wait for You* 2014); and Nue Comme Nuit (*Naked like Night* 2015). In 2016, Serhani published his first novel entitled Il n'y a pas de Barbe Lisse (*There is no Smooth Beard*) and his first philosophical essay, L'Islam au Risque de l'Interprétation (*Islam at the Risk of Interpretation* 2016). The poems here are taken from his book, Folle Encre (*Crazy Ink* 2013).

The Left-Handed Woman*

You like only the blackness of the bed
Crumpled sheets
Humid creases
Where day and night meet in you
You prefer only escape
After timid kisses
Your dunes crying
Foam and lightning
From a jaded water
From this nocturnal rain
My revolt is born

---

* After a novel by Peter Handke

Ashes

Night stirs the blood
And love in throes
Purges
Words from buried wounds
To the salt of hells
Padded heart
Defiant
Reborn
In forgetfulness

Desert Night

I like the perfumed night
Of desert
Thunder and tempests
A night
Of blues scrutinizing me
From their phallic mist
They denounce the sand
Cursing the height
The neighboring sun

Simple Shore

Your hand is the sister
Of dreams
The night is dark in you
Bastard bird
Your timid shoulders
Frightened
Of my torso
And this double din
Burns with travel
In square spirals
Sloping from my body
I confide to you, « don't put out my lights.
Be my igneous water on the loose in rage »

Souag, Moha

Moha Souag is a headmaster at a secondary school in Ait Chaker, Aoufous. His publications include: La Semaine Où J'ai Aimé (*The week when I Loved* 2016); Un Barrage de Sucre (*A Barrage of Sugar* 2011) and Nos Plus Beaux Jours (*Our Most Beautiful Days* 2014).

Prayer to Saint IMF

Saint IMF, you who has tamed the GATT and the Serpent
Accept us in your saintly politics
In the name of OPEP and OPEC united
Grant us your credit
Give us our daily dollar
To consume all the goods
Give to our leaders
their whisky and gin
their Volvo and Limousine
In the name of Saint BIRD
(with nothing of the bird but a name)
Protect our coffee
our brass
our cobalt
our cocoa and company
Bless our non-convertible currency
Devalue our money as you have devalued our culture
Pray for us poor unemployed
that we may avoid cops and their fury

In the name of dollars invested in the void
Be our guide
Direct our footsteps
Show us our options
so that we may avoid inflation and deflation
Accept the blood of our children
to sell yourself our diamonds so that at last your reign will prevail
May your will be done
May the schools and the hospitals close
Only your spirit will heal our sick and instruct our ignorant
In the name of Sin Marks
           Sin Francs
           Sin Euros
Saint Dior and MacIntosh
of Ice Cream and MacDonalds
You, God of Consumption
You brought down the Berlin Wall and the Wall of Bamboo
And with their bricks and with ours
You built the anti-missile Shield, arms of mass destruction, lateral and
    collateral damage
surgical strikes and desert storms
Have Mercy upon us
We who have the misery
and you the miser of
Bitterness.

honk honk

A driver of poetry in a Cairo taxi
holds forth with dry words on how a wind of sabers
has shattered our lives.
Spears, arrows and tapered swords
bodies pruned
heads, hands, legs of the presumed enemy, bloodied with his words,
metaphors and alternating rhymes.
A memory topped forever with the glories of yesteryear

that this submissive slave still sings
proud of the conquests of his ancestors
he subjects the world to his eight-cylinder machine
with a lying speedometer
crying about a past he had nothing to do with
but that makes him noble by default
These words gathered in schoolyards
that no one eats
satisfying a truncated ego
losing the battle for his daily bread
he gains on the lonely pedestrians
on the crowded streets
in his second-hand steed
trotting at the red light
stinking CO_2 through his nostril
blaring his horn at any enemy that moves
the war for a few copper pennies
continues.

Tebbal, Abdelkrim

Abdelkrim Tebbal (born in 1931 in Chefchaoun) is a Moroccan poet who attended Al Qaraouiyine University. He obtained a bachelor's degree in Islamic Studies. He worked as a high school teacher before he retired. He received an award for his book عابر سبيل (*A Passerby* 1994). His works include الطريق إلى الإنسان (*A Way to Man* 1971); البستان (*The Garden* 1988).

A Friend

My friend hasn't come back
since he first arrived
in the blazing heat
So I asked the drizzle
falling now
on his umbrella
and I asked the sobs
breathing
in his chest
I asked the marble
writing
his last poems
and I asked the evening
that will pass here
tomorrow
they all wept
and left
for the cemetery

An Andalusian Alley

I bow
to the shadow in front of you
before the beginning
and after the end
as if I were your shadow
walking towards you
I cast a pallor on your walls
Silence disperses me in you
like ashes
on cloudy stones
In the glitter of a window
in the hovel of fog
in a low moan
it flows from dejected doorsteps
from ripples on invisible
ceilings
A phantom
it sneaks
from the darkness of morning
or from the light of evening
to the open square
or to a field in the sky
****

****

oh you cradle of mine
this open space
and that sky
are but rain and gravel
in the alley
oh inhabitant who finds
tranquility
in me. In you
Why
does the earth bow over you
Do you journey secretly
to the country of gypsy poets?

(March 10th, 2004)

Another Skin

In the remote sands
some green
and some of the moon's breath
whoever passes by there
sees
in the glassy mirrors
the frothing
of water
premonitions
of jasmine
and then forms
in a new skin
even finer than water
more splendid than prophetic words
unexpected
a specter
with many faces
behind the sands

Strangers

Strangers
come here and
inhabit the shirt
as if they were family
they sleep and wake up in it
like its buttons
it doesn't cramp them
light, easy going
as if they were a dream
they don't mind if I cough
and they don't scoff if I laugh
they don't complain if I cry
thin and kind

If I strip myself of it in the evening
they remain on my chest
and below the pants
they moan
from the heat of doubt
and the chill of certainty
they may ascend to a hill on the forehead
the sky breeze blows on them
to delight them a little
and they may descend to the abyss
between two temples
damp like crying
there they discover
on a blue stone
or in the deep air
the roots of the shirt
the flowers of the shirt
and they don't come back.

Supplication

I fill up my pocket with water
knotting it together like beads
If she returns from her extreme
sobriety
I will present it to her

I will plant flowers in my palm
watering them with my tears
I will present them to her
If she rises like a sun
in the dark of night

I tress a silver laurel
from the grass of the heart
I will present it to her
If she lets me be her slave
in the kingdom of passion

I safeguard a rainbow
in my book of poetry
I will present it to her
if she wants to climb
the gate of the palace

My lady
lily that never wilts
If however the leaves of age whither
the one standing before you
is your shade
and will always be

The Sea

If in my yearning for you
I go out of my mind
It's all right
Because I was drawn to you
By fire
If I get lost
On my way to you
It's all right
Because I journeyed to you across all time
If I die
On coming to you
It's all right
It's like a river that comes
To you
Don't rescue me
From the suffering of the journey
And don't revive me
From the drowning of death

(March 1999)

The Words of a Paint Brush

From my blood
the deserters fell to earth
trembling with fear
then I talked like wild pigeons
and my faithful and melodic words were
a prelude to prayer
to a door
to the house of morning
they were a voice for the winds
my words were
the butterfly's wing
the deer's crown
and the evening's tattoo
And there was
talk without words
wine without vines
and the first ink
with which you wrote songs
and it was the light
in the blue of the sea
in the yellow of the glass
you were its shade
in the green of the river
in the red of the clay
it was in the beginning
and it was in the end
and it was in the finished painting

Then the paintbrush let down its plait of hair
to say:
if you are not
accustomed to words
and you don't flash
twilight on the canvas
if you don't gush forth

a star on the whiteness
you'll vanish from sight
and from everything else

A Solo Performance

If I were able
In a drop of light
To make two opposites one
Then a rose would sit
On the right side of a rose
And the grasshopper would dance
At the court of the sea
And whiteness would pour down
In the play of night
If I were able
I would seize the lightning
From its eyelids
And would make peace with myself
And would be no one else

Zrika, Abdallah

Abdallah Zrika, (born 1953) grew up in the poor neighborhood of Ben Msik, Casablanca. At the age of twelve, he wrote his first poem. In 1977, he published رقصة الرأس و الوردة (*Dance of the Head and the Rose*). Six of his poems were deemed morally dangerous, and he spent two years in jail. In 1978, he obtained a degree in Sociology. Zrika is also a playwright.

The Grapes of the Desert's Thirst

1.

Some travelers measure the earth
with a patch of text

some philosophers go to
a carpenter to lathe a question

some poets head to a tailor
to escape the rips widening within them

As for me, I run towards the rubble of emptiness or a heap
of shade in order to erase what is.

2.

There is no grave that can contain
the flavor of death pouring forth from the wooden bed

no grave that can gather what is left of words
sticking to the lips of a dead body

no room that can absorb the cold solitude
of a paper from which a poem has turned away

3.

The narrator doesn't walk in the funeral procession
but listens only to what is said at the dinner for the dead
and collects what falls from the crumbs of words

4.

I didn't understand then
how the head can be in the horizon
and the leg in the grave

or how the gate of a graveyard can lead
to the courtyard of a poem

5.

In the end
I felt the desert's thirst
for the grapes of Dionysus

and the cries of the ruins for
the dying embers

and the sadness of gazelles for
the silence of poets

6.

Instead of fleeing the blackness in my chest
towards the white of the paper
                    I threw myself in a field of yellow daisies
and fell
asleep.

from Loss of the Needle of Time

1.

Go, just go away. The needle with which time sews the cloth of days is lost.
The rain doesn't erase anything when it falls. You'll laugh with the tooth you
found in the earth. And when you cry your eyes will hang down to where your
tears fall. You will see that the entire ocean is smaller than any sadness in you.
You want to scream but no sound comes out. And even if you die forgetfulness
will roam in your body instead of worms.

2.

Come back oh come back! The face that you leave with in the morning is not
the one that returns at night. The bed sheet you left behind will soon be your
shroud. Time leaks from a rusty and lonely water tap. There is nothing for
you but writing with closed eyes until the ink that is in you absorbs all this
darkness. Until you enter the graveyard in your head. You close your ears so as
not to hear the snoring of the dead filling up the damp room that survived the
earthquake.
      Come back oh come back to yourself.

3.

Tell me tell me. Where are you going with your head a rusty fountain? Who
shares the bitterness of sunset with you now that electrical poles are the only
things left standing? No mouthful of bread will drive away this hunger. No
poetry will dispel the darkness that sips water from your eyes. Keep a last tear
to shed tomorrow when everything in you is dry. What have you done to reach
the hell of yourself? Don't comb your hair, don't leave for death what it can
trifle with. And don't say anything else that silence will devour after you leave.

4.

Like a carriage my donkey head draws me forward and the wind around me
brays and the words on the earth are straw so that I fear my head will bend
down to eat them

            I amuse myself with little devils
that dance in the circus of illusion

5.

Nothing is more important in this huge vast expanse than that extremely small
ant that flits past the way this poem flits through this wide world.

6.

Yesterday I let a little rain into my heart and shut the window between me and
the wind so that the solitary piece of paper that sips me when I write would not
fly away
      then I firmly closed the door for good so it wouldn't go back
from where it came.

7.

Hey the smell of bananas didn't lessen the smell of death in those old clothes.
Fear still tick-tocks in the grandfather clock. The darkness that comes in
through the window eats away at the edges of the photo of the white woman. In
fact no one dared open that room. There where the water to wash the dead man
still hasn't evaporated under the bed.

Nobody opened the door to drive death out of that room.

8.

Only the typewriter pecks on the papers like drops of rain and forgets the
words that gather around the lamp like flies while a moon like a night beggar
looks through the window

        No one has ever seen a poet enter that room.

9.

Hey what do you say. The snoring of poets covers beds packed with bugs.
The seller of old papers flees the mouse of poetry that nibbles what darkness
remains of yesterday.
        And I'm the only one in the cold alley putting my fingers
in my ears so as not to hear my own shouts

10.

and when I say the sky
I only mean
that black space
where I see
some dreams
at night

11.

Oh a word slips out over the smoothness
of description and does not fall

and the mirror's mercury sticks
to a face that hasn't yet awoken

and the wing of a butterfly
is under a poet's armpit

12.

In the beginning there was zero
then the desert when zero filled with sand
then the word when the desert couldn't bear
                to be alone

13.

Let everything I've seen end
and only this remain:
          the sound of water dripping from pine
          the sizzle of a wet candle
          the barking of a dog at night
          the sound of a pen fidgeting
          on this paper
            without writing